CRIMINAL PRACTICE

For 2027 exams

Mark Thomas and James J Ball

Series editors: Amy Sixsmith and David Sixsmith

REVISE SQE

First published in 2022 by Fink Publishing Ltd
This edition published in 2026

Impression number 10 9 8 7 6 5 4 3 2 1

British Library Cataloguing in Publication Data
A catalogue record for this book is available from the British Library
ISBN: 9781917183949

This book is also available in various ebook formats.
Ebook ISBN: 9781917183963

Production and typesetting by Westchester Publishing Services (UK)
Cover and text design by BMLD (bmld.uk)

Fink Publishing Ltd
E-mail: hello@revise4law.co.uk
www.revise4law.co.uk

Notes from the publisher

1. This book reflects the SQE1 assessment specification (updated April 2026) applicable for assessments from 1 September 2026.

2. While Fink Publishing has made every attempt to ensure that advice on the qualification and its assessment is accurate, the official specification and associated assessment guidance materials are the only authoritative source of information and should always be referred to for definitive guidance. See the SRA website at https://sqe.sra.org.uk. Note that the SRA may amend their assessment guidance (including the contents of the assessment specifications) at any point.

3. Fink Publishing has robust editorial processes to ensure the accuracy of the content in this publication, and every effort is made to ensure this publication is free of errors. We are, however, only human, and occasionally errors do occur. Fink Publishing is not liable for any misunderstandings that arise as a result of errors in this publication, but it is our priority to ensure that the content is accurate. If you spot an error, please do contact us at revise4law.co.uk so we can make sure it is corrected.

Contents

Contributors

THE AUTHORS

Mark Thomas is a practising barrister and has taught law for several years at both undergraduate and postgraduate levels, including the Legal Practice Course. Mark has published academic textbooks in the field of criminal law and evidence, and has extensive experience in writing revision-style books for law students. He is the co-author of *Revise SQE: Criminal Law* and *Revise SQE: Oral Skills for SQE2: Advocacy*. He is also the editor of *Revise SQE: Ethics and Professional Conduct*, *FLK1 Practice Assessments* and *FLK2 Practice Assessments*. Mark acts as MCQ adviser and reviewer for the Revise SQE series.

James J Ball is a practising barrister on the Midland Circuit and teaches on the undergraduate and postgraduate courses, including the SQE-preparation courses, at Nottingham Law School, Nottingham Trent University. He is the co-author of *Revise SQE: Criminal Practice* and *Revise SQE: Oral Skills for SQE2: Advocacy*.

SERIES EDITORS

Dr Amy Sixsmith is associate professor in law at the University of Sunderland and a senior fellow of Advance HE.

Dr David Sixsmith is assistant professor in law at Northumbria Law School and a senior fellow of Advance HE.

Introduction to Revise SQE

Welcome to *Revise SQE*, a series of revision guides designed to help you in your preparation for, and achievement in, the Solicitors Qualifying Examination 1 (SQE1) assessment. SQE1 is designed to assess what the Solicitors Regulation Authority (SRA) refer to as 'functioning legal knowledge' (FLK); this is the legal knowledge and competencies required of a newly qualified solicitor in England and Wales. The SRA has chosen single best answer multiple-choice questions (MCQs) to test this knowledge, and *Revise SQE* is here to help.

PREPARING YOURSELF FOR SQE

The SQE is the relatively new route to qualification for aspiring solicitors introduced in September 2021 as one of the final stages towards qualification as a solicitor. The SQE consists of two parts:

SQE1
- **Functioning legal knowledge (FLK)**
  - two x 180 MCQs
  - closed book; assessed by two sittings, over 10 hours in total.

SQE2
- **Practical legal skills**
  - 16 written and oral assessments
  - assesses six practical legal skills, over 14 hours in total.

In addition to the above, any candidate will have to undertake two years' qualifying work experience. More information on the SQE assessments can be found on the SRA's dedicated SQE website; this revision guide series will focus on FLK and preparation for SQE1.

It is important to note that the SQE can be perceived to be a 'harder' set of assessments than the Legal Practice Course (LPC). The reason for this, explained by the SRA, is that the LPC is designed to prepare candidates for 'day one' of their training contract; the SQE, on the other hand, is designed to prepare candidates for 'day one' of being a newly qualified solicitor. Indeed, the SRA has chosen the SQE1 assessment to be 'closed book' (ie without permitting use of any materials) on the basis that a newly qualified solicitor would know all of the information tested, without having to refer to books or other sources.

With that in mind, and a different style of assessments in place, it is understandable that many readers may feel nervous or wary of the SQE. This is especially so given that this style of assessment is likely to be different from what readers will have experienced before. In this *Introduction* and revision guide series, we hope to alleviate some of those concerns with guidance on preparing for the SQE assessment, tips on how to approach single best answer MCQs and expertly written guides to aid in your revision.

What does SQE1 entail?

SQE1 consists of two assessments, containing 180 single best answer MCQs each (360 MCQs in total). The table below breaks down what is featured in each of these assessments.

Assessment	Contents of assessment ('functioning legal knowledge')
FLK assessment 1	• Business law and practice • Dispute resolution • Contract • Tort • The legal system (the legal system of England and Wales and sources of law, constitutional and administrative law and European Union law and legal services)
FLK assessment 2	• Property practice • Wills and the administration of estates • Solicitors accounts • Land law • Trusts • Criminal law and practice

Please be aware that in addition to the above, ethics and professional conduct will be examined pervasively across the two assessments (ie it could crop up anywhere).

Each substantive topic is allocated a percentage of the assessment paper (eg 'legal services' will form 12–16% of the FLK1 assessment) and is broken down further into 'core principles'. Candidates are advised to read the SQE1 Assessment Specification in full (available on the SQE website). We have also provided a *Revise SQE checklist* to help you in your preparation and revision for SQE1 (see below).

HOW DO I PREPARE FOR SQE1?

Given the vastly different nature of SQE1 compared to anything you may have done previously, it can be quite daunting to consider how you could possibly prepare for 360 single best answer MCQs, spanning 11 different substantive topics (especially given that it is 'closed book'). The *Revise SQE FAQ* below, however, will set you off on the right path to success.

Revise SQE FAQ

Question	Answer
1. Where do I start?	We would advise that you begin by reviewing the assessment specification for SQE1. You need to identify what subject matter can be assessed under each substantive topic. For each topic, you should honestly ask yourself whether you would be prepared to answer an MCQ on that topic in SQE1. We have helped you in this process by providing a *Revise SQE checklist* on our website (revise4law.co.uk) that allows you to read the subject matter of each topic and identify where you consider your knowledge to be at any given time. We have also helpfully cross-referenced each topic to a chapter and page of our *Revise SQE* revision guides.
2. Do I need to know legal authorities, such as case law?	In the majority of circumstances, candidates are not required to know or use legal authorities. This includes statutory provisions, case law or procedural rules. Of course, candidates will need to be aware of legal principles deriving from common law and statute. There may be occasions, however, where the assessment specification does identify a legal authority (such as *Rylands v Fletcher* in tort law). In this case, candidates will be required to know the name of that case, the principles of that case and how to apply that case to the facts of an MCQ. These circumstances are clearly highlighted in the assessment specification and candidates are advised to ensure they engage with those legal authorities in full. In each of our texts in the *Revise SQE* series, we detail clearly which authorities are required for that subject. Any authorities provided in addition are designed to assist in your revision by acting as an aide-mémoire.
3. Do I need to know the history behind a certain area of law?	Whilst understanding the history and development of a certain area of law is beneficial, there is no requirement for you to know or prepare for any

Revise SQE FAQ (continued)

Question	Answer
	questions relating to the development of the law (eg in criminal law, candidates will not need to be aware of the development from objective to subjective recklessness). SQE1 will be testing a candidate's knowledge of the law as it stands four calendar months prior to the date of the first assessment in an assessment window. The SRA on the SQE website has helpfully provided the exact cut off date for each assessment in the cycle; it is worth checking this when you are preparing for your assessment.
4. Do I need to be aware of academic opinion or proposed reforms to the law?	Candidates preparing for SQE1 do not need to focus on critical evaluation of the law, or proposed reforms to the law either.
5. How do I prepare for single best answer MCQs?	See our separate *Revise SQE* guide on preparing for single best answer MCQs below.

Where does *Revise SQE* come into it?

The *Revise SQE* series of revision guides is designed to aid your revision and consolidate your understanding; the series is not designed to replace your substantive learning of the SQE1 topics. We hope that this series will provide clarity as to assessment focus, useful tips for sitting SQE1 and act as a general revision aid.

There are also materials on our website to help you prepare and revise for the SQE1, such as a *Revise SQE checklist*. This *checklist* is designed to help you identify which substantive topics you feel confident about heading into the exam – see below for an example.

Revise SQE checklist

Criminal Practice

SQE content	Corresponding chapter	*Revise SQE checklist*		
Rights of a suspect being detained by the police for questioning • Right to legal advice	Chapter 1, Pages 4–6	I do not know this subject and I am not ready for SQE1 ☐	I partially know this subject, but I am not ready for SQE1 ☐	I know this subject and I am ready for SQE1 ☐

Criminal Practice (continued)

SQE content	Corresponding chapter	*Revise SQE checklist*		
Rights of a suspect being detained by the police for questioning • Right to have someone informed of arrest	Chapter 1, Pages 6–7	I do not know this subject and I am not ready for SQE1 ☐	I partially know this subject, but I am not ready for SQE1 ☐	I know this subject and I am ready for SQE1 ☐
Rights of a suspect being detained by the police for questioning • Reviews and detention time limits under PACE 1984, Code C	Chapter 1, Pages 7–13	I do not know this subject and I am not ready for SQE1 ☐	I partially know this subject, but I am not ready for SQE1 ☐	I know this subject and I am ready for SQE1 ☐

PREPARING FOR SINGLE BEST ANSWER MCQs

As discussed above, SQE1 will be a challenging assessment for all candidates. This is partly due to the quantity of information a candidate must be aware of in two separate sittings. In addition, however, an extra complexity is added due to the nature of the assessment itself: MCQs.

The SRA has identified that MCQs are the most appropriate way to test a candidate's knowledge and understanding of fundamental legal principles. Whilst this may be the case, it is likely that many candidates have little, if any, experience of MCQs as part of their previous study. Even if a candidate does have experience of MCQs, SQE1 will feature a special form of MCQs known as 'single best answer' questions.

What are single best answer MCQs and what do they look like?

Single best answer MCQs are a specialised form of question, used extensively in other fields such as in training medical professionals. The idea behind single best answer MCQs is that the multitude of options available to a candidate may each bear merit, sharing commonalities and correct statements of law or principle, but only one option is absolutely correct (in the sense that it is the 'best' answer). In this regard, single best answer MCQs are different from traditional MCQs.

A traditional MCQ will feature answers that are implausible in the sense that the distractors are 'obviously wrong'. Indeed, distractors in a traditional MCQ are often very dissimilar, resulting in a candidate being able to spot answers that are clearly wrong with greater ease.

In a well-constructed single best answer MCQ, on the other hand, each option should look equally attractive given their similarities and subtle differences. The skill of the candidate will be identifying which, out of the options provided, is the single best answer. This requires a much greater level of engagement with the question than a traditional MCQ would require; candidates must take the time to read the questions carefully in the exam.

How are single best answer MCQs structured?

For SQE1, single best answer MCQs will be structured as follows:

A woman is charged with battery, having thrown a rock towards another person intending to scare them. The rock hits the person in the head, causing no injury. The woman claims that she never intended that the rock hit the person, but the prosecution allege that the woman was reckless as to whether the rock would hit the other person.

The factual scenario. First, the candidate will be provided with a factual scenario that sets the scene for the question to be asked (known as the 'stem').

Which of the following is the most accurate statement regarding the test for recklessness in relation to a battery?

The lead in. Next, the candidate will be provided with the question that they must find the single best answer to.

A. There must have been a risk that force would be applied by the rock, and that the reasonable person would have foreseen that risk and unjustifiably taken it.
B. There must have been a risk that force would be applied by the rock, and that the woman should have foreseen that risk and unjustifiably taken it.
C. There must have been a risk that force would be applied by the rock, and that the woman must have foreseen that risk and unjustifiably taken it.
D. There must have been a risk that force would be applied by the rock, and that both the woman and the reasonable person should have foreseen that risk and unjustifiably taken it.
E. There must have been a risk that force would be applied by the rock, but there is no requirement that the risk be foreseen.

The possible answers. Finally, the candidate will be provided with **five** possible answers. There is only one single best answer that must be chosen. The other answers, known as 'distractors', are not the 'best' answer available.

It will be beneficial to guide you through each aspect of the MCQ to further your understanding of the writing process.

The stem

The stem (ie scenario) will differ according to each MCQ and what it is seeking to test. If the MCQ is seeking simply to test a candidate's basic knowledge of the law, without application, then the stem is likely to be short. Where, however, the MCQ is seeking to have a candidate analyse a factual pattern, and apply it to the options available, the stem will be significantly longer.

In general, however, a stem should be a concise and clear introduction to the issue at hand. A well written stem should contain all material facts relevant to answering the question about to be asked (new facts should not be introduced in the lead in or the distractors). The stem should not be ambiguous or open to interpretation.

The lead in

The lead in will be a short question and can be phrased in a variety of ways. The lead in should provide the candidate with everything they need to answer the question. There should be no ambiguity or double meanings.

The length and nature of the lead in will vary dependent on the type of question being asked. These categories of MCQ are detailed in the table below.

Categories of MCQs	Explanation and example
'Knows' MCQs	To *recall* a specific answer (eg the author of X is Y)
'Shows How' MCQs	To *analyse* a fact pattern and *apply* (eg the application of X in this case is Y)
'Knows How' MCQs	To *know* the answer, and *show* the reason *why* (eg the purpose of X is Y because ...)

Most commonly, a lead in may be phrased as:
- Which of the following statements best describes ...?
- Which of the following statements best summarises ...?
- Which of the following best explains ...?

A lead in will not, however, be phrased as:
- Which of the following is true?
- What is the rule for X?
- Which one of the following is not correct?

The options

You will be provided with five possible answers and only one is correct (whether that be outright correct, or the single best).

The options will not ask a candidate to identify multiple options as being correct (eg 'A, C and D are correct; B and E are wrong'). Nor will the options feature an 'all of the above' option.

A well written MCQ will avoid vague language in the options. Words such as 'rarely', 'usually' etc should be avoided as they present too much ambiguity. On the other hand, absolute words such as 'only', 'always' and 'never' should equally be avoided because they are often obvious distractors (there rarely being a circumstance in English and Welsh law where the legal position is absolute without exception).

If written well, each option should be plausible (meaning that some candidates would choose it). Plausibility can come from drawing on faulty reasoning and common misconceptions. It may be the case that some options share identical wording save for one word (eg a change from 'may' to 'must'). You therefore need to pay close attention to the wording of the options.

To achieve that, all options will be of a fairly equal length to ensure that they are consistent with one another. It is often said that the correct answer is likely to be the longest; so the writers of the MCQs will have that in mind.

In addition, to ensure plausibility, each option is either likely to be a variation of the other, or each option will be entirely different to the others. MCQ drafters will often rely on the rule of 'Three and Two'. The idea behind this rule is that three options will be fairly similar to each other (eg starting with 'Yes'), whilst the remaining two answers will be equally similar to each other (eg starting with 'No'). If you know the answer is definitely 'Yes', that therefore removes the 'No' options immediately. If the MCQ has not adopted the rule of Three and Two, it is likely that you will be able to pick out the 'obvious' distractor.

Now that you know what the MCQs will look like on SQE1, let us talk about how you may go about tackling an MCQ.

How do I tackle single best answer MCQs?

No exact art exists in terms of answering single best answer MCQs; your success depends on your subject knowledge and understanding of how that subject knowledge can be applied. Despite this, there are tips and tricks that may be helpful for you to consider when confronted with a single best answer MCQ.

1. Read the question twice	2. Understand the question being asked	3. Select the answer if you know it outright	4. If not, employ a process of elimination	5. Take an educated and reasoned guess	6. Skip and come back to it later	7. Random guess

These tips and tricks are essential for preparing you to sit the SQE1 assessment. Each session will involve 90 MCQs, to be answered over 2 hours, 33 minutes. Answering 90 MCQs in that timescale allows *1 minute, 42 seconds per question*, under exam conditions. Of course, some questions will take more or less time to answer than others.

Please take a moment to think about that: on average, within 1 minute and 42 seconds you will have to:

- read the MCQ, including the various answers
- distil from that MCQ what the question is assessing
- work out which of the five possible answers is the correct (or 'single best') answer.

This will be an intensive assessment. You must ensure that you are properly prepared for it, in terms of your subject knowledge and also your mental resilience and time management. Your ability to navigate MCQs will also assist greatly.

1. Read the entire question at least twice

This sounds obvious but is so often overlooked. You are advised to read the entire question once, taking in all relevant pieces of information, understanding what the question is asking you and being aware of the options available. Once you have done that, read the entire question again and this time pay careful attention to the wording that is used.

- **In the factual scenario:** Does it use any words that stand out? Do any words used have legal bearing? What are you told and what are you not told?
- **In the lead in:** What are you being asked? Are there certain words to look out for (eg 'should', 'must', 'will', 'shall')?
- **In the answers:** What are the differences between each option? Are they substantial differences or subtle differences? Do any differences turn on a word or a phrase?

You should be prepared to give each question at least two viewings to mitigate any misunderstandings or oversights.

2. Understand the question being asked

It is important first that you understand what the question is asking of you. The SRA has identified that the FLK assessments may consist of single best answer MCQs that, for example:

- require the candidate to simply identify a correct legal principle or rule
- require the candidate to not only identify the correct legal principle or rule, but also apply that principle or rule to the factual scenario
- provide the candidate with the correct legal principle or rule, but require the candidate to identify how it should be properly applied and/or the outcome of that proper application.

By first identifying what the question is asking you to do, you can then understand what the creators of that question are seeking to test and how to approach the answers available. Many candidates actually find it beneficial to start with the lead in, before reading the scenario. This gives them the opportunity to understand what the scenario will likely entail. You need to decide what works best for you, so take the opportunity to try both ways.

3. Select the answer if you know it outright

You may feel as though a particular answer 'jumps out' at you, and that you are certain it is correct. It is very likely that the answer is correct. Whilst you should be confident in your answers, do not allow your confidence (and perhaps overconfidence) to rush you into making a decision. Review all of your options one final time before you move on to the next question.

4. If you do not know the answer outright, employ a process of elimination

There may be situations in which the answer is not obvious from the outset. This may be due to the close similarities between different answers. Remember, it is the 'single best answer' that you are looking for. If you keep this in your mind, it will thereafter be easier to employ a process of elimination. Identify which answers you are sure are not correct (or not the 'best') and whittle down your options. Get rid of the distractors. Once you have only two options remaining, carefully scrutinise the wording used in both answers and look back to the question being asked. Identify what you consider to be the best answer, in light of that question. Review your answer and move on to the next question.

5. Take an educated and reasoned guess

There may be circumstances, quite commonly, in which you do not know the answer to the question. In this circumstance, you should try as hard as possible to eliminate any distractors that you are positive are incorrect and then take an educated and reasoned guess based on the options available. 'Always select C' will not work in this assessment; the correct answers will be randomly distributed amongst the MCQs as options A–E.

6. Skip and come back to it later

If time permits, you may think it appropriate to skip a question that you are unsure of and return to it before the end of the assessment. The assessment portal will highlight any questions that have not been answered, and you are also able to 'flag' questions for your review later on in the assessment (time permitting). If you do so, we would advise that you:

- make a note of what question you have skipped or click 'Flag for Review' on your screen, and

- ensure you leave sufficient time for you to go back to that question before the end of the assessment.

The same advice is applicable to any question that you have answered but for which you remain unsure.

7. Random guess

As a matter of absolute last resort, being unable even to take an educated and reasoned guess, you should simply choose an answer. There is no negative marking in the SQE1 assessments, so it is better for you to select an answer with the possibility, by sheer luck, of answering it correctly than it is to leave the answer blank and have no chance of scoring a point. The advice is simple: answer all of the questions, even if you have to guess at the end.

We hope that this brief guide will assist you in your preparation towards, and engagement with, single best answer MCQs.

GUIDED TOUR

Each chapter contains a number of features to help you revise, apply and test your knowledge.

Make sure you know Each chapter begins with an overview of the main topics covered and why you need to understand them for the purpose of the SQE1 assessments.

SQE assessment advice This identifies what you need to pay particular attention to in your revision as you work through the chapter.

What do you know already? These questions help you to assess which topics you feel confident with and which topics you may need to spend more time on (and where to find them in the chapter).

Key term Key terms are highlighted in bold where they first appear and defined in a separate box.

Exam warning This feature offers advice on where it is possible to go wrong in the assessments.

Revision tip Throughout the chapters are ideas to help you revise effectively and be best prepared for the assessment.

Summary This handy box brings together key information in an easy to revise and remember form.

Practice example These examples take a similar format to SQE-type questions and provide an opportunity to see how content might be applied to a scenario.

Procedural link Where relevant, this element shows how a concept might apply to another procedural topic in the series.

Key point checklist At the end of each chapter there is a bullet-point summary of its most important content.

Key terms and concepts These are listed at the end of each chapter to help ensure you know, or can revise, terms and concepts you will need to be familiar with for the assessments.

SQE-style questions Five SQE-style questions on the chapter topic give you an opportunity to test your knowledge.

Answers to questions Check how you did with answers to both the quick knowledge test from the start of the chapter and the SQE-style questions at the end of the chapter.

Key cases, rules, statutes and instruments These list the key sources candidates need to be familiar with for the SQE assessment.

SQE1 TABLE OF LEGAL AUTHORITIES

The SQE1 Assessment Specification states the following in respect of legal authorities and their relevance to SQE1:

> On occasion in legal practice a case name or statutory provision, for example, is the term normally used to describe a legal principle or an area of law, or a rule or procedural step (eg *Rylands v Fletcher*, CPR Part 36, Section 25 notice). In such circumstances, candidates are required to know and be able to use such case names, statutory provisions etc. In all other circumstances candidates are not required to recall specific case names, or cite statutory or regulatory authorities.

This *SQE1 table of legal authorities* identifies the legal authorities you are required to know for the purpose of the SQE1 Functioning Legal Knowledge assessments for *Criminal Practice.*

Legal authority	Corresponding *Revise SQE* chapter/pages
Police and Criminal Evidence Act 1984	**Chapter 1: Advising clients, including vulnerable clients, about the procedure and processes at the police station, page 1**
Code C	**page 4**
Code D	**page 14**

Legal authority	Corresponding *Revise SQE* chapter/pages
Magistrates' Courts Act 1980	**Chapter 4: Plea before venue and allocation of business between magistrates' court and Crown Court, page 88**
s 19	**page 96**
s 20	**page 98**
s 22A	**[page 68]**
Crime and Disorder Act 1998	**Chapter 4: Plea before venue and allocation of business between magistrates' court and Crown Court, page 84**
s 50A	**page 101**
s 51	**page 102**
R v Turnbull [1977] QB 224	**Chapter 6: Principles and procedures to admit and exclude evidence, page 132**
Criminal Justice and Public Order Act 1994	**Chapter 6: Principles and procedures to admit and exclude evidence, page 132**
s 34	**page 137**
s 35	**page 138**
s 36	**page 138**
s 37	**page 138**
s 38	**page 139**
Police and Criminal Evidence Act 1984	**Chapter 6: Principles and procedures to admit and exclude evidence, page 132**
s 76	**pages 151**
s 78	**page 151**
Criminal Justice Act 2003	**Chapter 6: Principles and procedures to admit and exclude evidence, page 151**
s 100(1)	**page 158**
s 101(1)	**page 153**
Sentencing Children and Young People Definitive Guideline	**Chapter 10: Youth Court procedure, page 261**

TABLE OF CASES

The SQE1 Assessment Specification requires you to know the cases in bold below.

TABLE OF STATUTES

The SQE1 Assessment Specification requires you to know the statutes in bold below.

1

Advising clients, including vulnerable clients, about the procedure and processes at the police station

MAKE SURE YOU KNOW

This chapter will cover the principles relating to the procedure and processes at the police station. For the purposes of the SQE1, you are required to know:

- the rights of a suspect being detained by the police for questioning
- identification procedures
- advising a client, including vulnerable clients, whether to answer police questions
- procedure for interviewing a suspect under the Police and Criminal Evidence Act (PACE) 1984.

The SQE1 Assessment Specification has identified that candidates are required to know and be able to use PACE 1984, Codes C and D.

SQE ASSESSMENT ADVICE

As you work through this chapter, remember to pay particular attention in your revision to:

- the time limits for detaining a suspect without charge, and the circumstances where those limits may be extended
- when an identification procedure must be carried out, the procedures to be followed when legal advice may be delayed, and the criteria for delaying said access.

WHAT DO YOU KNOW ALREADY?

Have a go at these questions before reading this chapter. If you find some difficult or cannot remember the answers, make a note to look more closely at that area during your revision.

1) True or false? A suspect is always entitled to free, in-person legal advice at the police station irrespective of their income.

   [Rights of a suspect being detained by the police for questioning, page 4]

2) What is the name of the identification procedure where an eyewitness is shown images of a suspect and individuals who resemble the suspect?

   [Identification procedures, page 13]

3) True or false? If a suspect claims to have relied on legal advice to remain silent during a police interview, they will automatically be protected from having adverse inferences drawn from their silence.

   [Advising a client, including vulnerable clients, whether to answer police questions, page 19]

4) In the case of a juvenile, what is the hierarchical order that the police must follow when identifying an appropriate adult?

   [Procedure for interviewing a suspect under PACE 1984, page 22]

INTRODUCTION TO CRIMINAL PROCEDURE

Where an individual is suspected of being involved in a criminal offence, they may be arrested and taken to an authorised place of detention (ie a police station). At this stage, the suspect has not been *accused* of committing or being involved in the commission of the offence. A suspect becomes an 'accused' when they are charged with an offence. In this guide, we refer to this individual, once charged, as the 'defendant'.

Arrival at the police station

On arrival at the police station following arrest, a suspect will be 'booked' into custody (ie their details are recorded) by the **custody officer.** This must be done as soon as practicable. It is worth noting that an individual may find themselves in a police station on a voluntary basis (ie they are not arrested and attend for a voluntary interview). The SQE1 Assessment Specification refers to persons 'detained' by the police for questioning, so it is unlikely your SQE1 assessment will require you to know the procedure for dealing with a voluntary attendee at the police station.

Key term: custody officer

An officer, independent of the investigation, holding the rank of at least sergeant, who is responsible for the welfare of a suspect who is in police custody.

The custody officer is responsible for opening a **custody record** as soon as practicable for any arrested person brought to the police station, and informing the suspect of their rights whilst in police detention and for the authorisation of detention.

Key term: custody record

A digital document opened and kept by the custody officer which is used to record details of the suspect and their welfare whilst in police detention. In particular, the custody record will include details as to the suspect's name, address, etc, the offence which they have been arrested for, the time of arrest, arrival at the police station, time of interview, confirmation that the rights of the suspect (eg to legal advice) have been provided to them, any requests made by the suspect or representations made by their legal representative, and compliance with PACE Codes.

The custody record should also document the risk assessment undertaken by the custody officer. This risk assessment will deal with any welfare issues relevant to the detention of the suspect. They include physical or mental health difficulties/vulnerabilities, any language barriers (and thus the need for an interpreter) or any risks to the safety of themselves or staff. The risk assessment will also include whether the suspect should be seen by a medical practitioner at the station, or if they would benefit from an appropriate adult.

Two key points to note about the custody record:

- a suspect's custody record can be inspected at the request of a suspect, their solicitor, or appropriate adult at any time whilst the suspect is in custody
- a copy of the custody record can be obtained when the suspect is released from custody, upon request.

Decision to charge, release or detain

Following the booking in of the suspect, the custody officer must decide, based on the details provided by the investigating officer, whether there is sufficient evidence already to charge the suspect with an offence, or whether detention of the suspect is required. **Table 1.1** details these courses of action.

Table 1.1: Sufficient evidence to charge

Status of the evidence	Action to be taken by custody officer
Sufficient evidence to charge the suspect	Custody officer should charge the suspect and either release them on bail, to appear before the magistrates' court at a later date, or remand them into police custody
Insufficient evidence to charge the suspect	Custody officer should release the suspect on bail (with or without conditions), or unconditionally, unless detention can be justified

The custody officer may detain a suspect in police custody if they have reasonable grounds for believing that the suspect's detention without being charged is necessary: (a) to secure or preserve evidence relating to an offence for which the suspect is under arrest; or (b) to obtain such evidence by questioning the person. This requirement will generally cause the custody officer no concern where those officers involved in the investigation need to interview witnesses or search premises, for example.

Discussion of the detention of a suspect is available below: see **Reviews and detention time limits under PACE 1984, Code C**.

RIGHTS OF A SUSPECT BEING DETAINED BY THE POLICE FOR QUESTIONING

Once a suspect's initial detention has been authorised, they will remain in police custody for questioning. The suspect has certain rights, primarily prescribed and preserved by Codes of Practice under PACE 1984, known as the **PACE Codes**.

Key term: PACE Codes

Under PACE 1984, there are eight Codes of Conduct (Codes A–H) which regulate how the police or other investigative agencies (eg HM Revenue & Customs (HMRC)) should conduct themselves before and during criminal proceedings. You can access all Codes of Practice from the gov.uk website. A breach of the PACE Codes will likely be challenged by a defence advocate in practice and may result in evidence being deemed inadmissible.

The treatment of suspects in police custody is governed primarily by **PACE 1984, Code C**.

Key term: PACE 1984, Code C

Code C of PACE 1984 provides, amongst other things, how suspects should be treated in police custody, their rights and how interviews are to be conducted.

In this section, we shall focus our discussion on the right to legal advice; right to have someone informed of arrest; and reviews and detention time limits under PACE 1984, Code C. Other rights of note, but seemingly not assessed on the SQE1, include the right to request an interpreter (if required) and the right to consult the PACE Codes of Practice.

Right to legal advice

When a suspect is detained in custody, the suspect has the right to consult legal advice, privately, at any time. A suspect must be *informed* of the right to seek free independent legal advice:

- on arrival at a police station
- on arrest following voluntary attendance at the police station
- immediately before the commencement, or recommencement, of any interview.

All suspects are entitled to free, in-person advice, unless the punishment for the offence for which the suspect is being held in police custody is non-imprisonable, for which only advice over the telephone may be available. Once legal advice has been accepted or requested, subject to the power to delay (see below, **Delaying access to legal advice**), a suspect should be permitted to consult with a solicitor *as soon as practicable*. It is also key to note that a custody officer should act with no delay in ensuring a solicitor is contacted.

Obtaining legal advice

In most cases, the custody officer will contact the **Defence Solicitor Call Centre** (DSCC).

> **Key term: Defence Solicitor Call Centre**
>
> The DSCC, once contacted, will determine whether telephone advice is sufficient, or whether a solicitor or police station representative should attend in person.

There are occasions when the suspect may wish to have a specific solicitor or firm contacted instead. In that situation, the suspect will be asked to identify the solicitor/firm. The suspect must be informed of the solicitor's arrival at the police station and must be asked whether they wish to speak with the solicitor. Both the solicitor's arrival and the decision of the suspect to see the solicitor must be noted in the custody record.

Delaying access to legal advice

In limited circumstances, an officer of the rank of superintendent may delay a suspect's access to consult with a solicitor. The officer may do so if the suspect has been arrested for an indictable offence (which includes indictable only and either way offences; see **Chapter 3**) and the officer has *reasonable grounds to believe* that exercising the right to legal advice will, for example:

- lead to interference with or harm to evidence connected with the offence, or interference or physical injury to other persons
- lead to alerting others suspected of having committed such an offence who have not yet been arrested for it.

If a suspect has been denied access to a particular solicitor, they must be permitted to choose another solicitor. In any event, the right to access legal advice may only be delayed for as long as the ground used to justify the delay in the first place continues to exist. A delay to access legal advice must not exceed 36 hours from the relevant time (see **Initial decision to detain**, below). When the right to consult a solicitor is delayed, the suspect must be informed of the reason for the delay, and the reason shall be noted in the custody record.

Declining legal advice

If a suspect declines to speak to a solicitor, they must be informed that the right to legal advice also includes the right to speak to a solicitor on the telephone. The suspect must be given this option. If they decline, the custody officer must ask why the suspect has declined and record any answer in the custody record. Even if a suspect declines legal advice initially, they may request to consult a solicitor at any time.

Right to have someone informed of arrest

Where a person has been arrested and is being held in custody at a police station/authorised place of detention, they have the right to have someone informed of their arrest *as soon as practicable* following their arrest. The individuals who may be informed are any:

- relative
- friend
- other person known to them, or who is likely to take an interest in the suspect's welfare.

The custody officer must inform the suspect of this right, and ask the suspect if they wish to exercise it.

Should the request be made, the chosen person will be informed of the fact that the suspect has been arrested, and of their place of detention. If the suspect is subsequently moved to another authorised place of detention, the suspect can request to have the person chosen informed of their new whereabouts. If the person chosen cannot be contacted, the suspect can nominate a maximum of two alternatives. If they cannot be contacted, the custody officer may allow further attempts.

Delaying notification

An officer of the rank of inspector or above may authorise a delay in exercising the right of a suspect to notify someone of their arrest for up to 36 hours. Such a delay may *only* occur if the suspect is detained for an indictable offence (ie such delay cannot be used for summary only offences), and there are *reasonable grounds to believe* that notifying an individual will, for example:

- lead to interference with or harm to evidence connected with the offence, or interference or physical injury to other persons
- lead to alerting others suspected of having committed such an offence who have not yet been arrested for it.

Revision tip

A full statement of law relating to the delay of legal advice and the right to have someone informed is available at Annex B to PACE Code C.

See **Practice example 1.1** to apply your understanding of the right to have someone informed.

Practice example 1.1

At the scene of the alleged offence, Mark is arrested on suspicion of burglary, contrary to s 9 Theft Act 1968. Mark was the only suspect present at the scene when the police arrived. The police spoke to residents who claim to be witnesses. The witnesses said that they think there was another person involved; they saw another male and offered his description to the police. The custody officer informs Mark of his right to have someone informed of his arrest. Mark requested James to be informed and when the custody officer asked Mark for a brief description of James, the investigating officer matched this with the description provided by the eyewitnesses.

What actions may the custody officer take in relation to Mark exercising his right to have someone informed of his arrest?

It is likely that the custody officer may seek to have this right delayed. The custody officer may now have reasonable grounds to believe that James is the other male identified by the witnesses – a potential suspect linked to this offence but who has not yet been arrested for it. Therefore, due to Mark's request, it is possible that contacting James may alert him to the fact that the police are investigating the offence.

In addition, a delay may also be authorised where the officer has reasonable grounds to believe that:

- the person detained has benefited from their criminal conduct
- the recovery of the value of the property constituting the benefit will be hindered by telling the named person of their arrest.

When the right to inform someone of a suspect's arrest and detention is delayed, the suspect must be informed of the reason for the delay, and the reason shall be noted in the custody record.

Reviews and detention time limits under PACE 1984, Code C

For the purposes of SQE1, you need to be familiar with two time periods:

- Period of detention: Often referred to as the 'detention clock', this prescribes how long a suspect may be kept in police custody.

- Period of reviews of detention: Often referred to as the 'review clock', this prescribes the time periods when the detention of a suspect must be reviewed.

We shall consider both detention and its review in this section.

Initial decision to detain

Generally, a person suspected of committing an offence may only be held without charge for a maximum period of 24 hours from the **relevant time** (see **Practice example 1.2**).

Key term: relevant time

The relevant time is the time when the detention clock starts. Usually, the relevant time is the time when the arrested suspect arrives at the police station, or 24 hours after the arrest, whichever is earlier.

Practice example 1.2

Mark is arrested on suspicion of robbery, contrary to s 8 Theft Act 1968. Mark was arrested at 11.05pm and is transported to his local police station, arriving at 11.20pm. Mark's detention is authorised by the custody officer at 11.30pm.

When will Mark's detention clock begin to run?

As Mark has been arrested away from the police station, the general rule is that the detention clock will begin at the time of arrival at the police station. As such, Mark may be detained in police custody for 24 hours, beginning at 11.20pm. Mark must therefore be released or charged before 11.20pm the next day, or his detention must be extended (see below: Expiry of the initial 24-hour period).

Expiry of the initial 24-hour period

Once the initial period of detention is due to expire, the police ultimately have two options: (a) seek to extend the suspect's detention; or (b) release the suspect.

Revision tip

It is relatively uncommon for the police to use the full 24-hour period. In most cases, the police will charge the suspect with the offence or release them under investigation (referred to as RUI). Only rarely will the police require an extension to the suspect's detention. For offences that can only be charged by the CPS, a charging decision will often be made by CPS Direct, who will have consideration for the detention clock.

Table 1.2 demonstrates the process of extending the detention of the suspect.

Table 1.2: Extending the suspect's detention

Type of extension and explanation
Extension from 24 to 36 hours Before the initial 24-hour period has expired, an officer of the rank of superintendent or above, who is responsible for the station at which the suspect is being held, may authorise a maximum 12-hour extension to detain the suspect, taking them to a maximum of 36 hours in detention (ie 24 + 12 = 36 hours) This may only be done if the officer has reasonable grounds to believe that the: • detention of that person without charge is necessary to secure or preserve evidence relating to an offence for which they are under arrest or to obtain such evidence by questioning them • offence for which the suspect has been arrested in connection with is an indictable offence, and • investigation is being conducted diligently and expeditiously. These reasonable grounds must be recorded on the custody record. Furthermore, before the officer extends the period of detention, they must afford the suspect or their representative the opportunity to make representations about the detention. These representations can be made orally or in writing and must be recorded on the custody record.
Extension for more than 36 hours: warrants from the magistrates' court If the police wish to extend the detention of a suspect *beyond* 36 hours from the relevant time, they *must* seek a warrant for further detention from the magistrates' court. If the police do not apply for an extension, the suspect must be charged or released (either on bail or under investigation). The magistrates' court may authorise further detention for such period of time as the magistrates think fit, but up to a maximum of 36 hours' detention. The conditions for extending the suspect's detention are: • the court is made up of a minimum of two lay magistrates, or a district judge • the application is made on oath by a warranted constable, supported by written information • the suspect is present in court (or appears via live link) and being detained in connection with an indictable offence, and

Table 1.2: (continued)

Type of extension and explanation
• the court is satisfied that there are reasonable grounds for believing that the further detention of the suspect is justified. Further detention is 'justified' if it is necessary to: - secure or preserve evidence relating to the offence - obtain such evidence through questioning the suspect, and - the investigation is being conducted diligently and expeditiously. The magistrates' court may issue a warrant for further extensions, up to a maximum of 36 hours for each extension. However, the magistrates' court cannot extend detention beyond 96 hours in total. This means, for example, that if the magistrates extend detention by 36 hours on the first occasion, they would be restricted to an extension of 24 hours on the second detention (ie 24 + 12 + 36 + 24 = 96 hours).

Exam warning

Remember, if the police wish to have detention authorised beyond 36 hours, the magistrates' court must warrant the extension for further detention. It is imperative that the police have an application listed and heard *before* the 36-hour period is up. A magistrates' court cannot authorise a warrant for further detention if the 36-hour period has already expired.

Use **Table 1.3** and **Practice example 1.3** to aid your revision on detention time limits.

Table 1.3: Detention time limits

Time limit	0–24 hours	24–36 hours	36–72 hours	72–96 hours	96 hours
Authorisation	Custody officer (subject to detention reviews)	Officer of the rank of superintendent or above (subject to satisfying the relevant criteria)	Magistrates' court (subject to satisfying the relevant criteria)	Magistrates' court (subject to satisfying the relevant criteria)	No further extensions permitted Suspect must be released or charged
Offence	Any	Indictable	Indictable	Indictable	

Practice example 1.3

James has been arrested in connection with an offence of common assault. He arrived into the police station at 9:30pm and his detention was authorised at 9:45pm.

Mark has been arrested in connection with an offence of assault occasioning actual bodily harm. He arrived at the same time as James and is also detained at 9:45pm.

Explain the relevant detention clock and review clock times.

James cannot be detained for longer than 24 hours, as the offence of common assault is summary only. He must therefore be released at 9:30pm the following day at the latest. A review must be undertaken in respect of James' detention no later than 3:45am, 12:45pm, and 9:45pm (upon which he must be released).

Mark can be detained for longer than 24 hours with the necessary extensions. His review clock will be the same as James' except it will continue at nine-hour intervals for as long as his detention is extended.

Exam warning

The ability to extend detention does not apply to summary only offences. Upon the conclusion of 24 hours, a suspect of a summary only offence *must* be released. Do not allow an MCQ to trick you into thinking that a suspect of a summary only offence (eg common assault) can be detained beyond 24 hours by way of extension.

Procedure on expiry of detention

If the limit on detention has been reached and an extension is neither authorised nor sought after, the police have three options:

- charge the suspect
- release the suspect under investigation
- release the suspect.

Table 1.4 details each of these options in turn.

Table 1.4: Options following expiration of detention

Option	Explanation
Charge the suspect (and bail or remand in custody)	Depending on the nature of the offence, the police will usually need authorisation from the Crown Prosecution Service (CPS) to charge the suspect. If there is sufficient evidence, the suspect will be charged, and the case will

Table 1.4: (continued)

Option	Explanation
	progress to the next stage. If a suspect is charged, they may be granted police bail to attend court at a date in the future, or, depending on the offence, the police may remand the defendant into custody and produce them before the remand court in the magistrates' court the same or following day.
Release the suspect under investigation	Where the suspect has not been charged at the police station, it is common practice for them to be released under investigation (RUI). When RUI, the police may grant the suspect police bail (conditionally or unconditionally). Releasing the suspect on bail will mean that they must return to the police station to answer bail at a specified date in the future. Alternatively, the suspect could be released without bail.
Release the suspect	If the police do not have enough evidence to charge the suspect, and do not intend to prosecute, the suspect will be released without charge (referred to as 'taking no further action' (NFA)). The custody officer will provide a written notice of the police's intention not to prosecute the suspect relating to the offence concerned, unless new evidence arises which supports a prosecution

Detention reviews

Irrespective of how long a suspect is detained for, custody officers are required to carry out **detention reviews**.

Key term: detention reviews

A detention review is where an officer, of at least the rank of inspector who has not been involved in the investigation (a 'review officer'), determines whether a suspect's continued detention is justified. The review clock begins when the custody officer has authorised the initial detention of the suspect. Detention reviews must be logged in the custody record.

The first detention review must be conducted no later than six hours after the custody officer first authorised the detention of the suspect. The second review, and any subsequent reviews, must be carried out no later than nine hours after the previous review. **Figure 1.1** illustrates what occurs during the first 24-hour period in police custody and what reviews must be undertaken whilst a suspect remains detained.

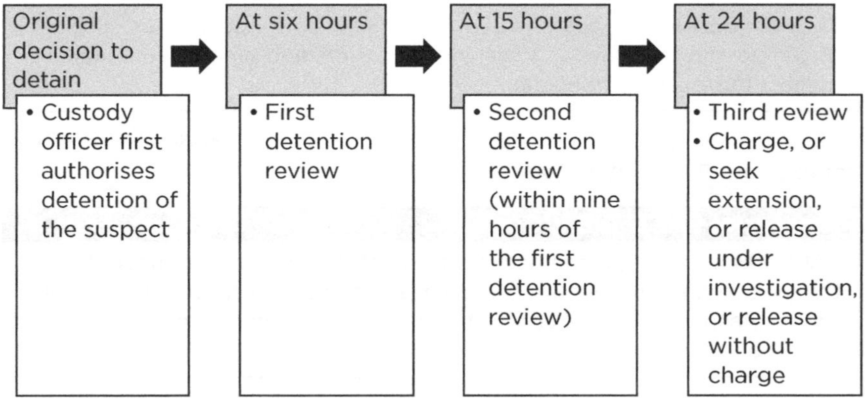

Figure 1.1: First 24 hours in police custody

Exam warning

Be aware! The detention clock and review clock start at different times. Do not confuse them. The detention clock begins at the point of arrival at the police station. The review clock begins when the custody officer first authorises the detention of the suspect. An MCQ may attempt to confuse the two points at which the clocks begin to run.

If the suspect has not been charged, the officer carrying out the detention review must determine whether the police have sufficient evidence to charge the suspect. If there is not enough evidence to charge, the review officer must decide if detention is still necessary. When conducting a review, the officer will:

- consult with the investigating officer to determine what documents and materials are essential for challenging the lawfulness of the arrest and detention, and these must be made available to the detained suspect
- allow the suspect, their solicitor, and if applicable, their appropriate adult, to make oral or written representations (ie submissions) about the detention.

IDENTIFICATION PROCEDURES

To assist the police in confirming that the suspect was involved in the alleged offence, or, in certain circumstances, potentially eliminating a suspect from an investigation, the police will usually carry out an **identification procedure**. For the purposes of SQE1, we shall only consider identification of a suspect by an eyewitness.

Key term: identification procedure

Identification procedures are methods of attempting to have a suspect positively identified by a witness, or witnesses, to an alleged offence.

They are designed to test the eyewitness's ability to identify the suspect as the person they saw on a previous occasion, and provide safeguards against mistaken identification.

Whenever the police carry out an identification procedure, they must comply with **PACE 1984, Code D**.

Key term: PACE 1984, Code D

PACE 1984, Code D, is the relevant Code of Practice for, amongst other things, carrying out identity procedures at the police station. This is not the only aspect of police conduct that is governed by Code D, but it is a significant part.

When an identification procedure must be held

There are some instances, prescribed in PACE 1984, Code D, where the police *must* carry out an identification procedure as soon as practicable. If *all* of the conditions in **Figure 1.2** are satisfied, an identification *must* take place.

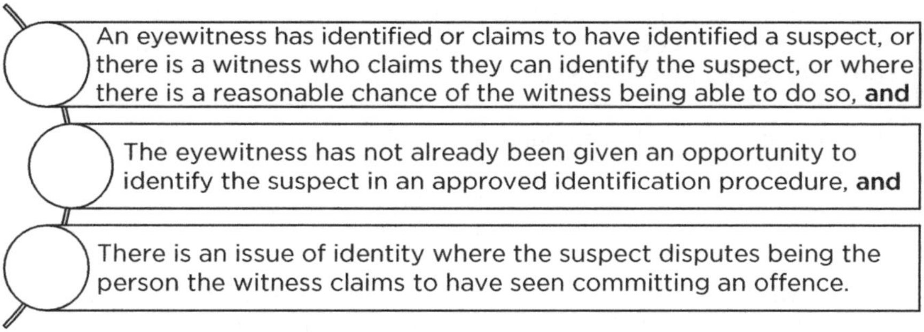

Figure 1.2: When an identification procedure must take place

There are exceptions to this general rule, however. An identification procedure need not be held if:

- it is not practicable to hold any such procedure, or
- any such procedure would serve no useful purpose in proving or disproving whether the suspect was involved in committing the offence.

Examples of where the procedure would serve no useful purpose are provided in Code D:

- where the suspect admits being at the scene of the crime and gives an account of what took place and the eyewitness did not see anything which contradicts that, or
- when it is not disputed that the suspect is already known to the eyewitness who claims to have recognised them when seeing them commit the crime.

An identification procedure may also be held if the officer in charge of the investigation, after consultation with the identification officer (see key term **identification officer**, below), considers it would be 'useful'.

Whether an identity procedure will be held depends on whether the suspect is **known and available**.

Key term: known and available

A suspect is considered 'known' for these purposes where the police have sufficient information to justify a person's arrest due to their suspected involvement in committing an alleged offence. A suspect is 'available' if they are immediately, or within a reasonably short period of time, willing to take part in an identification procedure.

Suspect's identity is unknown

In circumstances where the suspect's identity is unknown, the police may take the eyewitness to a particular area in an attempt to identify the alleged offender. The eyewitness may, complying with relevant guidelines, also be shown photographs of potential suspects.

Suspect's identity is known, and they are available

The police will likely want to carry out an identification procedure when a suspect is known and available. See below: **Different types of identification procedure**.

Suspect's identity is known, but they are not available

Where a suspect is known but is either not immediately available, or likely to be available in a reasonably short period of time, the identification officer may proceed to conduct covert identification procedures, or identification procedures without the suspect's consent (such as group identification or confrontation). If a suspect refuses to participate in an identification procedure, they will be treated as 'known but not available'.

Consequences of refusing to participate

If a suspect refuses to participate, their refusal may be adduced in evidence at any subsequent trial, and the police may conduct a covert procedure (ie carrying out an identification procedure without the suspect's consent or knowledge). See **Practice example 1.4** for application of this principle.

Practice example 1.4

With some incriminating evidence, James is arrested on suspicion of theft, contrary to s 1 Theft Act 1968. He is taken to a police station, interviewed and detained further after telling the police that he was nowhere near the scene of the alleged theft, disputing his involvement.

An eyewitness told police at the scene that they observed the alleged offence and provided the police with a description of the alleged offender which somewhat matches James. The eyewitness, who has not carried out an identification procedure, says that they could identify the alleged offender if given the opportunity and lives ten minutes from the police station. James was asked to consent to his participation but refuses.

What are the potential consequences relating to James' refusal to consent to an identification procedure?

Initially, James would have been considered as known and available: he would be 'known' due to the police having enough evidence to arrest him on suspicion of theft and detain him for questioning. As he was at the police station, he would have been considered 'available' for an identity procedure. As the eyewitness claims to be able to identify the suspect and has not previously been given an opportunity to do so at an identification procedure, and the issue of identity is disputed by James, an identification procedure must take place. However, as James has refused to consent to a procedure, he will now be considered as known but not available. The police may now carry out a covert identification procedure without James' consent, and James' refusal may be given in evidence at a subsequent trial.

Different types of identification procedure

The primary types of identification procedure where a suspect is known and available are as follows:

- video identification
- identification parade
- group identification
- confrontation.

Before we consider each in turn, it is important to appreciate the approach adopted by the police when dealing with the types of identification procedures. The choice can be summarised as follows:

- The suspect shall initially be invited to take part in a video identification.
- This is so unless:
  - a video identification is not practicable
  - an identification parade is both practicable and more suitable than a video identification, or
  - the officer in charge of the investigation considers group identification is more suitable than a video identification or an identification parade, and the identification officer considers it practicable to arrange.

The identification officer and the officer in charge of the investigation shall consult each other to determine which option is to be offered.

Video identification

The police may conduct a video identification, ordinarily with the suspect's consent.

This is where an eyewitness is shown a selection of portrait images on a computer screen, including an image of the suspect. The individuals whose images make up the selection will visually resemble the suspect, and the witness indicates if and when they see the image of the person they believe they saw commit the offence.

A video identification procedure is usually carried out when the suspect is known and available, or known but not available but photographs have been previously obtained.

Identification parade

When an identification parade takes place, the suspect is lined up with others who are visually similar to the suspect. The eyewitness will indicate which individual, if any, is the person they believe they have seen.

Group identification

Similar to an identification parade but without the same control, group identification is when an eyewitness sees the suspect in an informal group of people. During the procedure, the identification officer must reasonably expect that over the period the witness observes the group, the witness will be able to see, from time to time, a number of others (in addition to the suspect) whose appearance is broadly similar.

Confrontation

A measure of last resort, confrontation is when the suspect is directly confronted by the eyewitness. A confrontation does not require the suspect's consent and is less controlled. This method may be adopted when the suspect refuses to consent to an identification procedure, and thus is considered known but not available.

Revision tip

When revising the different types of identification procedures, think about the relative advantages and disadvantages of those procedures. That will help you to understand which procedures are likely to be offered to a suspect. For example, PACE 1984, Code D, provides that '[a]n identification parade may not be practicable because of factors relating to the witnesses, such as their number, state of health, availability and travelling requirements. A video identification would normally be more suitable if it could be arranged and completed sooner than an identification parade'.

Procedure for carrying out an identification procedure under PACE 1984, Code D

All identification procedures must be presided over by an **identification officer.**

> **Key term: identification officer**
>
> Independent from the main investigation, the identification officer oversees the identification procedure and ensures that PACE 1984, Code D, is complied with. The identification officer must be of the rank of at least inspector and any duties imposed must be performed as soon as practicable.

Regardless of the type of procedure carried out, all suspects who may be subject to an identification procedure will need to be provided with 'notice'. Prior to any identification procedure being undertaken, the identification officer must explain to the suspect (amongst other things):

- the purpose of the procedure
- the relevant process for the procedure, including the right to legal advice and to have a solicitor or friend present
- the right to refuse to participate
- the consequence of refusing to take part
- if appropriate, any special arrangements for juveniles or vulnerable persons
- the fact that their solicitor will be provided with the initial description of the suspect, as first given by eyewitnesses.

This information must then be recorded in a written notice and handed to the suspect.

The process to be followed for carrying out particular identification procedures, for example video identification, is detailed and complex. You are strongly advised to refer to PACE 1984, Code D, for a full breakdown of the procedure to be adopted. **Table 1.5** details where you can find the relevant rules, and gives examples of the procedure to be adopted (though you should read the Annexes in full).

Table 1.5: Specific procedure for carrying out an identification procedure

Type of identification procedure	Location of rules of procedure	Examples of procedure from the Code
Video identification	PACE 1984, Code D, Annex A	The set of images must include the suspect and at least eight other people who, so far as possible, resemble the suspect in age, general appearance and position in life

Table 1.5: (continued)

Type of identification procedure	Location of rules of procedure	Examples of procedure from the Code
Identification parade	PACE 1984, Code D, Annex B	May take place either in a normal room or one equipped with a screen permitting witnesses to see members of the identification parade without being seen
Group identification	PACE 1984, Code D, Annex C	The place where the group identification is held should be one where other people are either passing by or waiting around informally (eg people leaving an escalator)
Confrontation	PACE 1984, Code D, Annex D	Confrontation must take place in the presence of the suspect's solicitor, interpreter or friend unless this would cause unreasonable delay

ADVISING A CLIENT, INCLUDING VULNERABLE CLIENTS, WHETHER TO ANSWER POLICE QUESTIONS

Before a suspect is interviewed, and if the suspect wishes to exercise their right to legal advice, it is likely that they will consult privately with a solicitor. At this stage, and following a conference with the suspect, the solicitor should review the custody record and speak with the custody officer, assess the evidence, take instructions, then advise the suspect primarily on whether they should answer police questions.

Factors relevant to assessing whether to answer police questions

There are many advantages and disadvantages to answering police questions. For example, a client may benefit from answering police questions in that it will allow them to set the record straight and put their case forward clearly. On the other hand, by answering police questions, a suspect may say something incriminating or undermine their own credibility.

For these reasons (amongst many others), a solicitor must weigh up a number of factors to determine whether it is appropriate for the client to answer police questions or whether they should remain silent. **Table 1.6** outlines some of these factors that may be relevant to a given case.

Table 1.6: Determining whether to answer police questions

Factor relevant to the solicitor's advice	Explanation
Case is weak and there is insufficient evidence to prove allegation	A 'no comment' interview may be appropriate here to avoid the risk of the client revealing any incriminating information, and will often involve the police choosing not to pursue the matter further (if their evidence is indeed weak)
Inadequate police disclosure to solicitor	A 'no comment' interview may be appropriate given the fact that the solicitor has been unable to form a proper view of the strength of the police's case
Client will likely perform poorly in interview	For many reasons, a client may be deemed by their solicitor as likely to perform badly in interview. The client's age, lack of maturity or vulnerability may mean that answering police questions will be detrimental to them

In addition to the above factors, the solicitor must advise their client as to:

- the right to silence
- potential adverse inferences that may be drawn from silence.

The right to silence

In criminal proceedings, it is for the prosecution to prove that someone is guilty of an offence, not for a defendant to prove their innocence. This provides an important starting point for the solicitor's advice, and the suspect must be informed of their **right to silence**.

Key term: right to silence

The right to silence is a term which means that a suspect has the privilege against self-incrimination. In practice, this means that a suspect is not obliged to answer police questions. The right to remain silent is the first limb of the police caution (see below): 'You do not have to say anything'.

In essence, a suspect does not need to say or prove anything which may assist the police. However, exercising the right to silence may have potential consequences (see **Adverse inferences**, below).

After consulting with a suspect, the solicitor may advise them to remain silent, answer questions, or make a **prepared statement**.

Key term: prepared statement

The suspect may, on advice from their solicitor, decide to make a prepared statement and offer it to the police instead of directly answering questions at interview. This is particularly common where the solicitor is concerned that the client will perform poorly in interview or if the client is particularly vulnerable. A prepared statement may be sparse or detailed, and usually sets out the suspect's position. The police will still ask the suspect questions even if a prepared statement has been read out, but a suspect will tend not to answer those questions if a prepared statement has been used.

In practice, a suspect may also offer a 'mixed comment' interview, by which they answer some questions but answer 'no comment' or remain silent for others.

Adverse inferences

We discuss the effect of adverse inferences in more detail in **Chapter 6**. However, it is important to understand the impact that legal advice may have. Simply put, a suspect may be liable to have inferences drawn from their silence at interview if they later rely on a fact in their defence at trial.

Legal advice to remain silent

If a suspect remains silent on the advice of a solicitor, but later relies on a fact at trial which was not mentioned, but was reasonable to mention when questioned under **caution** before or on charge, the suspect is not necessarily immune from having adverse inferences drawn. If the suspect genuinely relied on the advice of a solicitor to remain silent but had a good defence, inferences may not be drawn. If, however, the arbiter of fact (eg the magistrates or jury) takes the view that the reliance on legal advice was not genuine, but merely used by the suspect as a screen to hide the fact that they have no defence (or no defence that would stand up to scrutiny), inferences may be drawn.

Key term: caution

The police caution, contained in PACE 1984, Code C, must be administered on arrest and before every interview. The standard police caution is:

> You do not have to say anything. But it may harm your defence if you do not mention when questioned something which you later rely on in Court. Anything you do say may be given in evidence.

Whilst minor deviation from the wording is permitted, the substance of the caution must be understood by the suspect. The caution must also be explained in ordinary terms to the suspect who will be asked whether they understood the terms of the caution.

Prepared statements and adverse inferences

Similarly, where a suspect offers a prepared statement to the police, this will not negate the possibility for adverse inferences to be drawn. If a statement has been prepared and used, and a constable has asked a question which the statement does not address, but the suspect later advances a fact at trial which they rely on, and which could have been given in response to that original question, inferences may still be drawn.

PROCEDURE FOR INTERVIEWING A SUSPECT UNDER PACE 1984

The procedure for interrogating suspects is governed primarily by PACE 1984, Codes C and E. The police, or investigating authority, will initially **interview** a suspect to further their investigation.

> **Key term: interview**
>
> In criminal proceedings, an interview is defined in Code C as the 'questioning' of a person regarding their involvement or suspected involvement in a criminal offence, which must be carried out under caution.

'Off the record' comments are comments made by a suspect outside of the formal interview. Where a suspect does make such a comment, the police officer should make a written record of that comment, which should be signed and dated. The suspect should then be given an opportunity to read the written record and to sign it as being an accurate record of what was said. Many suspects will decline to sign such records.

Requirements of a lawful interview under PACE 1984 Code C

PACE Code C prescribes the requirements for a lawful interview. This includes when a suspect may be interviewed, where the interview must take place, how the interview is to be conducted, and when the interviewed must be ended. In this section, we shall consider some of the essential aspects of a lawful interview pursuant to Code C. Where relevant, we will quote sections of Code C, or make reference to particular provisions (though you will not be expected to remember these exact provisions in the SQE1 assessment).

Fitness to be interviewed

Before a suspect is interviewed, it is imperative that they are deemed fit for interview. A suspect is considered unfit to be interviewed if it appears that they are unable to:

- appreciate the significance of the questions which are put to them, or their answers to the questions, or
- understand what is happening due to the influence of drugs, alcohol, or any medical illness, ailment or condition.

Any concerns regarding a suspect's fitness to be interviewed should be noted in the custody record, and steps should be taken to ascertain a suspect's fitness for interview.

Where interviews may be conducted

If a police officer arrests a person, the arrest should not be delayed in order to question the suspect beforehand. Following an arrest, therefore, the suspect will be interviewed, which *must* take place at a police station or authorised place of detention unless the delay in taking the suspect to a police station or an authorised place of detention would likely:

- lead to interference with or harm to evidence connected with an offence, or interference with or physical harm to other persons, or serious loss of, or damage to, property
- lead to the alerting of other persons suspected of having committed an offence but not yet arrested for it, or
- hinder the recovery of property obtained in consequence of the commission of the offence.

Exam warning

If an interview takes place anywhere but a police station or authorised place of detention due to one of the factors mentioned, the interview *must* cease once the relevant risk has been averted or the necessary questions have been put forward to avert the risk. Look out for this in an MCQ.

Interview records

Code C details strict rules on records of interviews. In short, an accurate record must be made of each interview, whether held in a police station or not. The record must state the place of the interview, the time it begins and ends, any breaks in the interview, and the names of those persons present. This rule is distinct from the rules on recording of interviews (ie audio and video recordings) which are contained in PACE Codes E and F.

How interviews are to be conducted

The conduct of an interview is dictated by PACE 1984, Code C, and can be summarised as follows:

- Interview room: As far as practicable, interviews should take place in interview rooms which are adequately heated, lit and ventilated.
- Reminder of right to legal advice: Immediately prior to the start of an interview, and unless it has been delayed for a valid reason, the suspect is to be reminded of the right to free legal advice and that the interview can be delayed for the suspect to obtain legal advice; any violation of a suspect's right to legal advice may lead to any evidence being excluded.
- Commencement of interview and caution (see key term **caution,** above): The interviewing officer will then begin the interview and will first caution the suspect and explain the terms of the caution in ordinary language.
- In the case of voluntary interviews, the suspect must be informed that they are not under arrest and that they may terminate the interview at any time.
- **Significant statement or silence:** Following the caution, the interviewing officer will put to the suspect any significant statement or silence (if applicable). The interviewing officer must ask the suspect whether they confirm or deny that earlier statement or silence and if they want to add anything.

Key term: significant statement or silence

In some instances, a significant statement is a statement which the suspect made in the presence and hearing of a police officer or other police staff, which has not been put in the course of a previous interview, that may be capable of being used in evidence and a possible admission of guilt. For example, a suspect may explain on arrest that they attacked the complainant but claim that they acted in self-defence. Equally, significant silence occurs when the suspect fails or refuses to answer a question or answer satisfactorily when under caution.

- Nature of police questioning: Whilst there is no particular guidance on how interviews are to be conducted, no officer must:
  - attempt to obtain answers through oppression (see **Chapter 6**)
  - indicate what action the police will take in the event of a suspect refusing to answer a question or make a prepared statement, unless the suspect directly asks such a question.
- Breaks from interview: It is important to note that those in police custody should have eight hours' undisturbed rest between interviews. 'Undisturbed rest' in this context means free from questioning, travel, or any interruption in connection with the investigation concerned (generally at night time). There are exceptions to this rule, including where there are reasonable grounds for believing not delaying or interrupting the period would involve a risk of harm to people or serious loss of, or damage to, property; delay unnecessarily the person's release from custody; or otherwise prejudice the outcome of the investigation. Breaks from interviewing should be made at recognised meal times or at other times that take account of when the suspect last had a meal. Short refreshment breaks must be provided at approximately two-hour intervals. Where any interview is paused and then recommenced, the interviewing officer should remind the suspect of their legal rights (eg to take legal advice etc), and should remind them that they remain under caution.
- Cessation of interviews: Generally, interviews should cease to continue when the officer responsible for conducting the investigation is satisfied that all of the questions which are deemed relevant to obtaining accurate and reliable information about the offence have been put to the suspect. This should be approached in conjunction with the other evidence available, and with consideration of whether there is sufficient evidence to provide a realistic prospect of conviction.

The role and appropriate conduct by a defence legal representative/solicitor

The conduct of a solicitor during an interview is an important consideration. The solicitor primarily has an ethical duty to represent the best interests of their client. In doing so, they can, for example:

- request that the police disclose evidence mentioned in interview
- challenge an improper question, or the manner in which the question is put
- advise their client not to answer a question.

Role of the solicitor

When a suspect is to be interviewed, the solicitor has a number of key roles to undertake. These roles are presented in **Table 1.7** with some examples of their application.

Table 1.7: Role of a solicitor at the police station

Prepare to meet the client On arrival, the solicitor should request to view the custody record of the suspect, should seek disclosure of evidence relating to the case, and should then consult with the suspect. In seeking disclosure, the solicitor must be aware that the police will be unlikely to provide full disclosure of evidence prior to interview. The solicitor must factor this into their advice to the client.
Prepare the client for interview The solicitor will meet with the suspect in private. The solicitor will aim to build a rapport with the suspect, and discuss the offence with them. They will want to take the instructions of the suspect and understand their position in respect of the offence. In respect of the interview, the solicitor should explain (inter alia): • How the interview will be conducted (eg the use of audible recordings and the general structure) • The seating arrangements (ie that the solicitor will sit beside the client at a table, whilst the interviewing officer will sit facing the client and solicitor) • That the interview can be stopped (by the client or solicitor) if further legal advice is required • That the solicitor will intervene where necessary to protect the client's interests • That the police will often use tactics to get the client to talk and, as a result, that they should remain calm • That if the client has chosen to remain silent, they should use the phrase 'no comment' in response to police questions
Take an active role in the interview A solicitor should not be passive in an interview. PACE 1984, Code C, provides that the solicitor may intervene in order to seek clarification, challenge an improper question to their client or the manner in which it is put, advise their client not to reply to particular questions or if they wish to give their client further legal advice. The solicitor should make an opening statement at the start of every interview explaining their role and involvement in the interview.

Conduct of the solicitor

It is important to remember, however, that a solicitor must not conduct themselves in an interview in a way which prevents the proper putting of questions to a suspect, for example:

- answering questions on a client's behalf
- providing written replies for a client to quote.

If an officer of the rank of superintendent or above takes the view that a solicitor is misconducting themselves, they may require the solicitor to leave the interview, on the grounds that they are impeding the interview being carried out. The suspect, in this situation, must be provided with the opportunity to consult another solicitor before the interview continues. For a discussion of the conduct of a solicitor in criminal practice, please refer to *Revise SQE: Ethics and Professional Conduct*.

The role of an appropriate adult and who can be an appropriate adult

It is not uncommon for a solicitor to represent a **juvenile** or **vulnerable person**. These individuals will present additional challenges to the solicitor's role and it is important to appreciate how the conduct of a police interview will vary according to the client's circumstances.

Key term: juvenile

A juvenile is anyone who is under the age of 18. In addition, in the absence of any clear evidence of a suspect's actual age, if they appear to be under the age of 18, they shall be treated as a juvenile. A juvenile is also regarded as being vulnerable (see below).

Key term: vulnerable person

An individual is treated as being vulnerable if because of a mental health condition or disorder:

- they may have difficulty understanding or communicating effectively about the full implications for them of any procedures and processes
- they do not appear to understand the significance of what they are told, of questions they are asked or of their replies
- they appear to be particularly prone to becoming confused and unclear about their position, providing unreliable, misleading or incriminating information without knowing or wishing to do so, accepting or acting on suggestions from others without consciously knowing, or wishing to do so, or readily agreeing to suggestions or proposals without any protest or question.

A juvenile or vulnerable person must not be interviewed regarding their involvement or suspected involvement in a criminal offence or offences, or asked to provide or sign a written statement under caution or record of interview, in the absence of an **appropriate adult**.

Key term: appropriate adult

An appropriate adult is an individual who generally must be present to safeguard the rights, welfare and entitlement of juveniles or vulnerable persons.

Who can be an appropriate adult?

Table 1.8 sets out who could, or could not, be considered an appropriate adult. As will be evident from **Table 1.8**, the law prescribes a hierarchical order that the police should follow when identifying the appropriate adult (see **Practice example 1.4**).

Table 1.8: Appropriate adults

Who can be an appropriate adult	Who cannot be an appropriate adult
For juveniles (a) Parents or guardians (or representatives from the local authority if the juvenile is in local authority care) (b) If not (a), then, a social worker from the local authority (c) If not (a) or (b), then, some other responsible adult aged 18 or over who is not connected to the police (eg a grandparent)	**Anyone who** • Is suspected of being involved in the suspected offence • Is a victim or a witness in the alleged offence • Is involved in the investigation (eg a police officer/police employee) • Has received admissions from the suspect before acting as an appropriate adult (this also applies to social workers and members of the Youth Offending Team)
For vulnerable persons (a) A relative, guardian or other person responsible for their care or custody (b) If not (a), then, someone experienced in dealing with vulnerable persons but who is not connected to the police (eg employed by the police) (c) If not (a) or (b), then, some other responsible adult aged 18 or over	• Is a solicitor representing the juvenile/vulnerable person • Is an estranged parent (if the juvenile/vulnerable person does not wish them to attend)

Practice example 1.4

James, a 16-year-old, is arrested on suspicion of assaulting his uncle, occasioning actual bodily harm, contrary to s 47 Offences Against the Person Act 1861. James' mother and aunt witnessed the alleged assault. James is taken to the police station. On arrival, the custody officer informed James of his rights, and asked for his age. James, being stubborn, refused to answer. As he appeared to be under the age of 18, the custody officer started to make arrangements for an appropriate adult to attend the police station. James is estranged from his father and informs the custody officer that he does not want him contacted. The solicitor, who also happens to be a close family friend of James, is on her way.

What action should the custody officer take in selecting an appropriate adult?

It is likely that the custody officer will initially ask James if there is anyone who could act as an appropriate adult. James' mother cannot be an appropriate adult as she witnessed the alleged assault, and for the same reason, nor can James' aunt. As James is estranged from his father, and James has made an express request not to contact him, the custody officer must not call James' father. Whilst James' solicitor is a family friend, she cannot act as an appropriate adult because she is acting as James' solicitor. As the uncle is the complainant, he cannot be an appropriate adult. If James does not provide the police with the contact details of anyone who could be an appropriate adult, it is likely that a social worker from the local authority would be contacted.

Role of the appropriate adult

An appropriate adult should not believe their role is simply to observe the interview take place; they should take an active role in assisting the suspect. PACE 1984, Code C, provides that an appropriate adult is generally expected, amongst other things, to:

- support, advise and assist the juvenile or vulnerable person in accordance with a PACE Code when they are required to provide information or participate in a procedure
- observe whether the police are acting properly and fairly, and to inform an officer of the rank of inspector or above if they consider that they are not
- assist detainees to communicate with the police whilst respecting their right not to say anything unless they want to
- help them to understand their rights and ensure that those rights are protected and respected.

Ethics and professional conduct

Be aware that an appropriate adult is not subject to the duty of confidential or legal professional privilege, like a solicitor is. Therefore, legal advice should generally be given in the absence of the appropriate adult.

■ KEY POINT CHECKLIST

This chapter has covered the following key knowledge points. You can use these to structure your revision, ensuring you recall the key details for each point, as covered in this chapter.

- Suspects under investigation reserve the right to have someone informed of their arrest, and the right to legal advice. These rights can only be delayed, not extinguished.
- The police have limited powers in authorising further detention. Once the police have exhausted their powers, any further extensions may only be authorised by the magistrates' court by means of a warrant.

- Identification procedures must only be carried out when the relevant criteria are satisfied. In any other case, a procedure may be carried out if the police deem it necessary.
- A client must appreciate the relative strengths and weaknesses of answering police questions and the consequences if they exercise their right to remain silent.
- An appropriate adult must be present when the police detain a juvenile or vulnerable person.
- Interviews should cease when all questions deemed necessary for obtaining relevant and accurate information have been put to the suspect, not necessarily answered.

■ KEY TERMS AND CONCEPTS

- custody officer (**page 2**)
- custody record (**page 3**)
- PACE Codes (**page 4**)
- PACE 1984, Code C (**page 4**)
- Defence Solicitor Call Centre (**page 5**)
- relevant time (**page 8**)
- detention reviews (**page 12**)
- identification procedure (**page 13**)
- PACE 1984, Code D (**page 14**)
- known and available (**page 15**)
- identification officer (**page 18**)
- right to silence (**page 20**)
- prepared statement (**page 20**)
- caution (**page 21**)
- interview (**page 22**)
- significant statement or silence (**page 24**)
- juvenile (**page 26**)
- vulnerable person (**page 26**)
- appropriate adult (**page 26**)

■ SQE1-STYLE QUESTIONS

QUESTION 1

A girl, aged 16, is arrested on suspicion of theft, contrary to s 1 Theft Act 1968, and is taken to a police station. On arrival, the custody officer books her in and opens a custody record. The custody officer asks the girl how old she is and who she lives with and informs her of her rights. The girl tells the custody officer that the only family she is aware of is her father, who she has not seen for five years, and that she is in the care of the local authority. The girl expressly informs the custody officer that she does not want her father involved. The girl asks to consult with a solicitor and insists that she wants to be interviewed immediately because she wants to go home.

Which of the following best describes the actions the custody officer should take?

A. The custody officer may arrange for an appropriate adult to attend the police station before interviewing the girl. As the girl has identified that she is in local authority care, her social worker or a representative of the local authority must be contacted. The girl must not be interviewed until the appropriate adult arrives and she has consulted with her solicitor.

B. The custody officer must arrange for an appropriate adult to attend the police station before interviewing the girl. As the girl has identified her father, he must act as the appropriate adult and attend the police station. The girl must not be interviewed until her father arrives and she has consulted with her solicitor.

C. The custody officer must arrange for an appropriate adult to attend the police station before interviewing the girl. As the girl has identified that she is in local authority care, her social worker or a representative of the local authority must be contacted. The girl must not be interviewed until the appropriate adult arrives and she has consulted with her solicitor.

D. The custody officer must arrange for an appropriate adult to attend the police station before interviewing the girl. The solicitor is able to act as an appropriate adult, and when the solicitor attends the police station, the girl must be able to consult with them in private.

E. The custody officer may arrange for an appropriate adult to attend the police station before interviewing the girl. As the girl has identified that she is in local authority care, her social worker or a representative of the local authority must be contacted. The girl may be interviewed before her solicitor and appropriate adult arrives if an officer of the rank of inspector or above is satisfied that the relevant conditions are met.

QUESTION 2

A woman is arrested on suspicion of common assault and is taken to an authorised place of detention. The woman did not say a great deal to the arresting officer but indicates that she may have acted in self-defence. At the scene, a witness claims to have seen the alleged assault, and even though they were standing at a distance, would recognise the suspect given the opportunity; a statement has been given to this effect. The woman, who is yet to be interviewed, is consulting with her solicitor, and the police are considering the appropriate course of action regarding an identification procedure.

Which of the following best describes the actions the police should take regarding carrying out an identification procedure?

A. The police must carry out an identification procedure, as a witness claims that they can identify the suspect who allegedly committed the assault and has not yet been given the opportunity to do so, and the identity of the suspect may be disputed.

B. The police may carry out an identification procedure but should wait until they have interviewed the woman. Whilst there is a witness who claims that they can identify the suspect who allegedly committed the assault and has not yet been given the opportunity to do so, the issue of identity may not be in dispute.

C. The police must carry out an identification procedure but must wait until they have interviewed the woman. Whilst there is a witness who claims that they can identify the suspect who allegedly committed the assault and has not yet been given the opportunity to do so, the issue of identity may not be in dispute.

D. The police must not carry out an identification procedure before the suspect is interviewed. There is a witness who claims that they can identify the suspect who allegedly committed the assault and has not yet been given the opportunity to do so, and as there is the potential for identity to be disputed, a procedure must be carried out.

E. The police may not carry out an identification procedure after the woman has been interviewed. As the witness has already provided a statement to the police purporting to recognise the woman, this is sufficient identification evidence and it is likely that the identification officer would conclude that it is unnecessary for a procedure to go ahead.

QUESTION 3

A woman is arrested on suspicion of murder. On arrival at the police station, the woman had her detention authorised by the custody officer. The woman confirmed that she wanted to speak to a solicitor, and the police waited until the solicitor arrived. The woman was very nervous and had never been in trouble with the police before. The solicitor spoke to the woman in private and requested disclosure of the evidence which the police had obtained. Before interview, the solicitor advised the woman to remain silent, which she did after trusting the solicitor. The woman is later charged and pleads not guilty. The woman gives evidence at trial and puts forward evidence not previously relied upon in response to police questioning. The woman is now concerned about the impact of any adverse inferences.

Which of the following best describes the position regarding whether adverse inferences will be drawn from the woman's silence during police questioning?

A. As the woman relied on the advice of the solicitor to remain silent, adverse inferences must not be drawn. There is no need to show that reliance on the advice was genuine, as remaining silent on legal advice is a permitted exception.

B. As the woman relied on the advice of the solicitor to remain silent, adverse inferences may not be drawn. If the jury are satisfied that reliance on the solicitor's advice was genuine, inferences may not be drawn.
C. As the woman remained silent at interview before charge, but put forward a positive defence at trial, inferences must be drawn irrespective of reliance on legal advice.
D. As the woman relied on the advice of the solicitor to remain silent, adverse inferences may not be drawn. If the trial judge is satisfied that the reliance on the solicitor's advice was genuine, inferences may not be drawn.
E. As the woman remained silent at interview before charge, but put forward a positive defence at trial, inferences must not be drawn irrespective of reliance on legal advice.

QUESTION 4

A man is arrested on suspicion of assault occasioning actual bodily harm, contrary to s 47 Offences Against the Person Act 1861. On arrest, the man was cautioned, and understood the caution. The man was interviewed, and then released on bail, still subject to investigation. The police obtained evidence from an eyewitness who claims that they could recognise the person who they believe committed the offence and gave a description which was similar to the man's appearance. The police asked whether the man would consent to an identification procedure. The man, who protests his innocence and denies any involvement, lives 20 minutes away from the police station and says that he will get to the police station as soon as he can.

Which of the following best describes the man's status for an identification procedure?

A. The man would be considered as known and unavailable, as whilst he is known to the police, he is not immediately available to participate in the identification procedure.
B. The man would be considered as known but unavailable, as whilst he is known to the police, he is not available within a reasonably short time to participate in the identification procedure.
C. The man would be considered as not known and available, as whilst he is reasonably available within a short period of time, he has not been positively identified by name. Therefore, his identity is not known to the police.
D. The man would be considered as known and available, as he is known to the police, willing to participate in the identification procedure and will be accessible within a reasonably short time.
E. The man would be considered as known and available, but as the eyewitness has given a detailed description of the alleged offender

to the police, there is no requirement to carry out an identification procedure.

QUESTION 5

A man is arrested at his home on suspicion of burglary, contrary to s 9 Theft Act 1968. The man is taken to an authorised place of detention and is booked into custody at 19:00 (7 PM). The man requested legal advice and consulted a solicitor before being interviewed. At the 24-hour period, an extension of 12 hours was granted for further detention. There are six hours left until the man will need to be charged or released, but the officers in the case are pursuing a new line of enquiry and seek to detain the man further.

Which of the following best describes the most appropriate course of action to detain the man further?

A. Authorisation for further detention can only be given by the magistrates' court, either with a single district judge or two lay magistrates, who may grant the police's request. The police will need to ensure that the application is listed and granted before the current 36-hour period expires.

B. Authorisation for further detention can only be given by an officer of the rank of superintendent or above, who is responsible for the station where the man is being held. The police will need to ensure that the extension is granted before the current 36-hour period expires.

C. Authorisation for further detention can only be given by the magistrates' court, either with a single district judge or two lay magistrates, who must grant the police's request. The police will need to ensure that the application is listed and granted before the current 36-hour period expires.

D. Authorisation for further detention can only be given by an officer of the rank of superintendent or above, who is responsible for the station where the man is being held. The police will need to ensure that the extension is granted after the current 36-hour period expires.

E. Authorisation for further detention can only be given by the magistrates' court, either with a single district judge or two lay magistrates, who may grant the police's request. The police will need to ensure that the application is listed before the expiry of the 36-hour period, but the magistrates' court may grant the extension after the expiry of the 36-hour period.

■ ANSWERS TO QUESTIONS

Answers to 'What do you know already?' questions at the start of the chapter

1) False. All suspects are entitled to free legal advice, but the advice is not always in person; suspects who are detained on suspicion of committing

an offence which is not punishable by imprisonment may receive free telephone advice.

2) Video identification procedure. This is where eyewitnesses are shown various images, including one of the suspect.
3) False. Suspects, who later become defendants, are not *automatically* immune from having adverse inferences drawn by simply claiming that they relied on legal advice to remain silent. If the arbiter of fact is satisfied that reliance on the advice was genuine, then inferences may not be drawn.
4) The police should first attempt to make contact with the parents or guardians of the juvenile (or representatives from the local authority if the juvenile is in local authority care). Failing that, the police should identify a social worker from the local authority to act as the appropriate adult. Failing that, the police should identify some other responsible adult aged 18 or over who is not connected to the police.

Answers to end-of-chapter SQE1-style questions

Question 1

The correct answer was C. This is because the police must contact an appropriate adult for the girl, and, as she has identified that she is in local authority care, the most appropriate individual would be a local authority representative. Options A and E are wrong because this is an instance where the police *must* obtain an appropriate adult; it is not optional. Option B is wrong because an estranged parent is not necessarily considered an appropriate adult. Option D is also wrong because solicitors are prohibited from acting as an appropriate adult when they are representing the juvenile or vulnerable person in their professional capacity.

Question 2

The correct answer was B. This is because at present, the issue of identity may not be in dispute (as the woman appears to be claiming self-defence). Before this is confirmed in interview, there is nothing compelling the police at this stage to carry out an identity procedure; therefore, option A is wrong. Option C is wrong because reliance on legal advice may prevent inferences being drawn where a fact was not mentioned before or on charge but was at trial. Option D is also wrong because whilst it would be practical to wait until the interview has concluded, there is nothing compelling the police to carry out a procedure after an interview. Option E is wrong because whilst the police retain the right not to hold an identity procedure if there is little purpose, that is not the case here, and the conditions *requiring* the police to carry out a procedure are satisfied.

Question 3

The correct answer was B. This is because if the woman's reliance on the advice was genuine, then inferences may not be drawn. However, there is nothing which says that inferences *must* not be drawn (therefore option C is wrong); it is for the arbiter of fact (in this case, the jury) to decide if the reliance was genuine. Option A is wrong because the woman will need to demonstrate that her reliance was genuine. Option D is wrong because the issue of reliance is for the jury, not the judge. Option E is wrong as it completely misrepresents the law relating to adverse inferences.

Question 4

The correct answer was D. This is because the correct term for a suspect who is known to the police and is willing and able to take part in an identity procedure is 'known and available'. Options A and B are wrong because a suspect is considered 'available' if they are immediately available or will be within a reasonably short time. Option C is wrong because the man is considered 'known' for these purposes. Option E is also wrong because there is a requirement to carry out an identity procedure in these circumstances.

Question 5

The correct answer was A. This is because the police have exhausted their powers of granting an extension to the period of detention, and the magistrates' court are the only body able to grant a further extension. The application must be listed and heard before the 36 hours expire; therefore, option E is wrong. The magistrates' court cannot extend custody time limits after the period expires. As previously mentioned, the police have exhausted their extension powers; therefore, options B and D are wrong. Option C is also wrong because the courts are not compelled to grant an extension; they *may* grant an extension if they consider the relevant criteria are satisfied.

■ KEY CASES, RULES, STATUTES AND INSTRUMENTS

The SQE1 Assessment Specification has identified that candidates are required to know and be able to use:

- PACE 1984, Code C
- PACE 1984, Code D.

The SQE1 Assessment Specification does not require you to know any case names, or statutory materials, for the topic of advising clients, including vulnerable clients, about the procedure and processes at the police station.

2

Bail applications

■ MAKE SURE YOU KNOW

This chapter will cover the procedures and processes involved in bail applications. For the purposes of SQE1, you are required to know:

- the right to bail and exceptions
- conditional bail
- procedure for applying for and opposing bail
- further applications for bail
- appeals against decisions on bail
- absconding and breaches of bail.

■ SQE ASSESSMENT ADVICE

As you work through this chapter, remember to pay particular attention in your revision to:

- the presumption in favour of bail, and when that presumption does not apply
- conditions that may be imposed on the granting of bail
- consequences of failing to comply with any bail conditions, or failing to surrender having been granted bail.

■ WHAT DO YOU KNOW ALREADY?

Have a go at these questions before reading this chapter. If you find some difficult or cannot remember the answers, make a note to look more closely at that area during your revision.

1) Fill in the blank: The right to bail does not exist post-conviction except where _____________.

   [Exceptions to the right to bail, page 41]

2) A defendant has been granted bail in the Crown Court. What right to appeal does the prosecution have against the grant of bail?

   [Appeals against decisions on bail, page 54]

3) True or false? A defendant who breaches their bail conditions is guilty of a criminal offence.

   [Absconding and breaches of bail, page 56]

4) Conditions may only be imposed on bail where it is 'necessary' to do what? **[Conditional bail, page 47]**

INTRODUCTION TO BAIL APPLICATIONS

The topic of **bail** is an unavoidable one in the criminal justice system. It is unlikely that any case, either in the magistrates' courts (except in GAP (guilty anticipated plea) courts) or the Crown Court, will be concluded at the first hearing (see **Chapter 3**). As a result, a decision is required as to whether the defendant should be remanded in custody (ie held in prison until their hearing/trial), or released on bail. That is the focus of this chapter.

Key term: bail

Bail refers to the situation where a defendant will remain out of custody whilst they await trial. Bail may be granted with conditions that have to be met, or without conditions. Bail must be distinguished from being remanded in custody.

Given that the SQE1 Assessment Specification refers to 'bail applications' it is doubtful that police bail will be assessed on SQE1. For that reason, police bail is not considered in this guide.

Remands

We must first consider the notion of a **remand**.

Key term: remand

A remand is a decision to adjourn (postpone) a case and dictate what will happen with the defendant. A remand decision will be necessary where a case is part-heard (eg a trial lasting numerous days), where the defendant is committed to the Crown Court for trial or sentence (see **Chapter 7**), where the court has adjourned for pre-sentence reports following a guilty plea or conviction (see **Chapter 8**) or where a case is appealed from the magistrates' court to the Crown Court (see **Chapter 9**).

A court, therefore, has two choices when it comes to a remand decision:
- remand the defendant in custody
- remand the defendant on bail (either conditionally or unconditionally).

Remand time limits

If the court chooses to remand a defendant in custody, time limits are set on the period of remand. These time limits are dependent on whether the decision is made before or after conviction and **Table 2.1** sets out these time periods.

Table 2.1: Time limits on remand

Pre-conviction
Three clear days in custody to a police constable
Eight clear days in custody to prison
28 clear days in custody to a prison where: • the next stage of proceedings is fixed to occur within that time • the defendant at the time of remand is before the court, and • the defendant has previously been remanded in custody by the court in the proceedings
28 clear days in custody to prison if the defendant is already serving a custodial sentence
Post-conviction
Three weeks in custody for enquiries or reports for sentencing
Four weeks on bail

Each of these periods is the maximum duration for a single remand. At the conclusion of the remand, the defendant will be produced before the magistrates' court, which may again remand them on bail or in custody.

Custody time limits

In addition to remand time limits, solicitors must also be aware of **custody time limits** that apply to defendants in criminal proceedings.

Key term: custody time limit

Custody time limit refers to the maximum amount of time that an individual may be remanded in custody during the progress of a criminal trial. These limits are designed to ensure that cases will be expedited where the defendant is in custody.

The custody time limits are as such (see **Chapter 3** for definitions):

- 56 days for summary only offences (from first appearance to trial)
- 70 days for cases sent to the Crown Court (from first appearance in the magistrates' court to committal (ie sending) to the Crown Court)
- 70 days for either way offences being tried in the magistrates' court (from first appearance to trial). This is reduced to 56 days if an allocation hearing is held within the first 56 days
- 182 days for indictable only offences sent to the Crown Court (from sending to arraignment (see **Chapter 5**) in the Crown Court).

The prosecution can apply for the deadline to be extended. To do so, it must show, on the balance of probabilities, that there is good and sufficient cause for the extension and that it has acted with due diligence and expedition. Once the time period has elapsed, the defendant *must* be released on bail pending their trial.

Revision tip

Always keep remand periods and custody time limits in your mind when considering an application for bail. If a defendant is remanded into custody, keep in mind the next time that they will be brought before the courts and when the next bail application may be made.

Now that we understand remands generally, including time limits, let us consider the right to bail.

THE RIGHT TO BAIL

Let us start with the general rule: A defendant charged with a criminal offence has a prima facie **right to bail**.

Key term: right to bail

Whilst it is more accurate to say that a rebuttable presumption in favour of bail exists for all persons charged with a criminal offence, it is common to say that there is a 'prima facie right to bail' (ie from the outset, there is a presumption of bail).

The right to bail applies to all persons, subject to a number of exclusions and exceptions; see **Table 2.2**.

Table 2.2: Exclusions and exceptions to the right to bail

Terminology	Explanation
Exclusion	This term is often used to describe the circumstances where the right to bail does not apply. 'Exclusion' is therefore used to demonstrate the circumstances where there is no right to bail
Exception	This term is used to describe the circumstances where the defendant *need not* be granted bail if there is a reason to refuse bail. The term 'exception' is therefore used when dealing with the grounds for refusing bail

We shall consider the exclusions to bail here, and the exceptions to bail in the next section.

Exclusions to the right to bail

There are a number of circumstances in which the presumption in favour of bail is removed. We shall deal with these in turn.

Following conviction

Where a defendant has been convicted of an offence, the right to bail ceases to exist. This is the case whether the defendant is convicted after trial, or enters a guilty plea, and applies equally in both the magistrates' court and the Crown Court. This means that a defendant who seeks to appeal against their conviction or sentence has no right to bail. Furthermore, a defendant who has been committed for sentence to the Crown Court following conviction in the magistrates' court has no right to bail.

It is important to note, however, that there is a proviso to this exception. The right to bail still remains where a defendant has been convicted of an offence but sentence has been adjourned by the court for the purpose of enabling inquiries or a report to be made to assist the court in dealing with the defendant for the offence. Therefore, where a defendant has been convicted for an offence and the court adjourns the case for a pre-sentence report, or psychological report in preparation for sentence, the presumption in favour of bail still remains.

Exam warning

An MCQ may seek to test your knowledge of when the right to bail is lost following conviction. Make sure you are not tricked into thinking that a defendant loses the right to bail immediately upon conviction; if their case is adjourned for a report for sentence, the right to bail remains.

The right to bail also applies to a defendant who is before the court having allegedly breached a requirement of their community order. However, the right does not exist for a defendant allegedly in breach of a suspended sentence order.

Homicide or rape cases if there is a previous conviction

The right to bail does not exist where the defendant:

- is charged with, or convicted of, murder, attempted murder, manslaughter, rape or attempted rape, and
- has previously been convicted of any of these offences.

In this circumstance, bail shall only be granted if the court is of the opinion that there are 'exceptional circumstances' justifying the grant of bail. This restriction only applies in manslaughter cases where the previous conviction resulted in a sentence of imprisonment.

Murder cases specifically

A further exclusion exists in respect of defendants charged with murder (in addition to the exclusion above). In cases of murder, bail may not be granted unless the court is satisfied that there is 'no significant risk' that, if released on bail, the defendant would commit an offence that would be likely to cause physical or mental injury to another person.

In cases of murder, only a Crown Court judge may grant bail; magistrates do not have the power to do so. As we will learn in **Chapter 3**, a defendant charged with murder will be sent 'forthwith' (ie immediately) to the Crown Court. A Crown Court judge must make a decision about bail as soon as reasonably practicable and, in any event, within the period of 48 hours beginning the day after the defendant appears or is brought before the magistrates' court (this 48-hour period excludes weekends, bank holidays and public holidays).

EXCEPTIONS TO THE RIGHT TO BAIL

The exceptions to the right to bail are listed in Schedule 1 Bail Act (BA) 1976. Whilst you are not required to know the BA 1976 for SQE1, you are highly advised to read Schedule 1 in full. The exceptions are defined according to the type of offence that the defendant is charged with, in particular:

- defendants accused or convicted of indictable imprisonable offences
- defendants accused or convicted of summary only imprisonable offences
- defendants accused or convicted of non-imprisonable offences.

Revision tip

If you keep the following simple list of questions in your mind, you should have little difficulty dealing with an MCQ on bail:

- Is there a right to bail (ie no exclusions)?
- What kind of offence is the defendant charged with? (This will determine your exceptions.)
- Are any of those exceptions made out? (Use the statutory factors to determine this.)
- Can any conditions be imposed to persuade the court to grant bail?

We shall consider each exception in turn before then considering the statutory factors.

Defendants accused or convicted of indictable imprisonable offences

This first heading applies in circumstances where the defendant is charged with, or convicted of, an indictable offence which is punishable by imprisonment. As we discuss in **Chapter 3**, an 'indictable' offence includes offences that are triable only on indictment, and offences triable either way. There are a number of exceptions that we must consider under this heading.

No real prospects test

Before we consider the exceptions to bail, it is important to note that a limitation exists in respect of *some* of the exceptions (see **Table 2.3**, below). Unless this limitation is met, the exceptions to bail will not apply (meaning that the prosecution cannot oppose bail using those exceptions, and the court cannot rely on their exceptions to withhold bail). Those exceptions to bail will not apply where:

- the defendant has attained the age of 18, and
- it appears to the court that there is no real prospect that the defendant will be sentenced to a custodial sentence (ie a term of imprisonment - see **Chapter 8**), other than a suspended sentence, in the proceedings.

Revision tip

Given that this limitation involves consideration of whether imprisonment is a likely sentence, a defence solicitor must be knowledgeable of the relevant sentencing guidelines and be prepared to make submissions on this during a bail application.

Risk of absconding, further offences or interference with witnesses

This is the most common ground upon which bail is opposed. In these cases, the defendant need not be granted bail if the court is satisfied that there are 'substantial grounds for believing' that the defendant, if released on bail (conditionally or not) would:

- fail to surrender to custody
- commit an offence whilst on bail, or
- interfere with witnesses or otherwise obstruct the course of justice.

Exam warning

This exception contains a relatively high threshold: the court must be satisfied that there are *substantial grounds* for believing that the defendant *would* do any of those things listed. This threshold will not be met where the court believes that the defendant *may* or *might* do any of those things. Look out for this wording in an MCQ.

Harm to an associated person

The defendant need not be granted bail if the court is satisfied that there are substantial grounds for believing that the defendant, if released on bail (whether conditionally or not), would commit an offence whilst on bail by engaging in conduct that would, or would be likely to, cause:

- physical or mental injury to an **associated person**, or
- an associated person to fear physical or mental injury.

Key term: associated person

For the purposes of this exception, an associated person includes a current or former spouse/civil partner, cohabitant, parent or someone with parental responsibility.

Offence committed whilst on bail

The defendant need not be granted bail if it appears to the court that the defendant committed the offence whilst they were on bail. This exception would apply where the defendant is, for example, on bail in connection with a charge of theft, and is subsequently charged with an unrelated offence whilst on bail.

Their own protection

The defendant need not be granted bail if the court is satisfied that the defendant should be kept in custody for their own protection or, if they are a child or young person, for their own welfare.

Already serving a custodial sentence

The defendant need not be granted bail if they are already serving a custodial sentence.

Arrested for absconding

The defendant need not be granted bail if, having previously been released on bail in, or in connection with, the proceedings, the defendant has been arrested for absconding or breaking conditions of bail.

Not practicable

The final exceptions apply:

- where it is not practicable to obtain sufficient information for the purpose of determining bail because of the shortness of time since proceedings began against the defendant, or
- where a case is adjourned for inquiries or a report, it is impracticable to complete inquiries or make a report without keeping the defendant in custody.

Summarising exceptions for indictable imprisonable offences

Given the complexity involved in these exceptions, **Table 2.3** summarises the law in a revision-friendly format, including when the limitation listed above applies. **Practice example 2.1** provides you with an example of the exceptions in operation.

Table 2.3: Exceptions to the right to bail for indictable imprisonable offences

Exception	Limitation applies?
Risk of absconding, further offences or interference with witnesses	✓
Harm to an associated person	×
Offence committed whilst on bail	✓
The defendant's own protection	×
Already serving a custodial sentence	×
Arrested for absconding	✓
Not practicable to bail	×

Practice example 2.1

James is charged with assault occasioning actual bodily harm, contrary to s 47 Offences Against the Person Act 1861. Before the first hearing, James visits the houses of different potential witnesses, attempting to persuade them not to give evidence, to the extent where reports have been made to the police. During the police investigation, James also made passing comments, stating that he will 'go after' the complainant before the trial. James is now brought before the magistrates, who are about to hear a contested bail application.

What course of action is the prosecutor likely to take?

Here, the prosecution will object to bail being granted, as the application is contested. Through James visiting potential witnesses, trying to persuade them not to give evidence and making comments to the police that he will 'go after' the complainant, the prosecutor will likely argue that these occurrences constitute *substantial grounds* for refusing bail. This is because the prosecutor will submit that James need not be granted bail because, if released, James would interfere with witnesses and/or commit further offences. The court, in refusing bail, does not need to be satisfied that it is *inevitable* that James will do what the prosecutor alleges; merely that there are *substantial grounds to believe* that he would.

Statutory factors

When the court is making a decision as to whether there are substantial grounds for denying bail, they *must* take into account any of the statutory factors (ie factors within the BA 1976) that appear to be relevant. These factors are laid out in **Table 2.4** with some explanations and examples to support them.

Table 2.4: Statutory factors

Factor	Explanation and examples
The nature and seriousness of the offence and the probable method of dealing with the defendant for it	The more serious the offence, the greater risk of a custodial sentence and greater risk the defendant will abscond
The defendant's character, antecedents, associations and community ties	Bad character (see **Chapter 6**) is admissible in bail hearings. Community ties include the defendant's family circumstances, residence, employment and other relevant factors

Table 2.4: (continued)

Factor	Explanation and examples
The fact that the defendant: (i) is pregnant, (ii) is the primary carer for another person, or (iii) has been the victim of an offence which involved behaviour by the offender amounting to domestic abuse.	This provision reflects the Government's ambitions to reduce the number of women going to prison. This provision represents common sense and factors that the court would ordinarily have considered in any event. However, they have been placed onto a statutory footing, ensuring that the court must consider these factors.
The strength of the evidence against the defendant (not relevant if already convicted)	The defence may contend that the prosecution's case is weak and thus there is no justification for refusing bail
The defendant's previous record on bail	Has the defendant previously complied with their bail conditions or obligations? Has the defendant previously failed to surrender?
Risk of harm to any person	If the court is satisfied that there are substantial grounds for believing that the defendant, if released on bail (conditionally or not), would commit an offence whilst on bail, the risk that the defendant may do so by engaging in conduct that would, or would be likely to, cause physical or mental injury to any person other than the defendant
Any other relevant factor	Relevant factors may include, for example, misuse of drugs

Defendants accused or convicted of summary only imprisonable offences

This second heading applies in circumstances where the defendant is charged with, or convicted of, a summary only offence which is punishable by imprisonment. As we discuss in **Chapter 3**, a 'summary only offence' refers to offences that can only be tried in the magistrates' court.

The exceptions under this heading are broadly similar to the above circumstance, but the criteria used are slightly different. The same limitation noted above applies to a number of the exceptions.

Under this heading, a defendant need not be granted bail if:

- they have previously been granted bail, failed to surrender and the court believes that they would fail to surrender to custody once more if released on bail (limitation applies)
- they were on bail on the date of the alleged offence and there are substantial grounds for believing that they would commit an offence if released on bail (limitation applies)
- the court is satisfied that there are substantial grounds for believing that the defendant would commit an offence on bail by engaging in conduct that would be likely to cause physical or mental injury to an associated person (or cause them to fear such physical or mental injury)
- they should be kept in custody for their own protection
- they were already serving a custodial sentence
- they have been arrested for absconding or breaching bail conditions and there are substantial grounds for believing that they would fail to surrender, commit an offence, interfere with witnesses or otherwise obstruct the course of justice if released on bail (limitation applies), or
- it is not practicable to obtain sufficient information for the purpose of determining bail because of the shortness of time since proceedings began against the defendant.

Defendants accused or convicted of non-imprisonable offences

This list of exceptions applies when a defendant is charged solely with an offence that is not punishable with imprisonment (eg something that can only be punished by way of a non-custodial penalty, such as a fine, discharge, or community order). Under this heading, a defendant need not be granted bail if:

- they have been convicted of the offence, have previously been granted bail and failed to surrender and the court believes that they would fail to surrender to custody once more if released on bail
- they should be kept in custody for their own protection
- they were already serving a custodial sentence
- they have been convicted of an offence, have been arrested for absconding or breaching bail conditions and there are substantial grounds for believing that they would fail to surrender, commit an offence, interfere with witnesses or otherwise obstruct the course of justice if released on bail, or
- they have been arrested for absconding or breaching bail conditions and there are substantial grounds for believing that they would commit an offence on bail by engaging in conduct that would be likely to cause physical or mental injury to an associated person (or cause them to fear such physical or mental injury).

Exam warning

Whilst there are no offences in the SQE1 Assessment Specification which are non-imprisonable, the SQE may still seek to test your knowledge on these exceptions by general reference to a non-imprisonable offence, as opposed to naming the offence. Do not overlook these exceptions simply because there are no non-imprisonable offences in the specification.

Revision tip

Draw yourself a table and divide it into the three classifications of offences covered in this chapter. Under each heading, focus on the key wording of the exceptions so that you can identify the subtle differences between them and avoid any mistakes in an MCQ.

Granting bail

If the court is of the view that the defendant does not pose a real risk in respect of any of the exceptions to the general right to bail, the court shall grant the defendant **unconditional bail**.

Key term: unconditional bail

The defendant is released on bail without being subject to any conditions, other than to surrender to the court at a time and place specified in their bail.

If, however, the court is not satisfied of such, the defence may attempt to reassure the court through the use of bail conditions; the court may thus grant **conditional bail**.

Key term: conditional bail

The court is entitled to grant bail to the defendant subject to one or more conditions. These conditions may *only* be imposed where it appears to the court that it is necessary to do so:

- to prevent the defendant from absconding
- to prevent them from committing further offences whilst on bail
- to ensure they do not interfere with witnesses or obstruct the course of justice
- for their own protection, or
- to ensure they make themselves available to enable inquiries or a report to be made to assist the court in sentencing.

We shall consider conditional bail in the next section.

CONDITIONAL BAIL

As noted above, in many circumstances the court will not be satisfied that the defendant does not pose a real risk to any of the exceptions to the right to bail. To allay its concerns, the court may choose to impose one or more conditions on the defendant's grant of bail. As the **Key term** above makes clear, the court may only impose conditions as are 'necessary' to allay its concerns.

Common conditions of bail

The most common conditions imposed are identified in **Table 2.5** with an explanation and examples of their use.

Table 2.5: Bail conditions

Condition	Explanation	Designed to allay what concerns?
Surety	A surety is a person who accepts that if the defendant fails to attend, they will be liable to forfeit a specified sum of money (known as a 'recognisance'). If the defendant fails to attend, the court may order full or partial forfeit of the specified sum. In considering the suitability of a surety, the court will consider the surety's financial resources, their character and any previous convictions and their proximity (whether in point of kinship, place of residence or otherwise) to the defendant. A surety is usually a friend or relative of the defendant; a solicitor should *never* act as a surety for their client.	• Risk of absconding
Security	A condition that the defendant deposit money or other goods as a 'security' for being released on bail. If the defendant fails to surrender, their security will be forfeited.	• Risk of absconding
Residence	A condition that the defendant be required to live and sleep at a specified address. Police will visit the address at random points in the day to monitor compliance. Residence may be set to a bail or probation hostel. The court may monitor compliance with this requirement through an electronically monitored tag.	• Risk of absconding • Committing offence on bail • Interfering with witnesses

Table 2.5: (continued)

Curfew	A condition that the defendant must be at a specified address between certain hours of the day (with no restriction on minimum and maximum periods). Court must consider the defendant's employment and care commitments. Police will visit the address at random points in the day to monitor compliance. The court may monitor compliance with this requirement through an electronically monitored tag.	• Committing offences on bail
Non-communication	A condition that the defendant must not make contact (directly or indirectly) with the complainant or any probable prosecution witness.	• Interfering with witnesses
Restriction on location/ whereabouts requirement	A condition that the defendant must not enter a certain area or building or go within a specified distance of a particular location or address. The court will define the 'zone' of exclusion. Additionally/alternatively, the court may include what is commonly referred to as a 'whereabouts' requirement, which means that a defendant must remain in a certain place (eg a condition to not leave South Yorkshire). The court may monitor compliance with either requirement through an electronically monitored tag.	• Committing offence on bail • Interfering with witnesses
Reporting	A condition that the defendant must report to the local police station. Such condition may require reporting daily, weekly or at other specified intervals.	• Risk of absconding
Surrender of passport	A condition that the defendant must surrender their passport to the police to prevent them from travelling abroad.	• Risk of absconding

Electronic monitoring requirements

As you can see from **Table 2.5**, the court may monitor a defendant's compliance with certain requirements by the use of an electronically monitored tag (EMT). There are detailed rules in place as to when an EMT may be imposed; we can break these rules down into two questions.

Does the defendant qualify for EMT?

In respect of adult defendants, a court may only impose electronic monitoring requirements where:

(a) the defendant has attained the age of 18, and

(b) the defendant has been released on bail in non-extradition proceedings, and

(c) it appears to the court that:

   (i) there is no real prospect that the person will be sentenced in the proceedings to a custodial sentence, other than a suspended sentence, and

   (ii) there is a real prospect that the person will be sentenced in the proceedings to a suspended sentence.

If the defendant does not meet these requirements, an EMT may only be imposed if the court is satisfied that, without the EMT, the defendant would not be granted bail (ie it is a direct alternative to custody).

Do any of the conditions for EMT apply to this defendant?

An EMT may be imposed for any offence, but the applicable conditions vary according to whether the offence charged is indictable or summary-only. In both cases, the court must be satisfied that the local justice area to where the defendant will be bailed is able to facilitate EMT.

In respect of indictable offences, an EMT may be imposed where either:

- the court is satisfied that there are substantial grounds for believing that without the EMT the defendant would fail to surrender to custody, commit an offence while on bail, or interfere with witnesses or otherwise obstruct the course of justice in relation to the person or any other person, or
- the court is satisfied that without the electronic monitoring requirements the person would not be granted bail.

In respect of summary-only offences, an EMT may be imposed where either:

- the defendant has previously failed to surrender, and the court believes that the defendant would fail to surrender again without an EMT,
- the defendant was on bail on the date of the alleged offence(s) and there are substantial grounds to believe the defendant would commit further offences without an EMT,
- the defendant had been released on bail and has been arrested for breach of bail, and there are substantial grounds to believe the defendant would fail to surrender, commit further offences, or interfere with witnesses without an EMT, or
- the court is satisfied that without the electronic monitoring requirements the person would not be granted bail.

Revision tip

Look ahead to **Chapter 8**: A defendant who has been subject to an electronically monitored curfew for a minimum period of nine hours per day is entitled to have half of that time count towards any sentence of immediate imprisonment.

Now that we have considered the right and exceptions to bail, and the conditions that can be imposed on bail, it is important to bring it all together and consolidate our understanding. **Figure 2.1** provides a step-by-step process for considering bail.

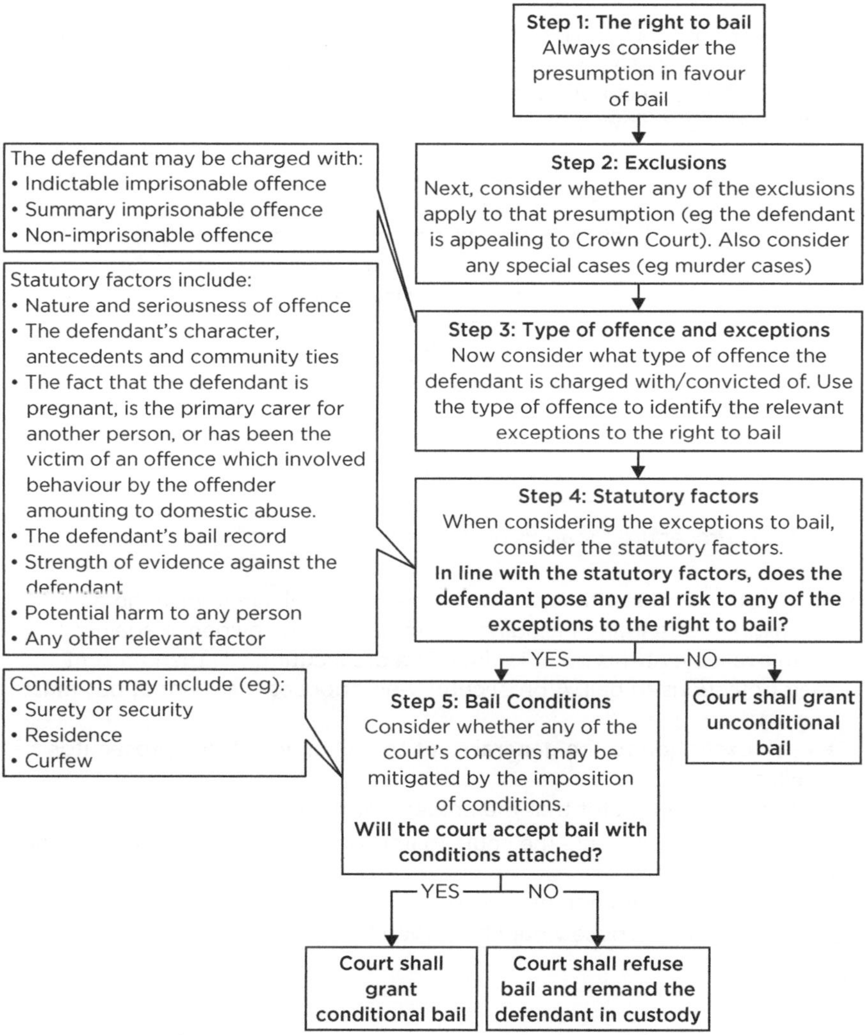

Figure 2.1: Bail: Step by step

PROCEDURE FOR APPLYING FOR AND OPPOSING BAIL

Now that we understand the substantive law relating to bail, we need to appreciate the procedure adopted when applying for bail and when bail is opposed by the prosecution. Before a decision is made as to bail, the prosecution must, as soon as practicable, provide the court and defendant with all the information in the prosecutor's possession which is material to what the court must decide. Bear in mind that bail applications are inquisitorial as opposed to adversarial in nature, which means that the court will gather sufficient evidence to make their determination (the strict rules of evidence seen in **Chapter 7** do not apply).

The defence solicitor should first speak with the prosecution to identify whether they intend to oppose bail or not. The following summary will proceed on the basis that the prosecution objects to bail. **Figure 2.2** outlines this procedure and the text that follows will explain the procedure in more detail.

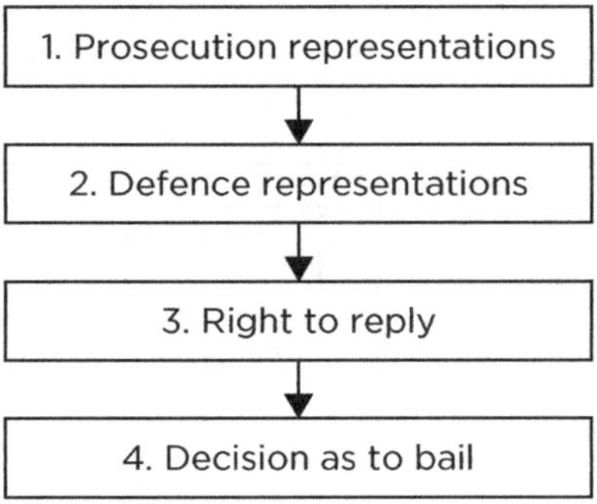

Figure 2.2: Procedure for applying for bail

- Prosecution representations: The prosecution will summarise the case against the defendant, including a summary of any evidence against them available at this point in time. The prosecution will then present their objections to bail. A prosecutor who opposes the grant of bail must specify:
  - each exception to the general right to bail on which the prosecutor relies
  - each statutory factor that the prosecutor thinks relevant.

  A prosecutor who wants the court to impose a condition on any grant of bail must:
  - specify each condition proposed
  - explain what purpose would be served by such a condition.

The court will be presented with the previous convictions (if any) of the defendant.

- Defence representations: The defence will then be permitted to make their representations as to the granting of bail. The defence will attempt to rebut the exceptions and mitigate any concerns raised by the prosecution in using the statutory factors. The defence advocate will try to persuade the court to grant unconditional bail or, where that is unlikely to be granted, will propose one or more conditions to bail which may persuade the court to grant it.
- Right to reply: The prosecution is permitted a right to reply if it is necessary to correct alleged misstatements of fact in what the defence have said. However, this right to reply is not normally utilised.
- Decision as to bail: The court will then announce its decision on the granting or withholding of bail. The court must explain its reasons for whatever decision it takes; a record of this decision will be made. If bail is granted, the court will inform the defendant where and when they should surrender to custody. As noted above, the court may impose conditions on the granting of bail. If bail is refused, the court will serve on the defendant a **certificate of full argument** (this will be relevant later when considering appeals - see **Chapter 9**).

Key term: certificate of full argument

This is merely a document which is issued by the magistrates' court to show that the court has heard a fully argued bail application. The certificate is necessary if the defendant wishes to appeal against their refusal of bail to the Crown Court - see below: **Appeals against decisions on bail**.

FURTHER APPLICATIONS FOR BAIL

If the court decides not to grant the defendant bail, it is the court's duty to consider the question of bail at each subsequent hearing. This duty only applies where:

- the presumption in favour of bail still applies, and
- the defendant remains in custody.

The nature of the bail application will vary depending on whether the application is being made at the first hearing following the refusal, or subsequent hearings thereafter (**Figure 2.3**).

First hearing	• At the first hearing after the hearing where the court refused to grant the defendant bail, the defendant is permitted to make a full application for bail. • The defendant may support an application for bail with any argument as to fact or law that they desire (whether or not they have advanced that argument previously).
Subsequent hearings	• However, at any subsequent hearings, the court need not hear arguments as to fact or law which it has heard previously. • This means that unless there has been a change in circumstances, the court may choose not to entertain an application for bail. A change in circumstances may arise due to the passage of time.

Figure 2.3: Further applications for bail

Exam warning

Be aware that the right to make a further full bail application is only available at the first hearing following the initial refusal of bail. If the defence advocate does not take the opportunity to make a full bail application at this hearing, the opportunity is lost, and the court may decline to hear a full bail application.

APPEALS AGAINST DECISIONS ON BAIL

For the purposes of SQE1, you will need to be familiar with appeals in two circumstances:

- appeals by the defence where bail is refused
- appeals by the prosecution where bail is granted.

Defence appeals

Where the magistrates' court has refused bail, the defendant may appeal to the Crown Court. The application process is as follows:

- The defendant must apply to the Crown Court in writing as soon as practicable after the magistrates' court's decision and serve that application on the Crown Court, magistrates' court and prosecution.
- The application must specify the decision that the defendant wishes the Crown Court to make, the reasons why bail should not be withheld, any proposed conditions of bail, and the application must attach a copy of the certificate of full argument (discussed above).

- Appeals will usually be heard within 48 hours after the magistrates' court initially refused bail.
- Appeals will be heard by a Crown Court judge in chambers (ie not in court). This will be a complete rehearing of a bail application, with the judge permitting both the prosecution and defence to make any necessary representations.
- The Crown Court judge may either withhold bail, and the defendant will continue to be remanded in custody, or grant bail (conditionally or unconditionally).

Exam warning

Whilst the ability to appeal against the refusal to grant bail exists, it is uncommon for the defence to immediately appeal against the refusal. Instead, it is more common for the defence to make a subsequent full application to the magistrates' court before then appealing. Look out for this practical consideration in an MCQ.

Prosecution appeals

The prosecution does not have an unfettered right to appeal against the granting of bail. Such prosecution appeals are only permitted where the defendant has been charged with, or convicted of, an imprisonable offence. If the offence is not punishable by way of imprisonment, the prosecution cannot appeal against a decision to grant bail.

The prosecution may appeal either to the Crown Court or to the High Court. **Table 2.6** identifies the procedure in each situation.

Table 2.6: Prosecution appeals against bail

Appeal to the Crown Court	Appeal to the High Court
Made where the prosecution is appealing against a decision of the magistrates' court to grant bail. This appeal must be held as soon as practicable and, in any event, no later than the second business day after the appeal notice was served	Made where the prosecution is appealing against a decision of the Crown Court to grant bail. This route does not apply where the Crown Court granted bail following an appeal from the magistrates' court by the defendant
In both cases, the prosecution must give oral notice to the court which has granted bail of the decision to appeal at the end of the hearing during which the court granted bail, and before the defendant is released on bail. The prosecution must serve written notice of appeal not more than two hours after informing the court of the decision to appeal. The defendant must be remanded in custody until the appeal has been determined	

The power to appeal should only be used in cases of grave concern and must be used judiciously and responsibly.

ABSCONDING AND BREACHES OF BAIL

This final section will consider the consequences of a defendant's conduct where they abscond and breach bail conditions.

Absconding

A defendant who has been released on bail must surrender to custody at the place and time specified by the court. If the defendant fails to do so, they are said to **abscond**.

Key term: abscond

Where the defendant, without reasonable cause, fails to surrender to the custody of the court, they are guilty of the offence of absconding.

Where a defendant fails to surrender, and there is no reasonable cause for such failure, the court will issue a warrant for their immediate arrest. This warrant will either be:

- Backed with bail: Meaning that once the defendant is arrested, they will be released by the police and informed to surrender at the next hearing.
- Not backed with bail: Meaning that the defendant will be arrested and held in custody until their next hearing (or, if the court has finished sitting on a Friday, will be presented before a remand court on the Saturday morning; no such courts sit on a Sunday).

Absconding is a criminal offence. A defendant will be liable in two circumstances (see **Practice example 2.2**):

- where, having been granted bail, they fail to surrender without reasonable cause, or
- where, having been granted bail, they fail to surrender as soon as is reasonably practicable after having had reasonable cause for failing to surrender initially.

Practice example 2.2

James is charged with theft and has consented to summary trial. James was granted bail at the first hearing before the magistrates' court with an obligation to surrender at 9 AM on Monday 2 July. Unfortunately, James is too ill to attend court, requiring hospitalisation. James recovers on the Wednesday and is discharged from hospital on Wednesday morning. James surrenders on Friday afternoon.

Is James likely to be charged with absconding?

In this circumstance, whilst there is a reasonable cause for James failing to surrender, he did not thereafter surrender as soon as is reasonably practicable (ie Wednesday afternoon or Thursday morning). The burden is on James to prove, on the balance of probabilities, that he had a reasonable cause to fail to surrender.

If the defendant is guilty of absconding, the court may sentence them immediately, or postpone that sentencing until the end of proceedings. The general principle is that the court should sentence 'as soon as practicable'. The punishment depends on the court that the defendant failed to surrender to:

- magistrates' court: punishable by up to three months' imprisonment/a maximum fine of £5,000
- Crown Court: punishable by up to 12 months' imprisonment/an unlimited fine.

As discussed above, a failure to surrender may mean that any surety made, or security deposited, will be forfeited.

Breaching bail conditions

When conditional bail is granted to a defendant, the importance of compliance with those conditions will be explained to them (by both the court and the defence solicitor). A breach of bail conditions is not a criminal offence, but can have unfortunate consequences for a defendant. A police officer has the power to arrest (without warrant) if they have reasonable grounds to believe that the defendant:

- has broken any conditions of their bail, or
- is likely to break any of the conditions of their bail.

If a defendant is arrested in either of these circumstances, they must be brought before the magistrates' court as soon as is reasonably practicable and in any event within 24 hours of their arrest. If they are not brought before the court within 24 hours, they have an absolute right to be released (ie they *must* be released).

The magistrates' court must decide whether to remand the defendant in custody or release them on bail. To do this, the magistrates will adopt a two-staged approach:

- Determine the breach: The magistrates will first determine whether there has in fact been a breach of any bail condition. The defence may make representations either accepting the breach or disputing it. If the defence dispute the breach, evidence will be called.
- Determine bail: If the court is satisfied that a breach did occur, the court must decide whether to remand the defendant in custody or on bail. If the court decides to release the defendant on bail, the court may maintain the same conditions imposed previously or vary them (with the opportunity to impose more stringent conditions).

Importantly, the magistrates may not remand a defendant into custody if they are an adult, have not yet been convicted in the present proceedings, and it appears to the court that there is no real prospect of the defendant being issued with a custodial sentence in the proceedings. This is similar to the limitation noted above, on **page 41**.

> **Revision tip**
>
> Keep the consequences of absconding and breaching bail conditions clear and separate in your mind. Absconding *is* a criminal offence and is punishable by the courts. Breaching bail conditions *is not* a criminal offence, though a person may be held in remand, or conditions varied, if they breach their bail. Do not confuse the two in an MCQ.

KEY POINT CHECKLIST

This chapter has covered the following key knowledge points. You can use these to structure your revision, ensuring you recall the key details for each point, as covered in this chapter.

- In general, a defendant has a prima facie right to (or presumption in favour of) bail.
- This right does not apply in certain circumstances or where the defendant is charged with a particular offence.
- A number of exceptions apply to the right to bail and these exceptions depend on whether the defendant is charged with an indictable imprisonable offence, a summary only imprisonable offence or a non-imprisonable offence.
- Where the court is of the opinion that the defendant poses no risk to any of the exceptions, they will grant unconditional bail.
- In any other cases, the court may impose one or a number of conditions on bail.
- A failure to surrender to custody will result in the defendant being liable for the criminal offence of absconding. A breach of bail conditions may result in the defendant being remanded in custody or having their conditions varied.
- A defendant may appeal to the Crown Court against a refusal to grant bail in the magistrates' court. The prosecution may equally appeal against the granting of bail, but only where the offence is imprisonable.

KEY TERMS AND CONCEPTS

- bail (**page 37**)
- remand (**page 37**)
- custody time limit (**page 38**)
- right to bail (**page 39**)
- associated person (**page 42**)
- unconditional bail (**page 47**)
- conditional bail (**page 47**)

- certificate of full argument (**page 53**)
- abscond (**page 56**)

SQE1-STYLE QUESTIONS

QUESTION 1

A man is charged with inflicting grievous bodily harm, contrary to s 20 Offences Against the Person Act 1861. The man is arrested and brought before the magistrates' court the following day. The prosecution object to bail on the grounds that the man would interfere with prosecution witnesses if released on bail. The prosecution concede that, on the facts of the case, no other objection could apply.

Which of the following best describes the legal position of the case?

A. The man has no right to make a bail application, as it is the first time the case has appeared before the magistrates' court.

B. The man has a right to be granted bail unless the magistrates are persuaded that there are substantial grounds for believing that he would interfere with prosecution witnesses.

C. The man has a right to be granted bail unless the magistrates are persuaded that there is a reasonable likelihood that he would interfere with prosecution witnesses.

D. The man has a right to bail; the objection that the man would interfere with prosecution witnesses does not apply to the type of offence that the man is charged with.

E. The man may only be granted bail if he persuades the magistrates that there is no reasonable prospect of him interfering with prosecution witnesses.

QUESTION 2

A woman is charged with theft, contrary to s 1 Theft Act 1968. The woman is to be tried in the magistrates' court and has been granted conditional bail. As part of her conditions, the woman must not enter the supermarket where she is alleged to have committed the offence. One day, the police are called to the supermarket and arrest the woman, found in the store. The woman claims that she had to enter the store to purchase goods for her young child that were unavailable at any other store in the local area.

Which of the following best describes the woman's situation?

A. The woman is in breach of her bail conditions and may be charged with an offence of breach of bail conditions.

B. The woman is in breach of her bail conditions and will be remanded into custody until her trial.
C. The woman is not in breach of her bail conditions as there was a reasonable cause for her to enter the supermarket.
D. The woman is in breach of her bail conditions and will be brought before the magistrates' court for bail to be reconsidered.
E. The woman is not in breach of her bail conditions as it was necessary for her to enter the supermarket.

QUESTION 3

A woman is charged with manslaughter. She has previously been convicted of manslaughter for which she was sentenced to three years' imprisonment. The defence solicitor makes an application for bail in respect of the current manslaughter proceedings.

Which of the following is the most accurate statement of bail in respect of the woman's case?

A. The woman may only be granted bail if the court is of the opinion that there are exceptional circumstances justifying the granting of bail.
B. The woman may only be granted bail if the court is of the opinion that there are no reasonable grounds for refusing the granting of bail.
C. The woman has the right to bail as the presumption is only removed where the woman was sentenced to five years or longer in imprisonment.
D. The woman has the right to bail as the presumption is only removed where the previous conviction is for murder or rape.
E. The woman has no right to bail; as the woman is charged with manslaughter, she must be remanded in custody.

QUESTION 4

A woman is charged with assault occasioning actual bodily harm, contrary to s 47 Offences Against the Person Act 1861. The woman appears before the magistrates' court, where she pleads not guilty and, following an allocation hearing, the matter is listed for summary trial. The woman has made two fully argued applications for bail in the magistrates' court, both of which have been refused. There has been no change in her circumstances, and no new information that she can put before the court since her last application.

Which of the following is the most accurate advice that can be given to the woman?

A. The woman should appeal against the refusal to grant bail to the Court of Appeal.

B. The woman should make another application for bail in the magistrates' court.
C. The woman has no further applications to make and must be held in remand until her circumstances change.
D. The woman should appeal against the refusal to grant bail to the Crown Court.
E. The woman should appeal against the refusal to grant bail to the High Court.

QUESTION 5

A man is charged with burglary, contrary to s 9 Theft Act 1968. The man is granted conditional bail by the magistrates' court. The magistrates impose the following conditions: that the man does not contact directly or indirectly any prosecution witness, that the man does not go within 100 metres of the burgled property and that the man provides a surety in the sum of £10,000.

Which of the following is the most accurate statement regarding any breach of the man's conditions?

A. The man can be arrested without a warrant by a police officer if he has broken any of his bail conditions.
B. The man can be arrested without a warrant by a police officer if the police officer has reasonable grounds to believe that he has broken any of his bail conditions.
C. The man can be arrested without a warrant by a police officer if the police officer has substantial grounds for believing that he has broken any of his bail conditions or is likely to break any of his conditions.
D. The man can be arrested without a warrant by a police officer if the police officer has substantial grounds for believing that he has broken any of his bail conditions.
E. The man can be arrested without a warrant by a police officer if the police officer has reasonable grounds to believe that he has broken any of his bail conditions or is likely to break any of his conditions.

■ ANSWERS TO QUESTIONS

Answers to 'What do you know already?' questions at the start of the chapter

1) The right to bail does not exist post-conviction except where the defendant's case is adjourned by the court for the purpose of enabling inquiries or a report to be made to assist the court in dealing with them

for the offence (for example, an adjournment for the production of a pre-sentence report or psychiatric report).

2) The prosecution may only appeal against the grant of bail to the High Court where the offence is punishable by imprisonment. This route does not apply where the Crown Court has granted bail following an appeal against a refusal of bail in the magistrates' court.
3) False. There is no criminal offence of breaching bail conditions. However, a defendant must be warned that breaching such conditions may mean that they are remanded into custody or their bail conditions may be varied (and made more stringent).
4) Conditions may only be imposed where it appears to the court that it is necessary to do so to prevent the defendant from absconding, to prevent them from committing further offences whilst on bail, to ensure they do not interfere with witnesses or obstruct the course of justice, for their own protection or to ensure they make themself available to enable inquiries or a report to be made to assist the court in sentencing.

Answers to end-of-chapter SQE1-style questions

Question 1

The correct answer was B. The man does possess the right to bail, but the magistrates may refuse bail where there are substantial grounds for believing that the man would interfere with witnesses. The test is 'substantial grounds'; reference to 'reasonable likelihood' and 'reasonable prospect' is wrong (thus options C and E, respectively, are incorrect). Option A is incorrect because the man does have a right to bail; it being his first appearance is irrelevant. Option D is wrong because the offence charged is an indictable imprisonable offence for which interference with witnesses is a ground for objection.

Question 2

The correct answer was D. The woman is in breach of her bail conditions as she has entered a supermarket that was excluded under her bail. The woman will be brought before the magistrates' court, which will determine whether the woman will be held in remand or released on bail. The magistrates may vary any bail conditions. Option A is wrong because there is no criminal offence of breaching bail conditions. Option B is wrong because the court is not obliged to remand the woman into custody; that is a matter for them to decide. Options C and E are wrong because the woman is in breach of bail and no defence of 'reasonable cause' or 'necessity' exists in respect of breach of bail conditions.

Question 3

The correct answer was A. The presumption in favour of bail is removed as the woman is charged with a homicide offence (manslaughter) and has a previous conviction for the same offence. In this case, the court need only grant bail where there are exceptional circumstances justifying it. Reference to 'reasonable grounds' is not a correct statement of law (thus option B is wrong). Option C is wrong as, whilst the law states that the presumption is removed where a manslaughter conviction results in a sentence of imprisonment, there is no period of time specified in law. Option D is wrong as the presumption is also reversed where the previous conviction is of manslaughter, but only where that conviction resulted in a sentence to imprisonment. Option E is wrong; whilst the presumption is reversed, the availability of bail is not completely removed.

Question 4

The correct answer was D. Given that the woman has made two full applications, and there is no change in her circumstances, there can be no further application for bail in the magistrates' court (therefore option B is wrong). The only route available to the woman now is to apply to the Crown Court for bail; this will take the form of a full re-hearing of the bail application. Options A and E are wrong because neither the Court of Appeal nor the High Court has jurisdiction in respect of bail in this circumstance. Option C is wrong as, although the woman has no further applications she can make in the magistrates' court, she can apply to the Crown Court.

Question 5

The correct answer was E. Where a police officer has reasonable grounds to believe that the man has either broken any of his conditions or is likely to break any of his conditions, he may arrest the man without a warrant. Option A is wrong because the man need not actually break any of his conditions before he can be arrested; the focus is on the police officer's reasonable belief. Option B is wrong as it does not include the fact that the police officer may also arrest the man where he has reasonable grounds to believe that the man is likely to break any of his conditions. Options C and D are wrong as they use the wrong test: 'substantial grounds' as opposed to 'reasonable grounds'.

■ KEY CASES, RULES, STATUTES AND INSTRUMENTS

The SQE1 Assessment Specification does not require you to know any case names, or statutory materials, for the topic of bail applications.

3

First hearings before the magistrates' court

■ MAKE SURE YOU KNOW

This chapter will cover the procedures and processes involved in an individual's first appearance before the magistrates' court. For the purposes of SQE1, you are required to know:

- classification of offences
- procedural overview – what will happen at the hearing
- applying for a representation order
- the role of the defence solicitor at the first hearing.

■ SQE ASSESSMENT ADVICE

As you work through this chapter, remember to pay particular attention in your revision to:

- the terminology used to classify criminal offences
- how the classification of criminal offences will affect the progression of a defendant's case
- the availability of public funding for a defendant accused of a criminal offence
- what will happen at the first hearing.

■ WHAT DO YOU KNOW ALREADY?

Have a go at these questions before reading this chapter. If you find some difficult or cannot remember the answers, make a note to look more closely at that area during your revision.

1) True or false? An indictable offence is one that can only be tried in the Crown Court.

   [Classification of offences, page 65]

2) A defendant is charged with an indictable only offence. What will happen at their first appearance before the magistrates' court?

   [Procedural overview – what will happen at the hearing, page 70]

3) A defendant is in receipt of welfare benefits and is charged with aggravated burglary. What advice would you give them regarding the provision of legal aid?

   [Applying for a representation order, page 74]

4) You are a defence solicitor meeting your client for the first time. Fill in the blank: My first steps include ______________________.
[Role of the defence solicitor at the first hearing, page 81]

INTRODUCTION TO FIRST APPEARANCE

When charged with a criminal offence, all adults will attend a magistrates' court for the first hearing. The procedure to be followed at that first hearing will be dictated by the type of offence charged and the plea entered by the defendant at that first hearing. For example, if a defendant remains in the magistrates' court, it is possible that their case may be dealt with in full at the first hearing. Further detail on the progression of a case is given in **Chapter 4**.

CLASSIFICATION OF OFFENCES

As noted above, the classification of an offence will determine how the case will progress in the criminal courts. It makes sense, therefore, for us to consider this first.

All criminal offences may be classified according to one of three descriptions (see **Table 3.1**).

Table 3.1: Classification of criminal offences

Classification	Explanation and examples
Summary only offences ('offences triable only summarily')	These are the least serious forms of offences and can only be dealt with in the magistrates' court (ie the case will start and end in the magistrates' court) Most road traffic offences are triable only summarily
Either way offences ('offences triable either way')	The severity of these offences is dependent on the facts of a particular case. An either way offence is one which is capable of being tried in either a magistrates' court or the Crown Court For example, fraud is an either way offence. Fraud which involves a relatively low amount of money will be less serious than fraud involving millions of pounds
Indictable only offences ('offences triable only on indictment')	These are the most serious forms of offences and can only be dealt with in the Crown Court. Murder, for example, is an indictable only offence Whilst a defendant will make their initial appearance in the magistrates' court when charged with an offence triable only on indictment, the magistrates will send the case to the Crown Court (see below: **Indictable only offences**)

A full list of examples is provided in **Table 3.2** below.

Revision tip

In order to determine the classification of an offence, you should look at the statute creating an offence (if there is one). The statute will usually prescribe the classification of the offence by reference to the nature of the punishment on conviction. For example, the offence of fraud is an offence triable either way. We know this because the Fraud Act 2006 offers different penalties according to whether a defendant is convicted summarily or on indictment.

Exam warning

Be aware that the term 'indictable only offence' is different to 'indictable offence'. The term 'indictable offence' technically includes both offences which are triable *only* on indictment and offences which are triable either way. It may be beneficial, therefore, to think that offences can be classified in two ways: 'Summary only' or 'indictable', and then 'indictable offences' can be further sub-divided into indictable only offences and either way offences.

Offences considered in SQE1

As part of SQE1, you will have to be prepared to answer an MCQ relating to a number of specified criminal offences. It is likely, therefore, that SQE1 may attempt to test your knowledge as to how those offences are classified for the purposes of criminal litigation. **Table 3.2** provides an overview of all specified criminal offences listed in SQE1, how they are classified and the court they will be heard in. See ***Revise SQE: Criminal Law*** for a discussion of the substantive elements of these offences.

Table 3.2: Classification of SQE1 criminal offences

Specified offence	Classification	Relevant court
Murder and manslaughter	Indictable only	Crown Court only
Assault and battery	Summary only*	Magistrates' court only
Assault occasioning actual bodily harm (Offences Against the Person Act 1861, s 47)	Either way	Magistrates' court or Crown Court
Malicious wounding/inflicting grievous bodily harm (Offences Against the Person Act 1861, s 20)	Either way	Magistrates' court or Crown Court

Table 3.2: (continued)

Specified offence	Classification	Relevant court
Malicious wounding/causing grievous bodily harm with intent (Offences Against the Person Act 1861, s 18)	Indictable only	Crown Court only
Theft (Theft Act 1968, s 1)	Either way*	Magistrates' court or Crown Court
Robbery (Theft Act 1968, s 8)	Indictable only	Crown Court only
Burglary (Theft Act 1968, s 9)	Either way*	Magistrates' court or Crown Court
Aggravated burglary (Theft Act 1968, s 10)	Indictable only	Crown Court only
Fraud	Either way	Magistrates' court or Crown Court
Simple criminal damage/ arson	Either way*	Magistrates' court or Crown Court
Aggravated criminal damage/ aggravated arson	Indictable only	Crown Court only

** See text for clarification.*

You will have noticed a number of offences being marked by an *. This is to indicate that special rules apply to these offences which may alter their classification. We shall briefly consider these special circumstances below.

Assault and battery

Whilst assault and battery are summary only offences, they are offences which are capable of being tried on indictment in circumstances where the assault/battery is (a) founded on the same facts or evidence as a count charging an indictable offence; or (b) is part of a series of offences of the same or similar character as an indictable offence which is also charged.

Whilst assault and battery can therefore be tried in the Crown Court in this limited circumstance, they remain summary only offences and thus the Crown Court would be restricted to the powers of the magistrates' court if the defendant were to be convicted on indictment.

Low-value shoplifting

Low-value shoplifting is not a separate offence; rather, it concerns the circumstances where a defendant has committed theft, contrary to s 1 Theft

Act 1968, the property stolen was offered for sale in a shop or any other premises, stall, vehicle or place from which there is carried on a trade or business and the value of the stolen goods (valued at the time they were offered for sale) does not exceed £200. The provisions relating to low-value shoplifting are contained in s 22A Magistrates' Courts Act (MCA) 1980. The SQE1 Assessment Specification has identified that candidates must know and be able to use this statutory provision.

On 29 April 2026, the Crime and Policing Act 2026 received Royal Assent. Amongst other provisions, the 2026 Act abolishes s 22A MCA 1980. This means that shop theft, regardless of the value, will remain an either-way offence, and will therefore proceed through the allocation procedure in the normal way.

However, at the time of writing, this provision had not yet been brought into force, nor was there a commencement date for the legislation. At the time of writing, therefore, low-value shoplifting remained a distinct principle.

The following will therefore describe the law as it stood at the time of updating this edition. Should the law relating to the removal of low-value shoplifting come into effect, we shall update the position on the Revise SQE website.

By s 22A(1), low-value shoplifting is an offence triable only summarily, meaning that offences of low-value shoplifting cannot be sent to the Crown Court for trial or committed there for sentence.

Exam warning

Whilst low-value shoplifting is a summary only offence, if the defendant pleads not guilty to the charge, they retain the right to elect trial by jury in the Crown Court (ie if the defendant pleads not guilty, the defendant can choose to be tried in the Crown Court, though he cannot be sent by the magistrates). See MCA 1980, s 22A(2).

Please also note that by s 22A(4) where a defendant is charged on the same occasion with multiple instances of low-value shoplifting, it must be the case that all instances fall under £200 in value *by aggregate*, to be treated as a summary only offence (see **Practice example 3.1**).

Practice example 3.1

Mark is charged with three allegations of theft, contrary to s 1 Theft Act 1968. Mark is alleged to have shoplifted from three separate stores, allegedly stealing £70 worth of goods from each store.

How will Mark's offences be classified?

Whilst each individual offence involves a figure below £200, the three offences taken together (as an aggregate) exceed the £200 threshold (£210, to be specific). The offences would, therefore, be dealt with on an either way basis. This means that Mark could be tried in either the magistrates' court or the Crown Court. If tried and convicted in the magistrates' court, Mark could be committed to the Crown Court for sentencing.

Exam warning

Be aware that the 'aggregate' rule only applies where the defendant is 'charged on the same occasion' in the magistrates' court. This means that all offences must appear at the same time in the magistrates' court. Should the defendant be charged with four offences of shop theft that exceed £200, all four offences will be triable either way. However, should the same defendant come back before the court the following day with a further offence of shop theft, not exceeding £200, it remains a summary only offence. Look out for this in an MCQ; they must be charged 'on the same occasion'.

Low-value criminal damage

Where the value of the property allegedly destroyed or damaged by the defendant does not exceed £5,000, the offence of criminal damage will be treated as a summary only offence. Unlike low-value shoplifting (see above), the defendant does not have a right to elect trial on indictment; they must be tried summarily. However, there are two exceptions to this rule, where the offence will be treated as an either way offence regardless of how inexpensive the property damaged or destroyed:

- where the property is damaged or destroyed by fire (ie arson), or
- where the property damaged or destroyed is a 'memorial'.

A 'memorial' is a building or other structure (or part thereof), or any other thing, erected or installed on land (or in or on any building or other structure on land); or a garden or any other thing planted or grown on land; which has a commemorative purpose ('commemorate' and 'commemorative' are not defined by the legislation and should be given their ordinary meaning). Note that this second exception only applies to offences committed on or after 28 June 2022.

Burglary

Burglary is an either way offence except in three circumstances, when it is regarded as being indictable only:

- where the ulterior offence (ie theft, assault or criminal damage) intended or committed whilst in the building or part of a building is indictable only
- where the burglary was in a dwelling and any person in the dwelling was subjected to violence or the threat of violence.

The third exception can be quite complex. It will be easier to break it down into further bullet points:

- where the defendant is charged with burglary of a dwelling (a 'domestic burglary')
- the defendant has two previous, and separate, convictions for domestic burglary
- the defendant is aged 18 or over on the date of this third offence, and
- those previous convictions occurred on or after 1 December 1999.

In such circumstances the third burglary currently charged will be treated as an indictable only offence. This is known as the 'three strikes rule'. Please note that attempted burglary is not a qualifying offence for the three strikes rule.

Revision tip

Third strike burglaries have the capacity to catch out candidates because of the strict nature of the rule. There is a set pattern that must be followed, so keep the rule simple:

> Commission of offence 1; conviction for offence 1; commission of offence 2; conviction for offence 2; commission of offence 3; conviction for offence 3.

If your MCQ does not follow that exact sequence, you do not have a third strike.

PROCEDURAL OVERVIEW - WHAT WILL HAPPEN AT THE HEARING

Now that we have an understanding for the classification of criminal offences, we can proceed to discuss how that classification will affect the progression of a case. We will consider each classification of offence in turn. Before that, it is necessary to consider what information the defendant should have before their first appearance.

Initial details of the prosecution case (IDPC)

For summary only and either way offences, the prosecution are required to serve **initial details of the prosecution case (IDPC).** This procedure applies whether the defendant is subsequently tried in the magistrates' court or in the Crown Court but, as noted below, it does not apply for indictable only offences.

Key term: initial details of the prosecution case (IDPC)

The IDPC is a form of pre-trial disclosure of evidence. This disclosure must be sufficient to assist the court in order to identify the real issues and to give appropriate directions for an 'effective trial'. In particular, the IDPC, to ensure an 'effective trial', should enable the court and defendant to take an informed view of plea, venue for trial, case management and sentencing at the first hearing.

Exam warning

The IDPC is not required for offences triable only on indictment (though the prosecution is still likely to provide it). When the magistrates send the case to the Crown Court, they will make standard directions as to when the prosecution must serve any relevant evidence on the defence. Disclosure is considered further in **Chapter 5.**

Contents of IDPC

The contents of the IDPC are initially dependent on whether the defendant was in police custody for the offence charged immediately before the first hearing in the magistrates' court, or not. A third alternative is also considered below. **Table 3.3** outlines what the IDPC must include in these circumstances.

Table 3.3: Contents of the initial details of the prosecution case (IDPC)

Defendant was in police custody	**Defendant was not in police custody**
(a) A summary of the circumstances of the offence (known as the 'MG5') (b) The defendant's criminal record, if any *However, do note that if the prosecution wish to rely on any information not contained in the list above, they must make it available to the defendant in the same time frame outlined below*	(a) A summary of the circumstances of the offence (MG5) (b) Any account given by the defendant in interview, whether contained in that summary or in another document (c) Any written witness statement or exhibit that the prosecutor then has available and considers material to plea, or to the allocation of the case for trial, or to sentence (d) The defendant's criminal record, if any (e) Any available statement of the effect of the offence on a victim, a victim's family or others

This list is expanded where the defendant has been released on bail after being charged, and where the prosecutor does not anticipate a guilty plea at the first hearing in a magistrates' court. In this circumstance and unless there is good reason not to do so, the prosecution should also make available the following material in advance of the first hearing in the magistrates' court:

- statements and exhibits that the prosecution has identified as being of importance for the purpose of plea or initial case management, including any relevant closed-circuit television (CCTV) footage that would be relied upon at trial and any streamlined forensic report
- details of witness availability, as far as they are known at that hearing
- an indication of any medical or other expert evidence that the prosecution is likely to adduce in relation to a victim or the defendant
- any information as to special measures, bad character or hearsay, where applicable.

Procedure for serving the IDPC

The procedure for serving the IDPC is fairly straightforward:

- The IDPC must be served on the magistrates' court as soon as is practicable and, in any event, no later than the beginning of the day of the first hearing (often in the remand court, prosecutors may themselves obtain the IDPC mere minutes prior to the hearing).
- If the defendant wishes to receive the IDPC before the first hearing, they must request it from the prosecution. Following such request, the prosecution must serve the IDPC on the defendant as soon as is practicable and, in any event, no later than the beginning of the day of the first hearing.
- If the defendant does not request the IDPC, the prosecutor must make them available to the defendant at, or before, the beginning of the day of the first hearing.

Where the prosecution fails to provide information in their IDPC, the court will not allow it to be introduced into evidence unless the court first allows the defendant sufficient time to consider it.

Summary only offences

Where a defendant is charged with a summary only offence, the court must read the charge to them and ask them whether they plead guilty or not guilty. The progression of the summary trial will then depend on the plea entered by the defendant:

- Guilty plea: Magistrates will proceed to sentence the defendant immediately or adjourn for any relevant reports.
- Not-guilty plea: Magistrates will normally adjourn and set a date for trial.

Case management in the magistrates' court is covered in **Chapter 5** and trial procedure in the magistrates' court is covered in **Chapter 7**.

Either way offences

Where a defendant is charged with an either way offence, the case may be dealt with by either the magistrates' court or the Crown Court. The magistrates will first ask the defendant to indicate whether they intend to plead guilty or not guilty; this will determine what happens next.

By way of brief summary:

- Guilty plea: The magistrates will consider whether their sentencing powers are adequate. If they are adequate, the magistrates will sentence the defendant. If the magistrates consider their sentencing powers to be inadequate, they will commit the defendant to the Crown Court for sentencing.
- Not-guilty plea: The magistrates must determine where the defendant's case will be tried, ie in the magistrates' court or the Crown Court (this is known as an 'allocation' hearing). A full consideration of plea before venue and allocation (formerly referred to as 'mode of trial') will be covered in **Chapter 4**.

Indictable only offences

Where a defendant is charged with an indictable only offence, the magistrates do not have jurisdiction to try the case or sentence the defendant. The following is a brief overview of the process:

- The defendant will be identified and the charge/allegation will be read to them.
- The court must explain the allegation, unless it is self-explanatory, and must explain that their case will be sent to the Crown Court due to the nature of the offence.
- The court must permit the prosecution and defence to make any necessary representations regarding the power to send the case to the Crown Court or any ancillary matters such as bail. Given that any case being sent to the Crown Court will be adjourned, a consideration of bail at this stage is vital.
- The court must seek an indication from the defendant as to whether they intend to plead guilty in the Crown Court (this is usually done by requiring the defendant to complete the Better Case Management (BCM) Form, which requires them to indicate a plea).
  - If the answer is 'yes', the court must make arrangements for the Crown Court to take the defendant's plea as soon as possible.
  - If the answer is 'no', or there is no answer, the court must make arrangements for the first hearing in the Crown Court (the plea and trial preparation hearing (PTPH)).

Case management in the Crown Court is covered in **Chapter 5** and trial procedure in the Crown Court is covered in **Chapter 7**. Sending indictable only offences without allocation to the Crown Court is covered in **Chapter 4**.

APPLYING FOR A REPRESENTATION ORDER

The majority of criminal cases are funded by legal aid. Legal aid is a form of public funding, authorised by the Legal Aid Agency (LAA). All individuals at a police station are entitled to free legal advice, through the Police Station Advice and Assistance Scheme, regardless of their financial means. This provision is available irrespective of whether the person has been arrested or is attending voluntarily.

Furthermore, a Duty Solicitor Scheme is available at the magistrates' court for free but is limited in scope. For example, whilst a duty solicitor may represent an individual applying for bail, they may not represent them at trial. If further assistance is required, a defendant will either have to pay for legal representation themselves, represent themselves or apply for a representation order. We shall focus on the last of these three.

An application for a representation order is made electronically (using the CRIM14 eForm) to the LAA. Whether such order is granted is determined by a two-stage test:

- interests of justice test (also known as the merits test)
- means test.

We shall consider each test in turn.

Interests of justice test

Firstly, it must be shown that the defendant has satisfied the **interests of justice test**.

Key term: interests of justice test

Criminal legal aid should, subject to means testing, be granted in cases only where it is in the interests of justice for the defendant to be represented. Each application will be determined by reference to a list of statutory factors.

There are a number of non-exhaustive statutory factors that must be considered in determining the interests of justice test. These factors, known as the 'Widgery criteria', are reproduced on the application forms. Applicants must make clear on application forms which factors they are relying on. Importantly, the LAA relies wholly on the information presented in the application (ie they will not have access to previous convictions or the nature of the prosecution's case, nor will they seek out that information for themselves); the form must therefore include all information relevant to the determination.

The statutory factors are laid out and explained in **Table 3.4.**

Table 3.4: Interests of justice factors

Interest of justice factor	Explanation and examples
'It is likely that I will lose my liberty if any matter in the proceedings is decided against me'	The test requires that custody is 'likely'. Where there is merely a 'risk' of custody, but custody is not likely, this does not meet the criteria. The Legal Aid Agency will pay regard to previous convictions and sentencing guidelines to determine whether custody is 'likely' in a given case NB 'custody' is not restricted to imprisonment; it could include, for example, suspended custodial sentences and hospital orders
'I have been given a sentence that is suspended or non-custodial. If I break this, the court may be able to deal with me for the original offence'	If the defendant would be in breach of a suspended custodial sentence if convicted (eg through the breach of its requirements), this is a relevant factor to be considered
'It is likely that I will lose my livelihood'	The defendant will almost always need to be in employment or be self-employed to argue that their livelihood would be lost. The risk of loss must be one that is directly attributable to the conviction or sentence (eg a conviction of theft from their employer, or a lorry driver disqualified from driving)
'It is likely that I will suffer serious damage to my reputation'	In every case two factors must be considered in deciding whether 'serious damage' would be caused: • The defendant's current reputation • The nature and seriousness of the offence If the defendant intends to plead guilty, this factor is unlikely to be relevant. Importantly, the likely damage must be 'serious' and previous convictions will likely prevent this factor from applying
'Whether the determination of any matter in the proceedings may involve consideration of a substantial question of law'	The defendant must identify the question of law which may arise, which aspect of the case it relates to (eg plea, trial, etc) and why it is substantial and beyond the remit of the duty solicitor. Substantial questions of law are likely to include issues relating to identification, bad character, special measures, dishonesty and abuse of process

Table 3.4: (continued)

Interest of justice factor	Explanation and examples
'I may not be able to understand the proceedings or present my own case'	This concerns cases where the defendant has a disability or their understanding of English is inadequate. The requirement for an interpreter will not only be sufficient to satisfy this factor; it must be proven that the defendant cannot present their own case. Disability alone is not sufficient; it must be proven that the disability has an impact on the defendant's ability to understand proceedings and present their case. The age of the defendant will also be relevant
'Witnesses may need to be traced or interviewed on my behalf'	The defendant must identify the relevance of the witnesses and why legal representation is necessary to trace and/or interview them
'The proceedings may involve the expert cross-examination of a prosecution witness (whether an expert or not)'	This factor is only relevant to the cross-examination of prosecution witnesses. This factor is not satisfied by the fact that a witness must be cross-examined; it must be proven that 'expert' cross-examining is required. This may be satisfied based on the nature and seriousness of the offence, the nature of the witness (eg a police officer or child), the number of witnesses and the nature/extent of the questioning involved
'It is in the interests of another person that I am represented'	The other person will most commonly be a prosecution witness in cases of sensitivity where it would not be appropriate for the defendant to cross-examine them in person (eg domestic abuse cases)
'Any other reason'	Other reasons may be taken into account as part of the interests of justice test beyond the statutory factors

Revision tip

Remember that the statutory factors relevant to the interests of justice test are not exhaustive. This means that you may have to consider factors outside those listed in **Table 3.4** and identify whether they are relevant to the interests of justice.

In summary, the more serious the charge or possible consequences for a client, the more likely that their case will satisfy the interests of justice test. Whilst only one ground needs to be satisfied, a representation order will more likely be granted where more than one ground is met.

Exam warning

Be aware that the interests of justice test is automatically met in respect of defendants under the age of 18, for trials in the Crown Court (ie indictable only and triable either way offences heard in the Crown Court), and following a committal for sentence. It is not automatically met, however, for appeals to the Crown Court against conviction or sentence. Look out for this in an MCQ to avoid reaching the wrong conclusion.

Means test

The second consideration is known as the **means test**.

Key term: means test

The means test is an assessment of the available funds and/or income of the defendant. The assessment undertaken differs according to whether the case is being heard in the magistrates' court or the Crown Court and some cases are 'passported'.

The means test takes into account the defendant's income, family circumstances, such as number of children, and essential living costs, such as mortgage or rent.

Passporting

In circumstances where a defendant automatically passes the means test, they are said to be 'passported'. Defendants will passport the means test if:

- they are under the age of 18, or
- they receive welfare benefits, including Income Support, income-based Jobseeker's Allowance, Universal Credit, State Pension Guarantee Credit and income-based Employment and Support Allowance (ESA).

The National Insurance number of the defendant will be needed to prove the receipt of one of these benefits. If a defendant does qualify for passporting, you will then need to consider the means test.

Initial means test

The initial means test is based upon the gross annual income of the defendant and their family circumstance. This initial assessment is weighted, taking account of the number and ages of family members. The operation of the assessment is dependent on the trial venue:

- Magistrates' court: The assessment is limited to the income of the defendant.
- Crown Court: The assessment includes the defendant's income, capital and equity. In addition, the defendant may be liable to contribute to the

funding (something not done in the magistrates' court). See below for rules on income contribution.

In order to determine whether a defendant satisfies the initial means test, one should consider a two-stage approach:

- calculate the gross annual income, and
- calculate any necessary weighting.

Once this approach is taken, the resulting value is known as 'adjusted annual income'. You should then take this adjusted annual income and compare it to the thresholds set by the LAA. The thresholds are laid out in **Table 3.5**.

Table 3.5: Legal Aid Agency (LAA) initial means thresholds

Adjusted annual income	Outcome
£12,475 or less	• In the magistrates' court: Means test passed; funding available • In the Crown Court: Means test passed; funding available. No contribution requirement
More than £12,475, less than £22,325	• In the magistrates' court: Depends on 'full means test' • In the Crown Court: Depends on 'full means test'. Contribution may also be required
£22,325 or more	• In the magistrates' court: Means test failed; no funding available • In the Crown Court: Depends on 'full means test'. Contribution may also be required
£37,500 of disposal income or more (Crown Court only)	• Means test failed; no funding available

Full means test

The full means test is used if the adjusted annual income (discussed above) was found to be more than £12,475 and less than £22,325. The full means test assesses the defendant's **disposable income.**

Key term: disposable income

Disposable income is calculated by deducting living costs from the defendant's gross annual income. Living costs include, for example, tax and National Insurance payments, annual housing costs, annual childcare costs, annual maintenance to former partners and any children, and an adjusted annual living allowance.

A similar calculation is undertaken to that of the initial means test. For the purposes of the full means test, you should:

- consider the 'annual living allowance' set by the LAA (£5,676), and
- calculate any necessary weighting.

These figures will then allow you to calculate the 'adjusted living allowance' of the defendant. You would then compare this amount to the threshold set by the LAA (**Table 3.6**).

Table 3.6: Legal Aid Agency (LAA) full means thresholds

Annual disposable income	Outcome
£3,398 or less	• In the magistrates' court: Means test passed; funding available • In the Crown Court: Means test passed; funding available. No contribution requirement
More than £3,398 (but no more than £37,500)	• In the magistrates' court: Means test failed; no funding available • In the Crown Court: Means test passed; funding available. Contribution will be required

Revision tip

For full guidance and helpful examples on how to assess the means of a defendant, see www.gov.uk/guidance/criminal-legal-aid-means-testing

Income contribution

As discussed above, there are no contributions to be made by a defendant in the magistrates' court. However, where the defendant is tried in the Crown Court, special rules apply regarding income contributions to be made:

- If the defendant's disposable income is above £3,398 but less than £37,500, they will have to make an income contribution towards their costs (either a full or part contribution).
- If the defendant has above £30,000 in capital and equity, and is convicted, they may have to contribute towards any remaining balance against their final defence costs.

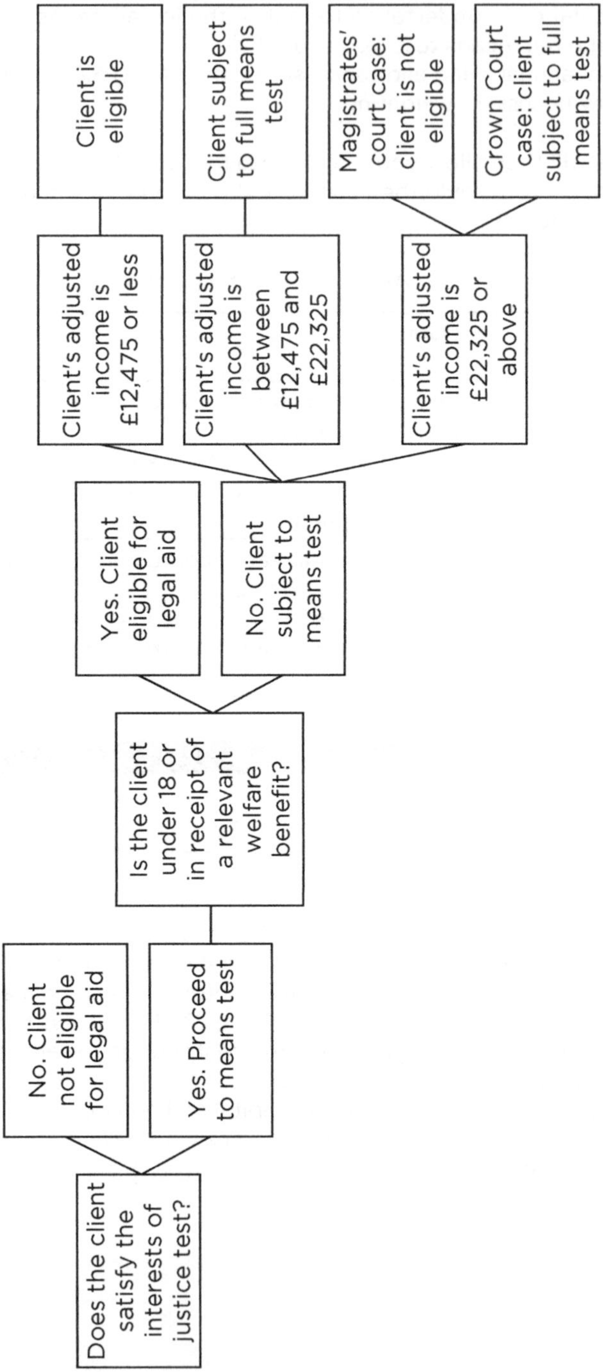

Figure 3.1: Process for assessing legal aid

Granting of the order

If the LAA is satisfied that the interests of justice test and the means test have been satisfied, the magistrates' court will grant the representation order, which will then be sent to the defendant's solicitor. If the application is refused, the defendant can resubmit another application, and further appeal to the magistrates' court.

Upon conclusion of the trial, the defence solicitor will claim their costs from the LAA (see **Practice example 3.2**).

Practice example 3.2

James has been arrested on suspicion of battery. James is a professional badminton player earning £150,000 per year. It is alleged that James punched another man in a nightclub. James has no previous convictions.

Will James be entitled to publicly funded legal representation in connection with the defence of his case?

James will be eligible for publicly funded legal representation at the police station as all persons, regardless of their means, are entitled to free legal advice at the police station. If charged with battery, James' case would be heard in the magistrates' court. He will not be able to get a representation order in the magistrates' court, because even if he passes the interests of justice test, he will fail the means test (due to his annual income) which applies in the magistrates' court.

ROLE OF THE DEFENCE SOLICITOR AT THE FIRST HEARING

In circumstances where the defendant is legally represented, the role of the defence solicitor can appear quite methodical. The defence solicitor should:

- obtain and review the IDPC, and using that evidence consider whether the charges against the defendant are appropriate and advise on the strength of the prosecution's case and any possible defences available to the client. In light of the strength of the prosecution's case, the defence solicitor should advise the client about whether to plead guilty or not guilty
- interview the client, obtain instructions, and take a proof of evidence from the client
- ascertain who is prosecuting and confirm they are acting on behalf of the client. The defence solicitor may need to raise any concerns about the nature of the charges, sufficiency of the evidence and, if the client is in custody, ascertain what objections there are to bail
- advise the client as to how the case will progress (dependent on the classification of the offence and the client's plea). This may require the solicitor to advise as to trial venue and case management (**Chapter 4**) and sentence (**Chapter 8**)

- advise the client as to prospects of bail, if in custody
- make any necessary representations to court, for example seeking a representation order, or an application for bail (see **Chapter 2**), as appropriate.

Many of these steps are largely common sense but this does not detract from the importance of a thorough understanding as to how the defence solicitor should proceed when acting on behalf of the defendant.

■ KEY POINT CHECKLIST

This chapter has covered the following key knowledge points. You can use these to structure your revision, ensuring you recall the key details for each point, as covered in this chapter.

- The procedure to be adopted in the courts system is dependent on the classification of offence charged and the plea of the defendant.
- A defendant may be charged with a summary only offence, an either way offence or an indictable only offence. The statute creating the offence (if relevant) should identify its classification.
- All defendants will make their first appearance in the magistrates' court. Summary only offences will remain in the magistrates' court. Either way offences may be tried in the magistrates' court or Crown Court, dependent on the plea indicated and the view of the magistrates as to suitability of the case. Indictable only offences will be sent to the Crown Court.
- In order to obtain public funding, a defendant must satisfy two tests: interests of justice test and means test.

■ KEY TERMS AND CONCEPTS

- initial details of the prosecution case (IDPC) (**page 71**)
- interests of justice test (**page 74**)
- means test (**page 77**)
- disposable income (**page 78**)

■ SQE1-STYLE QUESTIONS

QUESTION 1

In 2025, a man is charged with domestic burglary, having stolen property from a house whilst the householders were away. The man indicates a not-guilty plea, and the magistrates proceed to an allocation hearing. At the allocation hearing, the prosecution provides evidence of the man's previous convictions. The man has two previous convictions for domestic burglary from 2018. The man was convicted of both 2018 burglaries on the same indictment.

Which of the following best describes the legal position of the case?

A. The 2025 burglary is to be treated as an indictable only offence and must be sent to the Crown Court for trial.
B. The 2025 burglary is to be treated as an either way offence, and the magistrates' court may retain jurisdiction to hear the case.
C. The 2025 burglary is to be treated as a summary only offence, and the magistrates' court must hear the case.
D. The 2025 burglary is to be treated as an either way offence and must be sent to the Crown Court for trial.
E. The 2025 burglary is to be treated as an indictable only offence, and the magistrates' court may retain jurisdiction to hear the case.

QUESTION 2

A woman has been charged with inflicting grievous bodily harm, contrary to s 20 Offences Against the Person Act 1861, and theft, contrary to s 1 Theft Act 1968. The woman is alleged to have pickpocketed a wallet from a man's trousers and then pushed another man out of the way in order to escape, causing the man to suffer a broken leg. The woman is a shop assistant, earning £16,000 per year. The woman has one previous conviction for theft ten years ago and lives alone. The woman's disposable income is around £800 once all bills have been paid.

Will the woman be entitled to publicly funded legal representation in connection with the defence of her case?

A. Yes; the woman is likely to meet interests of justice test and has satisfied the initial means test.
B. No; whilst the woman is likely to meet interests of justice test, she will not satisfy the initial means test.
C. No; the woman is unlikely to meet the interests of justice test given that she has a previous conviction and lives alone.
D. No; whilst the woman is likely to meet the interests of justice test, she will not satisfy the full means test.
E. Yes; the woman is likely to meet the interests of justice test and has satisfied the full means test.

QUESTION 3

A man is charged with theft from a supermarket, contrary to s 1 Theft Act 1968. It is alleged that the man stole fresh packaged meat to the value of £150. The man intends to plead not guilty.

Which of the following is the best description for the procedure that follows?

A. The theft of the meat is treated as an either way offence and the magistrates' court will proceed with an allocation hearing to determine trial venue.
B. The theft of the meat is treated as an indictable only offence and the Crown Court will hear the case, unless the man elects trial in the magistrates' court.
C. The theft of the meat is treated as a summary only offence and the magistrates' court will hear the case, unless the man elects trial by jury.
D. The theft of the meat is treated as an either way offence and the magistrates' court will likely retain jurisdiction given the low value involved.
E. The theft of the meat is treated as a summary only offence and the magistrates' court will hear the case.

QUESTION 4

A woman is charged with robbery. The woman makes her first appearance in the magistrates' court and has met with her defence solicitor.

What advice would the defence solicitor give the woman as to court procedure?

A. The magistrates will ask the woman to enter her plea. If the woman pleads guilty, the magistrates will sentence the woman immediately, or commit her to the Crown Court for sentence. If the woman pleads not guilty, the magistrates will proceed to an allocation hearing.
B. The magistrates will not ask the woman any questions relating to her plea and will immediately send the case to the Crown Court.
C. The magistrates will ask the woman to enter her plea. If the woman pleads guilty, the magistrates will send the woman to the Crown Court for sentence. If the woman pleads not guilty, the magistrates will send the woman to the Crown Court for a case management hearing.
D. The magistrates will ask the woman whether she intends to plead guilty. If the woman indicates a guilty plea, the magistrates will send the woman to the Crown Court for a plea to be formally taken. If the woman indicates a not-guilty plea, the magistrates will send the woman to the Crown Court for a case management hearing.
E. The magistrates will ask the woman whether she intends to plead guilty. If the woman indicates a guilty plea, the magistrates will consider whether their sentencing powers are adequate or whether the woman should be committed to the Crown Court for sentence. If the woman pleads not guilty, the magistrates will proceed to an allocation hearing.

QUESTION 5

A man is charged with aggravated criminal damage. The man is alleged to have damaged a wall, causing it to collapse, endangering the neighbours in doing so. The man is a single parent, with three young children, all under the age of ten. The man was previously a successful banker, before his drug addiction caused him to lose all of his money. The man receives Universal Credit and has five previous convictions for dishonesty-related offences.

Will the man be entitled to publicly funded legal representation in connection with the defence of his case?

A. Yes, the interests of justice test is automatically satisfied, and the man automatically passes the means test as he receives Universal Credit.

B. Yes, the interests of justice test is likely to be satisfied as the man is likely to lose his liberty if convicted, and the man automatically passes the means test as he receives Universal Credit.

C. No, the interests of justice test is unlikely to be satisfied given that the man is not employed, and thus is not likely to lose his livelihood, and the man has several previous convictions, meaning that he will not suffer serious damage to his reputation.

D. No, the interests of justice test is unlikely to be satisfied given that the man will be able to understand proceedings and is to blame for his own financial situation.

E. Yes, the interests of justice test is likely to be satisfied as the man has three young children for whom the man is the sole carer, and the man automatically passes the means test as he receives Universal Credit.

■ ANSWERS TO QUESTIONS

Answers to 'What do you know already?' questions at the start of the chapter

1) False. An 'indictable offence' is an umbrella term generally encompassing offences both triable only on indictment, and either way offences. An indictable offence, therefore, may be tried in the Crown Court or the magistrates' court dependent on whether it is triable only on indictment or whether it is an either way offence.
2) The allegation will be read to the defendant, who will be asked to indicate whether they would plead guilty or not guilty. In either event, the magistrates' court must 'send' the defendant to the Crown Court (either to enter a plea of guilty, or for their first preparation hearing).
3) Given that aggravated burglary is an indictable only offence, the defendant will automatically pass the interests of justice test. As the

defendant receives welfare benefits, they may also automatically pass the means test (however, this would depend on the type of welfare benefits received).

4) My first steps include obtaining initial details of the prosecution case, meeting with my client, including the taking of instructions and a proof of evidence, considering the strength of the prosecution's case, advising my client as to the appropriate plea and advising them on the procedure that will follow dependent on their plea and the offence charged.

Answers to end-of-chapter SQE1-style questions

Question 1

The correct answer was B. This is because the man does not have three *separate* convictions for domestic burglary. The three strikes rule only applies where the man has two separate convictions for domestic burglary, and a third charge of domestic burglary against him. Given that the three strikes rule does not apply (the 'commission; conviction' sequence has not been followed), the 2025 burglary remains an either way offence (therefore options A and E are incorrect), for which the magistrates may retain jurisdiction or send the man to the Crown Court. Option C is incorrect because burglary is generally an either way offence. Option D is wrong on the basis that where an offence is triable either way, the magistrates are not obliged to send the case to the Crown Court; they may retain the case.

Question 2

The correct answer was E. This is because the woman is likely to lose her liberty given the nature of the offence charged. Given the dishonesty offence, the woman is also likely to lose her livelihood if convicted. As the woman earns over £12,475, she does not satisfy the initial means test (therefore option A is wrong). However, using the full means test, the woman's disposal income is less than £3,398 and thus she satisfies the full means test (therefore option D is wrong). Whilst option B is correct in some way, it fails to deal with the full means test; option B is therefore wrong. Option C is wrong as although her previous convictions will be relevant to the interests of justice test, they are only factors to be considered.

Question 3

The correct answer was C. This is because the man is charged with low-value shoplifting (ie theft of goods, offered for sale in a store, with a value of less than £200). Whilst theft is generally an either way offence, low-value shoplifting is treated as a summary only offence (therefore options A, B and D are wrong) and will be dealt with by the magistrates' court. However, the man retains the right to elect trial by jury (therefore option E is wrong). Note: This MCQ is correct as of May 2026. On a date to be specified, the law will change to remove the low-value shoplifting distinction. Option D will be the single best answer following the introduction of the new law.

Question 4

The correct answer was D. This is because robbery is an indictable only offence and must be sent to the Crown Court (options A and E are therefore incorrect). At the first hearing, the woman will be required to indicate whether she intends to plead guilty; this is different from asking the woman to enter a plea. A plea will only be entered at the first hearing in the Crown Court (therefore option C is incorrect). Option B is wrong because whilst the magistrates will not ask the woman to enter a plea, they will ask her to indicate a plea (to allow them to dispose of the case in the most efficient way).

Question 5

The correct answer was A. This is because aggravated criminal damage is an indictable only offence, which automatically passes the interests of justice test, and is 'passported' through the means test as the man is in receipt of Universal Credit. Options B, C, D and E are incorrect as they all ignore the fact that the interests of justice test is automatically satisfied.

■ KEY CASES, RULES, STATUTES AND INSTRUMENTS

The SQE1 Assessment Specification does not require you to know any case names, or statutory materials, for the topic of first hearings before the magistrates' court.

4

Plea before venue and allocation of business between magistrates' court and Crown Court

■ MAKE SURE YOU KNOW

This chapter will cover the procedures and processes involved in a plea before venue and the allocation of business between the magistrates' court and the Crown Court.

For the purposes of SQE1, you are required to know:

- plea before venue
- allocation of business between magistrates' court and Crown Court.

The SQE1 Assessment Specification has identified that candidates are required to know and be able to use:

- ss 19–20 Magistrates' Courts Act 1980
- s 22A Magistrates' Courts Act 1980
- ss 50A and 51 Crime and Disorder Act 1998.

It is likely that an MCQ may be asked making direct reference to the statute, as opposed to the procedure itself. For example, you may be asked whether a defendant can be 'sent to the Crown Court using s 50A of the Crime and Disorder Act 1998' as opposed to whether they can be sent without allocation.

■ SQE ASSESSMENT ADVICE

As you work through this chapter, remember to pay particular attention in your revision to:

- the procedure adopted at the plea before venue
- the circumstances in which a defendant chooses whether their case is tried summarily or on indictment
- the process involving indications of sentence
- the circumstances in which a defendant will be sent to the Crown Court without allocation.

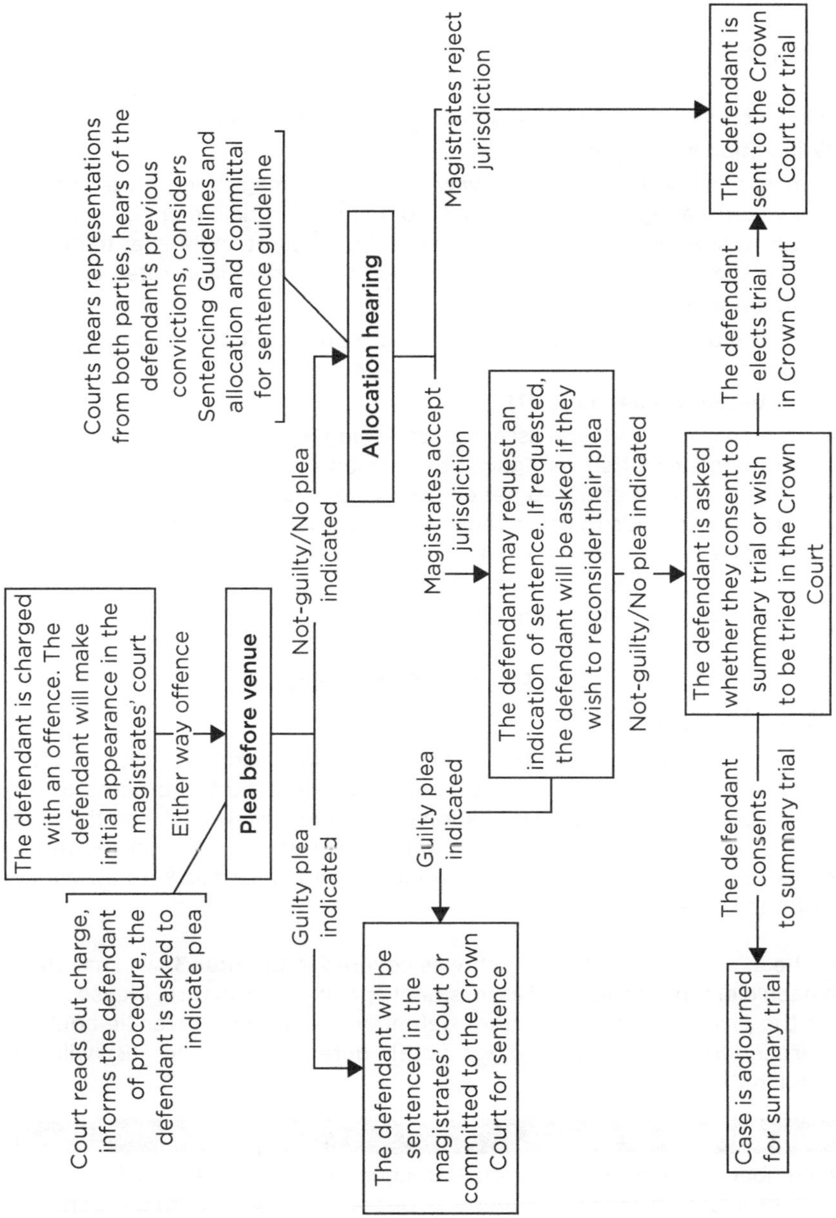

Overview of plea before venue and allocation

■ WHAT DO YOU KNOW ALREADY?

Have a go at these questions before reading this chapter. If you find some difficult or cannot remember the answers, make a note to look more closely at that area during your revision.

1) True or false? Where an indication of sentence is given during an allocation hearing, any court is bound by that indication.
   [Allocation hearing, page 96]
2) A man is charged with an either way offence. The magistrates have held an allocation hearing and have determined that trial on indictment is suitable. The man does not wish to be tried in the Crown Court and wishes to be tried in the magistrates' court. May he elect trial in the magistrates' court?
   [Allocation hearing, page 96]
3) Fill in the blank: The magistrates' court is a preferable trial court because ________________ .
   [Plea before venue, page 91]
4) A woman is charged with assault occasioning actual bodily harm, contrary to s 47 Offences Against the Person Act 1861. The allegation is that the woman attacked her ex-boyfriend, causing injury. The prosecution intends to call a young witness, aged 12, who watched the attack take place. The woman intends to plead not guilty. Where is the woman's trial likely to take place?
   [Sending without allocation, page 100]

INTRODUCTION TO PLEA BEFORE VENUE AND ALLOCATION

In **Chapter 3**, we introduced you to the process involved in the defendant's first appearance in the magistrates' court. We discussed the process to be adopted dependent on the classification of the offence charged, and the plea of the defendant. In this chapter, we will focus our attention on the more complex procedure involved when an individual is charged with an either way offence (see **Chapter 3**).

With the exception of s 22A, which was covered in **Chapter 3**, we shall deal with each element of the SQE1 assessment specification in turn. Please note, this is the process to be applied for defendants aged 18 or over (ie adults). The procedure to be adopted for youth defendants (under 18) will be covered in **Chapter 10.**

Exam warning

Remember, in **Chapter 3** we discussed a number of offences which, whilst ordinarily charged as either way offences, are subject to different procedures (eg third strike burglars). Do not forget these special rules as they will affect the course of proceedings.

Summarising the allocation of business between the magistrates' court and the Crown Court

Whilst this chapter is focused largely on allocation of either way offences, **Table 4.1** briefly summarises the position for all three categories of offences.

Table 4.1: Allocation of business between the magistrates' court and Crown Court

Classification	Court
Summary only	Magistrates' court only. Proceed to trial or sentence, dependent on plea. See **Chapter 3, page 72**.
Either way	Magistrates' court or Crown Court. Proceed to plea before venue and allocation. See **pages 91–100** of this chapter.
Indictable only	Crown Court only. Send the case forthwith to the Crown Court. See **page 102** of this chapter.

Exam warning

A common mistake made by candidates is not understanding the circumstances where a defendant's plea is taken, dependent on the classification of offences. Keep each classification distinct:

- Summary only offences: the court will take the defendant's plea to the charge(s).
- Either way offences: the court will ask the defendant to indicate a plea to the charge(s).
- Indictable only offences: the court will ask the defendant whether they intend to plead guilty to the charge(s).

PLEA BEFORE VENUE

As discussed in **Chapter 3**, all defendants will make their first appearance in the magistrates' court, regardless of the classification of offence charged. Where a defendant is charged with an offence triable either way, the magistrates will adopt the process identified in the **overview figure** (at the start of the chapter).

The first stage of this process is known as a **plea before venue** (PBV).

Key term: plea before venue

This process, specific to either way offences, is designed to allow the defendant to indicate their intended plea. The procedure that follows will be dependent on the plea indicated by the defendant.

The prosecution is required to serve initial details of the prosecution case (IDPC) on the defence prior to their first appearance to enable a plea to be indicated. IDPC was discussed in full in **Chapter 3.**

Procedure on defendant entering plea

The procedure to be followed at the PBV is detailed in statute, and the Criminal Procedure Rules (CrimPR) 2025.

> **Revision tip**
>
> Make use of the CrimPR 2025 - they are the rules that must be followed by participants in the criminal justice system, cross-referencing, where appropriate, statutory materials. Whilst you do not need to be aware of it for the purposes of SQE1, Part 9 of the CrimPR 2025 deals with allocation proceedings and sets the process out in an accessible manner.

The procedure can be summarised as follows:

- The charge must be written down (if it has not already been) and read to the defendant.
- The court must explain to the defendant:
  - the allegation, unless it is self-explanatory
  - that the offence is one which can be tried in a magistrates' court or in the Crown Court
  - that the court is about to ask whether the defendant intends to plead guilty
  - that if the answer is 'yes', then the court must treat that as a guilty plea and must sentence the defendant or commit the defendant to the Crown Court for sentence
  - that if the defendant does not answer, or the answer is 'no', then the court must decide whether to allocate the case to a magistrates' court or to the Crown Court for trial, and if the court allocates the case to a magistrates' court for trial, the defendant can nonetheless require trial in the Crown Court.
- The court must then ask whether the defendant intends to plead guilty.

Upon being asked to indicate a plea, a defendant has three options:

- indicate a guilty plea
- indicate a not-guilty plea
- remain silent (ie do not give an indication of plea).

> **Exam warning**
>
> Be aware that the defendant is not obliged to indicate a plea; it is their choice as to whether they wish to do so. Where a defendant does not indicate a plea, they will be treated as having indicated a not-guilty plea. Do not think that the defendant must indicate a plea at this stage.

Guilty plea indicated

Where the defendant indicates an intention to plead guilty, the magistrates will treat that as a guilty plea and will proceed as if the defendant has been convicted of a summary offence. This means that the magistrates will proceed to the sentencing stage of proceedings. The magistrates may either sentence the defendant immediately, or adjourn the case for pre-sentence reports.

The procedure upon sentencing a defendant is covered in **Chapter 8**. For the purposes of this chapter, we need to consider the powers available to the magistrates. In summary, the magistrates may choose to:

- sentence the defendant in the magistrates' court
- commit the defendant to be sentenced in the Crown Court, if they consider their sentencing powers to be inadequate. In this situation, the magistrates must be of the opinion that the offence was so serious that the Crown Court should have the power to deal with the offender in any way it could deal with them if they had been convicted on indictment.

Exam warning

In **Chapter 3**, we learned that criminal damage of property valued less than £5,000 must be tried summarily. In addition, it is important to know that the magistrates do not have the power to commit the defendant for sentence to the Crown Court in this particular instance. Watch out for this in an MCQ.

Where the magistrates adjourn the case for reports or commit the defendant to the Crown Court for sentence, they should consider whether the defendant should be held in remand or on bail (see **Chapter 2**). Where a defendant, who was on bail at the time of the PBV, enters a guilty plea, the usual practice is for bail to continue unless there is good reason to refuse bail. On the other hand, a defendant held in remand when indicating their plea at the PBV will ordinarily continue to be held in remand.

Not guilty/no plea indicated

Where the defendant indicates a not-guilty plea, or does not indicate a plea, the magistrates will proceed to the **allocation hearing.**

Key term: allocation hearing

An allocation hearing is a formal process whereby the magistrates determine whether the defendant is to be tried in the magistrates' court or sent to the Crown Court for trial. The magistrates will take a number of matters into account when determining trial venue and the defendant needs to be aware of the respective advantages/disadvantages of each trial venue.

Before we proceed to deal with the procedure involved in an allocation hearing, you must be prepared to advise a client as to trial venue.

Advising the client on trial venue

In **Chapter 3**, we discussed the role of the defence solicitor at the first hearing. This included an assessment of the strength of the prosecution's case and the appropriate plea of the defendant in a given case. Their role also involves advice regarding trial venue, a matter we shall discuss in further detail here.

SQE1 requires you to be able to '[advise] the client on trial venue'. This is because, as we will shortly see, the defendant retains the right to elect trial by jury where the magistrates accept summary jurisdiction. Given the right available to the defendant, you must be able to advise your client as to the respective pros and cons of trial in the magistrates' court and trial in the Crown Court. **Table 4.2** seeks to assist you in this advice.

Please note, an advantage in the magistrates' court will obviously be a disadvantage in the Crown Court, and vice versa.

Table 4.2: Advising the client on trial venue

In favour of magistrates' court	In favour of Crown Court
Sentencing powers: Magistrates have limited sentencing powers when compared to the Crown Court (though the defendant can be committed for sentence)	**Conviction rates:** There is a higher likelihood of conviction in the magistrates' court compared to the Crown Court. Magistrates are 'case-hardened'; juries are seemingly more sympathetic
Appeals: Appeal routes are more favourable in the magistrates' court: a convicted defendant may appeal, without leave, to the Crown Court against conviction or sentence for a full rehearing of the case. Appeals from the Crown Court proceed to the Court of Appeal and require leave to appeal	**Questions of law:** In the Crown Court, the functions of the judge and jury are separated, the judge being the arbiter of law and the jury the arbiter of fact. A judge in the Crown Court is better placed to deal with a point of law, including the exclusion of evidence, than a lay magistrate. Furthermore, where evidence is inadmissible, the jury will never hear of it, unlike in the magistrates' court
Delay: Summary trials are listed quicker than trials on indictment. The trials themselves are also faster	**Preparation for trial:** Whilst delay is a factor against choosing a Crown Court trial, it can also have a positive spin to it: delay means that the defence have longer to prepare their case and gather evidence
Stress: Summary trials are less formal than trials on indictment and thus may be less stressful (particularly relevant for a vulnerable defendant)	
Publicity: Trials in the Crown Court will usually garner more publicity and attention from the media. Where the defendant is a public figure, or public perception is important, summary trial may be more appropriate	

Table 4.2: (continued)

In favour of magistrates' court	In favour of Crown Court
Cost: Trial in the magistrates' court will be much cheaper in comparison to the Crown Court, where the defendant is not legally aided. No income contributions are required for summary trial	
Disclosure: There is no requirement to serve a defence statement on summary trial, meaning that more of the defence's case may be hidden from the prosecution	

Revision tip

Whilst the factors in **Table 4.1** are beneficial, you must always remember that no two cases are the same. A particularly advantageous factor to one defendant may not be so advantageous to another defendant. Make sure you maintain a practical oversight of these factors and keep in your mind: What is best for this particular client? See **Practice example 4.1**.

Practice example 4.1

James is charged with burglary of a warehouse, contrary to s 9 Theft Act (TA) 1968. James was allegedly spotted leaving the warehouse in the early hours of the morning by a passer-by. James claims that this is a case of mistaken identification and wishes to challenge the admissibility of the ID procedure, claiming it was carried out in breach of Code D of Police and Criminal Evidence Act (PACE) 1984 (see **Chapter 1**). James is unemployed and in receipt of Universal Credit. James has a previous conviction for theft, contrary to s 1 TA 1968. James indicates a not-guilty plea at the PBV and the magistrates' court accepts summary jurisdiction.

Should James elect trial in the Crown Court or consent to summary trial?

James must decide which trial venue is most suitable for him; the defence solicitor cannot decide for him, they can only advise. Advice may include the fact that in the magistrates' court, the maximum sentence for a single offence is 12 months' imprisonment, whereas in the Crown Court, it is ten years' imprisonment (though the magistrates may commit James for sentence). James has previous convictions so it is questionable whether he would feel stress from the process. James would automatically qualify for legal aid if the case proceeded to the Crown Court but would have to prove the interests of justice test if the case was heard in the magistrates' court. The magistrates' court has a statistically

higher rate of conviction, and James' previous conviction will be relevant to that. James wishes to challenge ID evidence, which may be best challenged in the Crown Court. As you can see, the advice is mixed.

At this stage, the client has indicated a not-guilty plea and has been advised on trial venue. With that, we may now turn to consider the allocation hearing.

ALLOCATION HEARING

The allocation hearing is designed to ensure that a case is dealt with at whichever venue is considered most suitable. The procedure to be adopted in determining trial venue is laid out in ss 19–20 MCA 1980. We shall now consider this procedure.

Decision as to allocation (MCA 1980, s 19)

Given that the SQE1 Assessment Specification has specifically identified s 19 MCA 1980 as a legal authority, it makes sense to take s 19, and thus the process involved, step by step.

Before making their decision:

- The court shall first give the prosecution an opportunity to inform the court of the defendant's previous convictions (if any) given that any relevant convictions will likely affect sentence (MCA 1980, s 19(2)(a)).
- The court shall then give the prosecution and the defendant an opportunity to make representations (ie submissions) as to whether summary trial or trial on indictment would be more suitable (MCA 1980, s 19(2)(b)).

Following this, the magistrates will then consider a number of statutory factors in making their decision:

- first, whether the sentence which a magistrates' court would have power to impose for the offence would be adequate (MCA 1980, s 19(3)(a))
- second, any representations made by the prosecution or the defendant (MCA 1980, s 19(3)(b))
- third, the allocation and committal for sentence guideline issued by the Sentencing Council (MCA 1980, s 19(3)(b)) - see **pages 97–98**.

We shall consider the statutory factors in s 19(3) now.

Adequacy of magistrates' sentencing powers

First, the magistrates will consider whether their sentencing powers are adequate. To do this, the magistrates will consider any relevant sentencing guidelines and the maximum sentence available for that offence. For example, a single offence of fraud is punishable by up to 12 months' imprisonment in the magistrates' court and ten years' imprisonment in the Crown Court.

Revision tip

The sentencing guidelines will provide an indication as to the starting point and category range of the sentence, based upon the severity of the offence, the culpability of the defendant, any aggravating and mitigating circumstances and any potential reduction for a guilty plea. Make use of the sentencing guidelines in your revision to experience the operation of the law in practical situations. See **Chapter 8** for a further discussion of sentencing.

Importantly, a defendant must be warned that even if the decision is made that summary trial is suitable, all sentencing options remain open and, if the defendant consents to summary trial and is convicted by the court or pleads guilty, the defendant may still be committed to the Crown Court for sentence.

Furthermore, a special rule applies in s 19(4). It provides that where a defendant is charged with two or more offences, and those offences can either be joined in the same indictment or arise out of the same or connected circumstances (eg multiple thefts from the same victim), then the magistrates will consider whether their sentencing powers are adequate in light of the maximum aggregate sentence which a magistrates' court would have power to impose for all of the offences taken together.

Representations by the parties

Each party involved is permitted to make representations as to the appropriate venue for trial. The prosecution will fully outline the allegation against the defendant and will provide the court with the defendant's previous convictions. In many cases, the parties will agree on trial venue and the prosecution will indicate this in their submissions. It is often the case that any dispute arises where the prosecution seeks to have the case sent to the Crown Court, but the defendant wishes to remain in the magistrates' court. The value of defence submissions cannot be understated here.

Allocation and committal for sentence guideline

Finally, the court will consider the **allocation and committal for sentence guideline.**

Key term: allocation and committal for sentence guideline

Produced by the Sentencing Council, the allocation and committal for sentence guideline (formerly known simply as the 'allocation guideline' prior to 1 June 2025) provides that in general, either way offences should be tried summarily. The guideline provides two exceptions to this rule, where Crown Court trial may be more suitable:

- where the outcome would clearly be a sentence in excess of the court's powers for the offence(s) concerned after taking into account personal mitigation and any potential reduction for a guilty plea
- for reasons of unusual legal, procedural or factual complexity, the case should be tried in the Crown Court. This exception may apply in cases where a very substantial fine is the likely sentence. Other circumstances where this exception will apply are likely to be rare and

case-specific; the court will rely on the submissions of the parties to identify relevant cases.

Visit the Sentencing Council's website to view the allocation and committal for sentence guideline in full.

In addition, the allocation and committal for sentence guideline provides that in cases with no factual or legal complications, the court should bear in mind its power to commit for sentence after a trial. In this regard, it may retain jurisdiction despite the fact that the likely sentence might exceed its powers.

Outcome of allocation

At the end of the allocation hearing, the magistrates must determine the outcome of the hearing. They have two options available to them:

- decline summary jurisdiction and deem trial on indictment to be more suitable
- accept summary jurisdiction and deem summary trial to be more suitable.

We shall consider the procedure to be followed according to each outcome.

Trial on indictment appears more suitable (MCA 1980, s 21)

If the court decides that the offence appears to be more suitable for trial on indictment, the court shall inform the defendant of this and send them forthwith to the Crown Court in accordance with s 51 of the Crime and Disorder Act (CDA) 1998 (see **page 102** for more details on s 51 as it applies to indictable only offences). A date will be set for the defendant's first appearance before the Crown Court at the plea and trial preparation hearing (PTPH) (see **Chapter 5**).

Exam warning

Be aware, where the magistrates have declined jurisdiction, that the defendant has no choice but to accept this decision. It is wrong to suggest, therefore, that the defendant has a right to elect summary trial in this instance. Avoid making this mistake in an MCQ.

Summary trial appears more suitable (MCA 1980, s 20)

Where the magistrates accept summary jurisdiction, the procedure to be adopted is set out in s 20 MCA 1980. As we did with s 19, let us consider s 20 step by step.

First, under s 20(2), the court will explain to the defendant:

- that it appears to the court more suitable for the defendant to be tried summarily for the offence

- that they can either consent to be so tried or, if they wish, be tried on indictment
- that if they are tried summarily and convicted by the court, they may be committed for sentence to the Crown Court.

At this stage in the process, the defendant may request an **indication of sentence.**

Key term: indication of sentence

An indication of sentence is where the magistrates identify whether a custodial sentence or non-custodial sentence would be more likely to be imposed if the defendant were to be tried summarily for the offence and to plead guilty (MCA 1980, s 20(3)).

An indication of sentence is a key part of allocation proceedings. Let us break the process down further:

- The court is not obliged to give such an indication (MCA 1980, s 20(4)).
- Where it does so, however, the court must ask the defendant whether they wish to reconsider their intended plea based upon the indication of sentence (MCA 1980, s 20(5)).
- If the defendant indicates an intention to reconsider their plea, the court will ask them again whether they would plead guilty or not guilty if the offence were to proceed to trial (MCA 1980, s 20(6)).

If the defendant wishes to reconsider their plea, and indicates a plea of guilty, the magistrates will proceed as if the defendant has pleaded guilty and shall convict them of the offence. Special rules outlined in s 20A of the MCA 1980 apply where the defendant indicates a guilty plea, based upon the indication of sentence.

In summary, s 20A provides that:

- No court (whether magistrates' court or not) is bound by the indication of sentence provided by the magistrates.
- No sentence may be challenged or be the subject of an appeal on the ground that it is not consistent with the indication of sentence.
- No court (whether magistrates' court or not) may impose a custodial sentence on the defendant, unless such a sentence was indicated in the indication of sentence.

Exam warning

Be aware that the procedure in s 20A *only* applies where the defendant has indicated that they intend to plead guilty. If the defendant does not reconsider their plea, the indication of sentence will have no bearing on the defendant's case if they are eventually convicted and sentenced. For example, if the magistrates indicate a non-custodial sentence, there is nothing to prevent the magistrates from imposing a custodial sentence if the defendant did not change their plea as the provisions of s 20A will not apply.

If no indication of sentence is given or requested, or an indication is given but the defendant does not wish to reconsider their plea, the court shall then seek the **defendant's choice**.

Key term: defendant's choice

Whilst not a legal term per se, it is important to highlight the choice available to the defendant. Under s 20(9) MCA 1980, the defendant must make a choice as to whether they consent to be tried summarily, or wish to be tried on indictment.

This choice is only available where the magistrates' court has accepted summary jurisdiction.

The defendant's choice will then affect the progression of the case:

- The defendant consents to summary trial: The magistrates will adjourn the case and set a date for summary trial. The magistrates' court will issue directions for case management (see **Chapter 5**).
- The defendant elects trial by jury: The magistrates will adjourn the case and send the defendant to the Crown Court. A date will be set for the defendant's first appearance before the Crown Court where their plea will be formally taken. The magistrates' court will complete the case management questionnaire when sending the defendant to the Crown Court (see **Chapter 5**).

Revision tip

It may be beneficial to break down the above process into three steps, to aid your revision:

- Step 1: PBV: The defendant indicates their plea.
- Step 2: Allocation hearing: Magistrates make their determination as to suitability.
- Step 3: Defendant's choice: If the magistrates accept summary jurisdiction, the defendant must decide whether to consent to summary trial or elect trial on indictment.

SENDING WITHOUT ALLOCATION

Finally, you must be aware of the circumstances where a case can be sent to the Crown Court without allocation. The first circumstance listed in the SQE1 Assessment Specification is where an either way offence is sent to the Crown Court, without an allocation hearing under s 50A of the CDA 1998. The second is where indictable only offences are sent to the Crown Court forthwith under s 51 of the CDA 1998.

Sending under the CDA 1998, s 50A

There are a number of provisions that you must be aware of under s 50A where the magistrates' court can send an either way offence to the Crown Court without allocation. We will consider each in turn here.

Notices in serious or complex fraud cases

First, s 50A(2) identifies that if notice is given under s 51B CDA 1998, a charge of fraud, whilst ordinarily an either way offence, must be sent forthwith to the Crown Court for trial, without allocation. Section 51B concerns circumstances where the prosecution is of the opinion that the evidence of the offence charged:

- is sufficient for the person charged to be put on trial for the offence
- reveals a case of fraud 'of such seriousness or complexity that it is appropriate that the management of the case should without delay be taken over by the Crown Court'.

Such notice can only be given by a 'designated authority', which refers to the Director of Public Prosecutions (DPP) (which includes the Crown Prosecution Service), the Director of the Serious Fraud Office, or the Secretary of State.

Notices in certain cases involving children

Second, s 50A(2) also identifies that if notice is given under s 51C CDA 1998, a case must be sent forthwith to the Crown Court for trial, without allocation. Section 51C concerns circumstances where the DPP, and anyone to whom the DPP delegates authority, eg a Crown Prosecutor, is of the opinion that:

- the evidence of the offence would be sufficient for the person charged to be put on trial for the offence
- a child would be called as a witness at the trial, and
- for the purpose of avoiding any prejudice to the welfare of the child, the case should be taken over and proceed without delay by the Crown Court.

Procedural link: substantive criminal law

Notice in cases involving children only applies to offences involving an assault on, or injury or a threat of injury to, a person, child cruelty, certain sexual offences, kidnapping, false imprisonment or child abduction. It also applies to attempting, conspiring and assisting or encouraging any of those offences (see ***Revise SQE: Criminal Law*** for more details on substantive criminal law).

Related offences and offenders

By s 50A(3), where a defendant (or a co-defendant) has been sent to the Crown Court for an offence triable only on indictment, or for an offence sent with notice given under ss 51B or 51C, the court must also send the defendant to the Crown Court for any related either way offence (for the definition of 'related', see **page 103**).

Sending under the CDA 1998, s 51

The second, and more common way, in which an offence is sent to the Crown Court without allocation is in accordance with s 51 CDA 1998. Whilst this provision applies to both indictable only offences and either way offences, the SQE1 Assessment Specification has cited s 51 in the context of 'sending *without* allocation'. As previously discussed, unless notice is given in certain cases, either way offences must be dealt with in accordance with ss 19–20 MCA 1980 (ie *with* allocation (see **page 96**)). Therefore, any reference to s 51 in SQE1 must relate to indictable only offences. It is those offences that we shall deal with here.

Sending indictable only offences

Where a defendant is charged with an indictable only offence, the magistrates' court must send them to the Crown Court **forthwith**.

> **Key term: forthwith**
>
> 'Forthwith' is a term simply used to describe the notion that the magistrates' court is sending the defendant to the Crown Court without delay (given the seriousness of the offence). 'Sending' is purely an administrative act; the magistrates are not concerned with the evidential sufficiency of the charges alleged against the defendant.

By way of procedure, the magistrates must set a date for a PTPH — within 28 days of sending (see **Chapter 5**), and determine the defendant's bail position (ie whether to remand them in custody or on bail — see **Chapter 2** for a discussion of bail). As discussed in **Chapter 3**, the magistrates should ask the defendant whether they intend to plead guilty or not (though this often does not happen in practice). This plea should be noted on the Better Case Management (BCM) form.

Where the defendant has indicated a guilty plea, the magistrates must make arrangements for the Crown Court to take the accused's plea as soon as possible, and should consider ordering a pre-sentence report at that stage, so that the Crown Court can proceed to sentence at the first hearing. Where a not-guilty plea is likely to be entered, the BCM should identify the likely issue that the defendant takes with the charge (ie their defence). Any further court directions, such as further disclosure of prosecution evidence, should also be recorded on the BCM to assist the parties in preparing for the PTPH.

Sending related offences without allocation

By s 51(3) CDA 1998, where a defendant appears before the magistrates' court charged with an indictable only offence, and other either way or summary only offences, the magistrates *must* send all offences to the Crown Court for trial without allocation.

Where, however, the magistrates have previously sent the defendant to the Crown Court for trial, and the defendant subsequently appears before the magistrates charged with related either way or summary only offences, the magistrates *may* send these subsequent offences to the Crown Court for trial without allocation (CDA 1998, s 51(4)).

Both rules only apply in circumstances where the either way or summary only offences are **related** to the indictable only offence.

Key term: related offences

An either way offence is 'related' if the charge for the either way offence could be joined on the same indictment as the charge for the indictable only offence. A summary only offence is 'related' if it arises out of circumstances which are the same as, or connected with, those giving rise to the indictable only offence (or to an either way offence also being considered) *and* is punishable with imprisonment or involves obligatory or discretionary disqualification from driving.

Practice example 4.2 demonstrates the application of this key term.

Practice example 4.2

James is charged with robbery, contrary to s 8 Theft Act 1968, after threatening Mark in his house and taking an expensive laptop. On his way out of Mark's house, James headed for his car to escape. A stranger, who saw James running from the house carrying the laptop and being closely followed by Mark, stood in front of James' car door, refusing to move. James hit the stranger, causing a black eye and knocking him to the ground. James was also charged with assault occasioning actual bodily harm, contrary to s 47 Offences Against the Person Act 1861. A passer-by shouted at James, ordering him to stop. James, walking towards the passer-by and waving his fists, shouted, 'You're going to get punched'. The passer-by feared that they would get hurt. James was charged with common assault.

How will these offences be dealt with?

The view may be taken that the robbery (an indictable only offence) and assault occasioning actual bodily harm (an either way offence) are related offences, as they arise out of the same facts. Both offences may be joined on the same indictment and subsequently sent to the Crown Court to be tried. In addition, even though a charge of common assault is a summary only offence, as it arises out of the same facts as the robbery, and is punishable by imprisonment, it can be sent to the Crown Court without allocation.

Sending related adult offenders without allocation

In circumstances where, say, there are two defendants (D1 and D2) and the magistrates send D1 to the Crown Court, charged with an indictable only offence, they *must* also send D2 to the Crown Court without allocation, where:

- D2 is jointly charged with D1 for an either way offence,
- the either way offence is related to the indictable only offence for which D1 has already been sent, and
- D1 and D2 appear together on the same occasion.

Where, however, D2 appears subsequent to D1 (ie not on the same occasion), jointly charged with an either way offence, related to the indictable only offence, the magistrates *may* send D2 to the Crown Court without allocation. Both of these circumstances are contained in s 51(5) CDA 1998 and s 51(6) provides that any either way or summary only offence related to the offence sent under s 51(5), may also be sent to the Crown Court without allocation. The term 'related' is the same as that used for related offences.

Practice example 4.3 will assist in understanding the scope and operation of s 51(5).

Practice example 4.3

Mark and James appear before the magistrates' court, jointly charged with inflicting grievous bodily harm contrary to s 20 Offences Against the Person Act 1861. Mark had, on a previous occasion, been sent to the Crown Court charged with robbery, contrary to s 8 Theft Act 1968. The prosecution alleged that the offences could be joined on the same indictment.

How will this case be dealt with?

The magistrates may send Mark to the Crown Court for trial as the offence is related; they are not obliged to do so, however. The magistrates may send James to the Crown Court for trial as a related offender. In neither case are the magistrates obliged to send Mark and James to the Crown Court because their appearance for the either way offence is subsequent to Mark's initial appearance for the indictable only offence. Should there be any additional either way or summary only offences related to the these matters charged, they too can be sent without allocation to the Crown Court.

Sending related child offenders without allocation

The position regarding the sending of children charged with an adult offender who has been sent to the Crown Court is dealt with in **Chapter 10**.

KEY POINT CHECKLIST

This chapter has covered the following key knowledge points. You can use these to structure your revision, ensuring you recall the key details for each point, as covered in this chapter.

- At the defendant's first appearance charged with an either way offence, they will be asked to indicate a plea. This is known as plea before venue (PBV). The court will advise the defendant of the procedure to be adopted dependent on their plea.
- If the defendant indicates a not-guilty plea, the court will proceed to an allocation hearing, to determine which trial venue will be most suitable for the defendant's case.
- If the magistrates accept summary jurisdiction, the defendant will then need to make a choice as to whether they consent to summary trial or elect trial by jury.
- A defence solicitor will need to be familiar with the relative advantages and disadvantages of trial in both the magistrates' court and Crown Court.
- Some either way offences may be sent to the Crown Court without allocation, and all indictable only offences must be sent forthwith to the Crown Court.

KEY TERMS AND CONCEPTS

- plea before venue (**page 91**)
- allocation hearing (**page 93**)
- allocation and committal for sentence guideline (**page 97**)
- indication of sentence (**page 99**)
- defendant's choice (**page 100**)
- forthwith (**page 102**)
- related offences (**page 103**)

SQE1-STYLE QUESTIONS

QUESTION 1

A man is charged with theft, contrary to s 1 Theft Act 1968. The man indicates a not-guilty plea at the plea before venue (PBV) and the magistrates identify that the offence is suitable for summary trial. The man requests an indication of sentence which is provided by the magistrates. The indication does not identify a custodial sentence. The magistrates are now ready to ask the man whether he wishes to reconsider his indication of a not-guilty plea.

Which of the following best describes the legal position of the indication of sentence?

A. The magistrates' court is bound by the indication of sentence, but the Crown Court is not bound by the indication of sentence if the magistrates commit the man for sentencing.

B. The magistrates' court and the Crown Court are bound by the indication of sentence and cannot impose a custodial sentence.
C. Neither the magistrates' court nor the Crown Court is bound by the indication of sentence but cannot impose a custodial sentence if it did not form part of the indication of sentence if the man changes his plea to guilty.
D. Neither the magistrates' court nor the Crown Court is bound by the indication of sentence and can impose a custodial sentence.
E. Neither the magistrates' court nor the Crown Court is bound by the indication of sentence but cannot impose a custodial sentence if it did not form part of the indication of sentence.

QUESTION 2

A woman is charged with malicious wounding, contrary to s 20 Offences Against the Person Act 1861. The woman had been sent, on a previous occasion, to the Crown Court for trial in respect of malicious wounding with intent, contrary to s 18 Offences Against the Person Act 1861, for which she pleaded not guilty. The allegation by the prosecution is that both offences were committed within a few days of each other against the same complainant. The woman indicates a not-guilty plea for the s 20 offence.

Which of the following best describes the likely trial venue for the s 20 offence?

A. The s 20 offence may be tried in either the magistrates' court or the Crown Court.
B. The s 20 offence must be tried in the Crown Court, alongside the s 18 offence, as it is a related offence.
C. The s 20 offence will be tried in the magistrates' court, as it is a summary only offence.
D. The s 20 offence will likely be tried in the magistrates' court.
E. The s 20 offence shall be tried in the Crown Court, as it is an indictable only offence.

QUESTION 3

A man is charged with two either way offences. The man has indicated a not-guilty plea at the plea before venue (PBV) to both charges.

Which of the following most accurately describes the process in s 19 Crime and Disorder Act 1998?

A. The prosecution will inform the court of the facts but is not permitted to present the man's previous convictions. The magistrates will then consider any representations by the man, but not the prosecution. The magistrates will also consider whether their sentencing powers are adequate, with reference to the aggregate sentence for the two offences and the allocation and committal for sentence guideline.

B. The prosecution will inform the court of the facts, including the man's previous convictions. The magistrates will then consider any representations by the prosecution and the man. The magistrates will also consider whether their sentencing powers are adequate, with reference to the aggregate sentence for the two offences and the allocation and committal for sentence guideline.
C. The prosecution will inform the court of the facts, including the man's previous convictions. No representations may be made by either the prosecution or defence. The magistrates will also consider whether their sentencing powers are adequate, focusing on the sentence for each offence and the allocation and committal for sentence guideline.
D. The prosecution will inform the court of the facts but is not permitted to present the man's previous convictions. The magistrates will then consider any representations by the man, but not the prosecution. The magistrates will also consider whether their sentencing powers are adequate, focusing on the sentence for each offence and the allocation and committal for sentence guideline.
E. The prosecution will inform the court of the facts, including the man's previous convictions. No representations may be made by either the prosecution or defence. The magistrates will also consider whether their sentencing powers are adequate, with reference to the aggregate sentence for the two offences and the allocation and committal for sentence guideline.

QUESTION 4

A man is charged with criminal damage. The value of the property damaged is assessed at £4,000. The man indicates a plea of not guilty.

Which of the following best describes the process that will be followed?

A. The man will be tried in the magistrates' court and, if convicted, can be committed to the Crown Court for sentence.
B. The man will be tried in the Crown Court and, if convicted, will be subject to the sentencing powers only available to the magistrates' court.
C. The man will be subject to an allocation hearing, which will determine whether he will be tried in the magistrates' court or the Crown Court.
D. The man will be tried in the Crown Court and, if convicted, will be subject to the ordinary sentencing powers of the Crown Court.
E. The man will be tried in the magistrates' court and, if convicted, cannot be committed to the Crown Court for sentence.

QUESTION 5

A woman is charged with burglary, contrary to s 9 Theft Act 1968. The woman indicates a plea of not guilty.

Which of the following is the most accurate description of the woman's choice in allocation proceedings?

A. The woman never has a choice as to which court her case will be heard in.
B. Where the magistrates accept summary jurisdiction, the woman has no choice as to which court her case will be heard in.
C. Where the magistrates reject summary jurisdiction, the woman has a choice as to which court her case will be heard in.
D. Where the magistrates accept summary jurisdiction, the woman has a choice as to which court her case will be heard in.
E. The woman always has a choice as to which court her case will be heard in.

■ ANSWERS TO QUESTIONS

Answers to 'What do you know already?' questions at the start of the chapter

1) False. No court is bound by the indication of sentence given during an allocation hearing. However, where the defendant changes their plea to guilty, following an indication of sentence, a custodial sentence cannot be imposed, unless such sentence was indicated in the indication of sentence.
2) No, if the magistrates conclude that trial in the Crown Court is suitable, the defendant has no choice but to accept that decision. The defendant only has a right to choose which court he would like his case heard in if the magistrates' court accept summary jurisdiction.
3) The magistrates' court is a preferable trial court because the sentencing powers are limited (though the magistrates do retain the power to commit to the Crown Court for sentence), the appeal routes are more accessible than appeals from the Crown Court and the proceedings are faster and less formal. These factors are case- and fact-specific, however.
4) Given that s 47 is an either way offence, it would normally be subject to an allocation hearing. However, given that the offence is one involving an assault on another person, and a child witness is to be called to give evidence, it is likely that this case will be sent to the Crown Court for trial following notice from the DPP.

Answers to end-of-chapter SQE1-style questions

Question 1

The correct answer was C. This is because whilst the indication of sentence is not binding, any court cannot impose a custodial sentence unless that was indicated in the indication of sentence, and the man has subsequently changed his plea. Options A and B are wrong because no court is bound by the indication of sentence. Option D is technically correct but fails to consider the circumstance where a custodial sentence is not indicated (therefore is not the best answer). Option E is also technically correct but does not deal with the fact that this rule only applies where the man reconsiders his plea. If the man continues to plead not guilty, a custodial sentence can be imposed.

Question 2

The correct answer was A. This is because, whilst the s 20 charge is seemingly related to the s 18 charge, the woman appeared before the magistrates at a subsequent hearing charged with s 20. As such, the magistrates have the discretion to send to the Crown Court without allocation; they are not obliged to do so (option B is therefore incorrect). Options C and E are wrong because s 20 is an either way offence. Whilst option D is a possibility, it is not the most accurate answer or advice that can be given. In fact, it is more likely for the charge to be sent to the Crown Court with the s 18 offence given the close factual connection (eg avoiding the need for two trials).

Question 3

The correct answer was B. This option lays out the full procedure set out in s 19 MCA 1980. The prosecution can present the man's previous convictions (as this will be relevant to the question of whether the magistrates' sentencing powers are adequate). Both parties may make appropriate representations and the magistrates will consider relevant sentencing guidelines and allocation and committal for sentence guideline. As the man is charged with more than one offence, the magistrates would consider the maximum aggregate sentence. All other options are therefore incorrect.

Question 4

The correct answer was E. This is because criminal damage of property valued less than £5,000 is a summary only offence, tried in the magistrates' court. The man has no right to elect trial by jury, and the magistrates have no power to commit the man for sentence (therefore option A is wrong). Options B and D are incorrect because low-value criminal damage is a summary only offence. Option C is incorrect as, whilst criminal damage is normally an either way offence, low-value criminal damage must be tried summarily.

Question 5

The correct answer was D. This is because a defendant will *only* have the choice as to which venue their case will be heard in when the magistrates deem summary trial as being suitable (ie they *accept* summary jurisdiction). Where the magistrates *reject* summary jurisdiction, and send a defendant to the Crown Court, the defendant has no choice in this allocation. Options A, B, C and E are therefore incorrect as they do not correctly identify the procedure.

■ KEY CASES, RULES, STATUTES AND INSTRUMENTS

The SQE1 Assessment Specification requires you to know ss 19–20 and 22A of the MCA 1980, and ss 50A and 51 of the CDA 1998.

5

Case management and pre-trial hearings

MAKE SURE YOU KNOW

This chapter will cover the rules and procedures relating to case management and pre-trial hearings in the magistrates' court and Crown Court. For the purposes of SQE1, you are required to know:

- magistrates' court case management directions
- plea and trial preparation hearing
- disclosure – prosecution, defence and unused material.

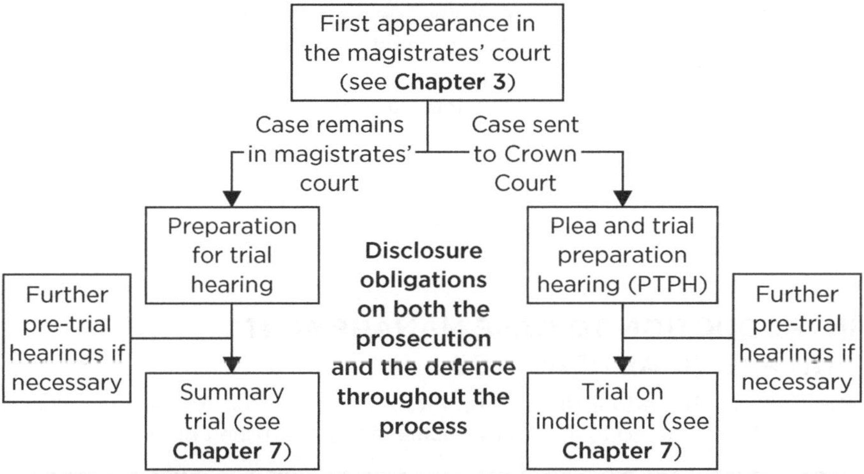

Overview of case management

SQE ASSESSMENT ADVICE

As you work through this chapter, remember to pay particular attention in your revision to:

- the case management obligations owed by all parties to a criminal case to further the overriding objective
- the standard directions issued by a magistrates' court in preparation for trial and the forms to be completed for pre-trial hearings in both the magistrates' court and Crown Court

- the content, structure and importance of the plea and trial preparation hearing in the Crown Court to ensuring an effective trial
- the obligations imposed on both the prosecution and defence regarding their duties to disclose evidence.

WHAT DO YOU KNOW ALREADY?

Have a go at these questions before reading this chapter. If you find some difficult or cannot remember the answers, make a note to look more closely at that area during your revision.

1) The court must further the overriding objective by actively managing the case. What sort of things does 'active case management' include?

   [Introduction to case management and pre-trial hearings, page 112]

2) What standard directions would you expect to see from the magistrates' court in order to prepare for an effective trial? List as many as you can think of.

   [Magistrates' court case management directions, page 113]

3) Fill in the blank: In general, there will be no further pre-trial hearings following a plea and trial preparation hearing. The court may hold further pre-trial hearings if ____________.

   [Plea and trial preparation hearing, page 115]

4) True or false? The prosecution is obligated to disclose evidence which might be reasonably considered capable of undermining the case for the defendant.

   [Prosecution disclosure, page 118]

INTRODUCTION TO CASE MANAGEMENT AND PRE-TRIAL HEARINGS

The Criminal Procedure Rules (CrimPR) 2025 provide a framework of rules that must be adhered to in order to achieve **the overriding objective**.

Key term: the overriding objective

The overriding objective is that criminal cases be dealt with justly. Dealing with a criminal case justly includes (amongst other things) acquitting the innocent and convicting the guilty, dealing with the prosecution and the defence fairly, and dealing with the case efficiently and expeditiously. All persons involved in the conduct of a case must further this overriding objective by complying with the CrimPR and associated directions.

The court must further the overriding objective by actively managing the case, and the parties to the case must actively assist the court in fulfilling that duty (eg through the early identification of issues).

For the purposes of SQE1, you are required to understand case management in both the magistrates' court and the Crown Court. The following sections will deal with those issues, before we then proceed to deal with the law relating to disclosure.

Revision tip

Whilst SQE1 does not require any candidate to know or be able to use statutory material or case law for the topic of case management, you are strongly advised to read the following materials for a full understanding of case management in practice:

- *The Better Case Management Revival Handbook* – January 2023 (Judiciary of England and Wales)
- CrimPR 2025, Part 3.

MAGISTRATES' COURT CASE MANAGEMENT DIRECTIONS

In **Chapter 3**, we considered the defendant's first appearance in the magistrates' court. Now, we shall turn our attention to further pre-trial hearings within that court, distinguishing cases that will remain in the magistrates' court and those that will be sent to the Crown Court.

Cases remaining in the magistrates' court

If the defendant is charged with a summary only offence, or an either way offence that is to be tried in a magistrates' court, the court will give such directions as are necessary to prepare for sentencing (following a guilty plea) or for a trial (following a not-guilty plea). If a defendant pleads 'not guilty', the magistrates must conduct a 'preparation for trial hearing' (this will generally take place during the first hearing).

Preparation for trial hearing

At a preparation for trial hearing, the court must give directions for an effective trial. As part of this process, the parties and court must complete a Preparation for Effective Trial (PET) form. This form records the contact details of the parties to the case, the evidence which will be relied upon by the prosecution at trial, the elements of the prosecution's case disputed by the defendant, and any decisions and directions for effective trial given by the court.

Further pre-trial hearings

Further pre-trial case management hearings may be conducted in limited circumstances. These are where:

- the court anticipates a guilty plea
- it is necessary to conduct such a hearing in order to give directions for an effective trial, or

- such a hearing is required to set ground rules for the conduct of the questioning of a witness or defendant.

Magistrates' court standard directions

Part 5 of the PET form lists a number of standard directions to be given by the court. **Table 5.1** provides a summary of some of the important case directions you may come across in an MCQ.

Table 5.1: Magistrates' court standard directions

Service of evidence and disclosure The court may direct that the prosecution must serve further evidence by a certain date, or must comply with their initial duty of disclosure (if they have not already done so) by a certain date. The disclosure of unused material will be relevant here
Witnesses and evidence The parties must provide the details of the witnesses that they intend to call. The obligation applies to both the prosecution and the defence. In respect of defence witnesses, the defence must supply the name, address and date of birth of the witness. This must be done within ten business days of the prosecution complying with the initial duty of disclosure The court will also direct parties to identify whether evidence from the witness is to be heard live, or (if uncontested) may be read in court. If the evidence is to be heard live in court, the court will direct that the parties note the time required to question each witness
Expert evidence If an expert witness is required by the defence for a particular issue, the court will direct that any witness statement or report from that expert be served on the prosecution
Securing attendance To secure the attendance of a witness at trial, a party to the case can apply to the court to issue a witness summons. In order to do so, the court must be satisfied that the evidence to be given by that witness would be material to the case at hand and that it would be in the interests of justice to issue a summons. A summons will not always be necessary, but is practically vital
Special measures, including intermediaries The court may direct for the use of special measures for a particular witness, and a particular form of special measures. The court may direct that there is a restriction of cross-examination by the defendant and for any use of an intermediary

Cases sent to the Crown Court

Where a defendant is to be sent to the Crown Court for trial (as a result of being charged with an indictable only offence or an either way offence), the magistrates will issue standard directions for the preparation of trial. The Better Case Management (BCM) form must be completed on sending for trial. The magistrates must set a date for a **plea and trial preparation hearing** (PTPH) at the Crown Court (which must be held within 28 days of sending). We shall consider PTPHs now.

PLEA AND TRIAL PREPARATION HEARING

Where a case is sent to the Crown Court, generally the first hearing in the Crown Court will be the PTPH (in some cases the defence will make a bail application that will precede the PTPH).

Key term: plea and trial preparation hearing

The PTPH is a pre-trial hearing designed to set the date for trial; identify, so far as can be determined at that stage, the issues for trial; provide a timetable for the necessary pre-trial preparation (known as 'stage dates') and give appropriate directions for an effective trial; and make provision for any further pre-trial case management hearings.

In any event, a PTPH *must* be held in every criminal case sent to the Crown Court.

Content of a PTPH

The PTPH will deal with a number of matters as part of the criminal case.

Arraignment

Once the defendant has been identified by the Court Clerk, the PTPH will begin with the **arraignment** of the defendant.

Key term: arraignment

Arraignment refers to when the charges on the indictment are read to the defendant in open court by the clerk of the court, and the defendant is asked to enter a plea in respect of each of those charges, eg 'guilty' or 'not guilty'.

If there are several counts on the indictment, a plea must be taken on each count separately. If two counts are in the alternative, and the defendant pleads guilty to the first count (eg murder), it is unnecessary to put the second alternative count (eg manslaughter) to them.

Guilty plea: sentencing

Where a guilty plea is entered at the PTPH, the court should ordinarily proceed to sentencing on the same day. Sentencing may be adjourned to a later date if reports are required (eg pre-sentence or psychological/psychiatric reports), or where the defendant disputes the factual basis of the prosecution's case (thus requiring a Newton hearing - see **Chapter 8**). If sentencing is adjourned, the court will need to determine whether to remand the defendant into custody or on bail (see **Chapter 2**).

Revision tip

As discussed in **Chapter 8,** a judge is permitted to give an indication of sentence following a request for such indication by the defendant. The indication is of the maximum sentence that would be imposed if the defendant were to plead guilty at that stage in the proceedings (known as a Goodyear indication). Be aware of this ability to request an indication as this may affect the plea of a defendant at the PTPH and forms part of your advice to your client. If, however, your client is adamant as to their innocence, there will be little use in requesting an indication of sentence.

Not-guilty plea: case management hearing

If a not-guilty plea is entered, case management will then take place in preparation for trial. In preparation for the PTPH, the PTPH form must have been completed by both the prosecution and defence. The form is intended to:

- gather necessary information from the parties
- monitor the extent to which the prosecution provides information prior to the PTPH
- allow the court to make and record clear orders timetabling case progression in areas where the need can be anticipated
- allow the court to provide for further hearings when they are going to be necessary and most useful.

On the PTPH form, the prosecution are required to confirm that the indictment properly sets out the offence(s), what evidence they seek to rely on, and whether there will be any applications as part of the trial (eg special measures, bad character etc). The defence are required, as part of the PTPH form, to identify the issue for trial (ie what the defendant's defence is) and what witnesses are required for trial.

See **Practice example 5.1** for an identification of what will be involved in a case management hearing.

Practice example 5.1

Mark is charged with murder. Mark is sent forthwith to the Crown Court and a PTPH is held. At the PTPH, Mark pleads not guilty and the court proceeds with case management.

What will happen as part of Mark's case management hearing?

As part of case management, the court will:

- **set the trial date (known as 'listing')**
- **identify, so far as can be determined at that stage, the issues for trial (eg if Mark argues that he acted in self-defence)**
- **consider with the parties the witness requirements that can be determined at that stage (eg if any witness to the alleged offence requires any special measures to assist them)**
- **provide a timetable for the necessary pre-trial preparation (ie 'set the stage dates') and give appropriate directions for an effective trial**
- **make provision for any further case management hearings (see immediately below) that are required to take place at the time when they can be of maximum effectiveness.**

Further case management hearings

Generally, there should be no further case management hearings (FCMH) following the PTPH. Ordinarily, the next hearing would be the trial itself. However, the court may conduct FCMH where:

- it is necessary to conduct such a hearing in order to give directions for an effective trial, or
- such a hearing is required to set ground rules for the conduct of the questioning of a witness or defendant.

This second circumstance is particularly important. Where a case is likely to feature one or more vulnerable witnesses (see **Chapter 7**), the court will hold a **ground rules hearing**.

Key term: ground rules hearing

A ground rules hearing is designed to establish the most appropriate way for vulnerable witnesses to give their best evidence. The hearing will address the management of questions to witnesses at trial, including the restrictions on the type and nature of questions to be asked, and whether any reasonable adjustments are required; for example, whether the witness could give evidence by live link (see **Chapter 7**).

At the conclusion of the PTPH, the defendant will either be remanded into custody or released on bail pending trial (see **Chapter 2**).

DISCLOSURE

The final matter to be considered in this chapter is the topic of **disclosure.**

Key term: disclosure

In criminal proceedings, disclosure refers to the legal duties imposed on the parties to a criminal case to provide evidence or information to the other side. Both the prosecution and defence possess legal duties relating to disclosure and those duties vary according to the type of case being dealt with and the court within which it is heard.

The following sections will consider the legal duties imposed on the prosecution and defence in both the magistrates' court and the Crown Court. Before then, it is important to understand the nature of material to be disclosed in a criminal case:

- First, the prosecution will need to disclose all evidence that they rely upon in the case. This is evidence that the prosecution will use in order to prove the defendant's guilt.
- Second, the defence may be under an obligation to disclose information regarding their case (eg the defence that they intend to run). The obligation on the defendant depends on the court where the case is tried.
- Third, the prosecution is also under an obligation to disclose **unused material**. This is a continuing duty until the end of the case.

Key term: unused material

Unused material refers to any evidence or information that the prosecution possesses but does not intend to use as part of its case against the defendant. The prosecution is under an obligation to disclose unused material in line with their initial and continuing duty of disclosure.

See **Table 5.3** on **page 124** for a summary of the time frames within which the various disclosure obligations must take place.

Prosecution disclosure

The rules relating to prosecution disclosure apply equally whether the case is being heard in the magistrates' court or the Crown Court. For that reason, we shall structure our discussion on prosecution duties relating to disclosure according to the time frame of disclosure. In **Chapter 3**, we discussed the rules relating to the initial details of the prosecution's case (IDPC). Our discussion of disclosure will follow on from that.

Revision tip

Whilst SQE1 does not require you to know any statutory materials relating to the rules on disclosure, you are strongly advised to read the *Attorney General's (AG) Guidelines on Disclosure 2024*, which outline the high-level principles that should be followed when considering the rules relating to disclosure.

Initial duty of prosecution to disclose

Following any IDPC, the prosecution must disclose to the defendant any prosecution material:

- which has not previously been disclosed to the accused, and

- which *might reasonably be considered* capable of undermining the case for the prosecution against the defendant or of assisting the case for the defendant.

This will include any evidence that the prosecution intends to rely on and any unused material. If there is no material to disclose of the description given above, then the prosecution must give the defendant a written statement stating such. In both circumstances listed above, the prosecution must also inform the court of any disclosure or written notice of no disclosure.

As should be evident, the duty of the prosecution is quite specific. Candidates often misunderstand the nature of the prosecution's disclosure duties. Use **Table 5.2** to solidify your understanding as to what must be disclosed and what need not be disclosed by the prosecution.

Table 5.2: Initial duty of the prosecution to disclose

What must be disclosed	What need not be disclosed
Material which might reasonably be considered capable of being adverse to the prosecution's case	Neutral material, not affecting either party positively or negatively
Material which might reasonably be considered capable of positively impacting the defendant's case	Material which is adverse to the defendant's case (though, of course, you would expect the prosecution to rely on this evidence and thus disclose it in the ordinary course of events)

In practice, the prosecution will produce a schedule of material not disclosed to alert the defendant of its existence (including a sensitive and a non-sensitive schedule). However, the *AG Guidelines on Disclosure* are clear that such evidence, if not within the legal obligation of the prosecution, should not be disclosed.

Paragraph 84 of the *AG Guidelines on Disclosure* provides a list of considerations that the prosecution must take account of in deciding whether material satisfies the disclosure test. These considerations include:

- the use that might be made of the material in cross-examination (see **Chapter 7**)
- the capacity of the material to support submissions that could lead to the exclusion of evidence, or a stay (pause) of proceedings
- the capacity of the material to suggest an explanation or partial explanation of the defendant's actions
- the capacity of the material to undermine the reliability or credibility of a prosecution witness

- the capacity of the material to have a bearing on scientific or medical evidence in the case.

Revision tip

Paragraph 86 of the *AG Guidelines on Disclosure* provides some examples of materials that are 'likely' to meet the test for disclosure and include such things as any incident logs relating to the allegation and any material casting doubt on the reliability of a witness (eg previous convictions). Please review paragraph 86 for the full list of examples.

Time frames for initial disclosure

The prosecution must ensure that they comply with their duties of initial disclosure within the time set by law. This time frame varies according to whether the case is tried in the magistrates' court or the Crown Court:

- Magistrates' court: Prosecution must comply *as soon as is reasonably practicable* after the defendant pleads not guilty.
- Crown Court: Prosecution must comply as soon as is reasonably practicable after the case is committed or transferred for trial, or after the evidence is served where the case is sent for trial, or after a count is added to the indictment.

Continuing duty of prosecution to disclose

The prosecution must keep under review the question of whether at any given time there is prosecution material which:

- might reasonably be considered capable of undermining the case for the prosecution against the defendant or of assisting the case for the defendant, and
- has not already been disclosed to the defendant.

If at any time there is any such material, the prosecution must disclose it to the defendant as soon as is reasonably practicable. This duty continues until the defendant is either convicted or acquitted, or the prosecution decides not to proceed with the case. This continuing duty will be most applicable following receipt of any defence statement (see below, **Defence disclosure**).

Withholding disclosure

The prosecution may apply to the court to prevent the disclosure of material where the prosecution (and the court) considers that it would not be in the public interests to disclose (also known as **public interest immunity**).

Key term: public interest immunity

In some circumstances, the prosecution may apply to the court to prevent the disclosure of material that is considered sensitive and that would be contrary to the public interests to disclose. Such material could include matters relating to national security or the identity of police informants, for example.

If the material is the sort that should be disclosed (under the rules identified above), then the prosecution may only withhold such material if the court considers it protected by public interest immunity (ie it is for the court to rule that public interest immunity applies to that evidence). Any such application must be made in writing and must describe the material to be withheld. Ordinarily, the prosecution will prepare a schedule of sensitive materials which they may provide to the defendant.

Defence application to disclose

If the defendant has at any time reasonable cause to believe that there is prosecution material which should be disclosed to them under the prosecution's continuing duty to disclose, and such material has not been disclosed, they may apply to the court for an order requiring the prosecution to disclose it to them. In this case, the defence *must* serve a defence statement before they are able to apply for disclosure.

Defence disclosure

Once the prosecution has disclosed evidence, in line with the above rules, the onus of disclosure passes to the defendant. The onus on the defendant is to give notice indicating whether they intend to call any witnesses (other than themselves), including the details of those witnesses, and may also require them to serve what is known as a **defence statement**.

Key term: defence statement

A defence statement is a written statement which sets out the nature of the defendant's defence, including any particular defences on which they intend to rely. The defence statement also indicates the matters of fact on which the defendant takes issue with the prosecution, setting out why they take issue with the prosecution, and indicates any point of law (including any point as to the admissibility of evidence or an abuse of process) which they wish to take, and any authority on which they intend to rely for that purpose.

Special rules apply where the defence statement discloses an alibi (ie evidence that tends to show that the defendant was not at the location when the crime occurred at the time in question). Where a defence statement discloses an alibi, it must give particulars of that alibi, including the name, address and date of birth of any alibi witness, or as many of those details as are known to the defendant when the statement is given.

The nature of the defendant's duty to disclose a defence statement is dependent on the trial venue. Our discussion will therefore focus on trial in the magistrates' court and Crown Court.

Defence statements in the magistrates' court

Where the case is tried in the magistrates' court, the defendant *may* give a defence statement to the prosecution, and if they do so they must also give such a statement to the court.

If a defendant chooses to serve a defence statement, they must do so not more than 14 days after the prosecution discloses material in line with their initial duty of disclosure, or serves notice that there is no such material to disclose. The defendant may apply for an extension to this time period if they can show that it would be unreasonable to require them to give a defence statement within that period.

Defence statements in the Crown Court

Where the case is tried in the Crown Court, the defendant *must* supply a defence statement to the prosecution and the court. This is often referred to as a 'compulsory disclosure'. If there are multiple defendants to be tried on the indictment, the court *may* order that the defence statement be served on those co-defendants also. Where a defendant fails to comply with the requirement of compulsory disclosure in the Crown Court, the court may be able to draw adverse inferences against the defendant (see below, **Faults with defence disclosure**).

A defendant must serve a defence statement in the Crown Court not more than 28 days after the prosecution discloses material in line with their initial duty of disclosure, or serves notice that there is no such material to disclose. As in the magistrates' court, the defendant may apply for an extension to this time period.

Exam warning

An MCQ may seek to test your knowledge of the rules relating to defence disclosure. Keep the rules simple in your mind:

- The defendant is tried in the Crown Court: The defendant *must* serve a defence statement.
- The defendant is tried in the magistrates' court: The defendant *may* serve a defence statement but need not do so.

Faults with defence disclosure

There may be circumstances where the defendant's disclosure does not comply with the relevant rules. For example, the defendant may fail to serve a defence statement in the Crown Court, or may do so, but not in time. Equally, the defendant may serve a defence statement that is inconsistent with the defence being run at trial, or may fail to update a defence statement.

Where any of these circumstances arise, the defendant may be subject to adverse inferences or comment at trial (see **Chapter 6** for a definition and more information on adverse inferences). In particular:

- the court or any other party may make such comments as appears appropriate
- the court or jury may draw such inferences as appear proper in deciding whether the accused is guilty of the offence concerned (see **Practice example 5.2**).

Permission is not generally required for the prosecution to make a comment on faults with the defence statement. The main exception is where the information that was not disclosed relates to a point of law.

Practice example 5.2

James is charged with burglary in the Crown Court, contrary to s 9 Theft Act 1968. At the PTPH, James enters a not-guilty plea. James fails to serve a defence statement. At trial, James claims that he was not involved in the burglary and that this is a case of mistaken identity.

What is the consequence of James failing to supply a defence statement?

By failing to supply a defence statement, the trial judge and prosecution may make any comments as appear proper (eg the prosecution may cross-examine the defendant on his failure to serve a defence statement). Furthermore, the jury can draw any inferences as appear proper (eg they can take account of James' failure to give a defence statement when they are making their decision on the guilt or innocence of James).

A jury is generally not permitted to see a defendant's defence statement, even though reference may be made to it. However, on application by any party or on the judge's own motion, the judge may direct that the jury be given a copy of any defence statement. However, such a direction may be made only if the judge is of the opinion that seeing a copy of the defence statement would help the jury to understand the case or to resolve any issue in the case.

A defendant cannot be convicted of an offence, however, solely on an inference drawn due to faults with the defence statement. In the Crown Court, the judge must expressly direct the jury as to this.

Revision tip

Adverse inferences is a popular topic to test. Be aware, therefore, of the different occasions in which an adverse inference may be drawn, and the extent to which that inference can impact the decision of the tribunal of fact (ie how much weight a magistrate or jury will give to the inference).

It is vital, therefore, that the defence complies with their disclosure obligations. See **Table 5.3** for all the relevant disclosure time frames.

Table 5.3: Time frames for disclosure in criminal cases

Disclosure obligation	Time frame
Prosecution initial duty of disclosure (magistrates' court)	As soon as is reasonably practicable after the defendant pleads not guilty
Prosecution initial duty of disclosure (Crown Court)	As soon as is reasonably practicable after the case has been sent for trial
Prosecution continuing duty of disclosure	If, following initial disclosure, further information or evidence becomes available which satisfies the disclosure test, then the prosecution must disclose it to the defendant as soon as is reasonably practicable
Defence statement (magistrates' court) *NB Not obligatory to serve a defence statement in the magistrates' court*	Not more than 14 days after the prosecution discloses material in line with their initial duty of disclosure, or serves notice that there is no such material to disclose
Defence statement (Crown Court)	Not more than 28 days after the prosecution discloses material in line with their initial duty of disclosure, or serves notice that there is no such material to disclose

■ KEY POINT CHECKLIST

This chapter has covered the following key knowledge points. You can use these to structure your revision, ensuring you recall the key details for each point, as covered in this chapter.

- The overriding objective is to deal with cases justly, and active case management is vital to further that objective. Parties to the case, including the court, must actively manage the case.

- Following a not-guilty plea in the magistrates' court, the court will hold a preparation for trial hearing where it will issue standard directions to ensure an effective trial.
- Where a defendant has been sent to the Crown Court for trial, the first hearing there will be a PTPH. This hearing is designed to take the plea of the defendant, identify any issues between the parties and set a date for trial.
- The prosecution is under a duty to disclose all evidence that they rely upon and, in certain circumstances, any unused material in their possession.
- The defendant must serve a defence statement when tried in the Crown Court, but is under no such obligation if tried in the magistrates' court.

■ KEY TERMS AND CONCEPTS

- the overriding objective (**page 112**)
- plea and trial preparation hearing (**page 115**)
- arraignment (**page 115**)
- ground rules hearing (**page 117**)
- disclosure (**page 117**)
- unused material (**page 118**)
- public interest immunity (**page 120**)
- defence statement (**page 121**)

■ SQE1-STYLE QUESTIONS

QUESTION 1

A man is charged with theft, contrary to s 1 Theft Act 1968. The man, who indicates a not-guilty plea, is subject to a plea before venue and consents to summary trial. At the preparation for trial hearing, the magistrates give a number of standard directions, including the requirement to ensure proper and full disclosure has taken place as required by law.

Which of the following best describes the obligation for disclosure by the man in the case in his defence?

A. The man is required to disclose the details of any defence witness to be called other than himself and must give a defence statement within 14 days following disclosure by the prosecution.

B. The man is required to disclose the details of any defence witness to be called other than himself and may give a defence statement. If the man chooses to give a defence statement, he must do so as soon as is reasonably practicable following disclosure by the prosecution.

C. The man is required to disclose the details of any defence witness to be called other than himself and must give a defence statement within 28 days following disclosure by the prosecution.
D. The man is required to disclose the details of any defence witness to be called other than himself and may give a defence statement. If the man chooses to give a defence statement, he must do so within 28 days following disclosure by the prosecution.
E. The man is required to disclose the details of any defence witness to be called other than himself and may give a defence statement. If the man chooses to give a defence statement, he must do so within 14 days following disclosure by the prosecution.

QUESTION 2

A woman is charged with assault occasioning actual bodily harm, contrary to s 47 Offences Against the Person Act 1861. At the plea before venue, the woman elects trial on indictment and is sent to the Crown Court. The prosecution complies with its initial duty of disclosure and the defence gives their defence statement in accordance with the time limit prescribed by law. The woman's defence is one of alibi, claiming that she was not involved in the incident. The prosecution is in possession of evidence from a witness who claims to have seen the offence being committed by the woman. The prosecution chooses not to rely on this evidence at trial, however, as the witness possesses a number of previous convictions and the prosecution cannot be sure that the evidence is reliable.

Which of the following best describes the prosecution's duty in respect of the unused evidence?

A. The prosecution is obliged to disclose the information as they are under a duty to disclose material which might reasonably be considered capable of undermining the case for the defence.
B. The prosecution is obliged to disclose the information as they are under a duty to disclose any material within their possession which is relevant to the proceedings.
C. The prosecution is not obliged to disclose the information as they are under no duty to disclose material which might reasonably be considered capable of undermining the case for the defence.
D. The prosecution is obliged to disclose the information as they are under a duty to disclose any material within their possession which is relevant to proceedings tried in the Crown Court.
E. The prosecution is not obliged to disclose the information as the witness is considered as being unreliable and the prosecution must not mislead the court.

QUESTION 3

A man is charged with murder and at his first appearance in the magistrates' court is sent forthwith to the Crown Court for trial. At the plea and trial preparation hearing (PTPH), the man enters a not-guilty plea, and the parties proceed with case management in preparation for the trial. Following the PTPH, and in line with their continuing duty of disclosure, the prosecution discloses the witness statement of an elderly woman who claims to have witnessed the murder. The woman initially refused to come forward with this information due to a fear for her own safety as she believes the man was aware of her presence at the scene when the alleged murder took place. The woman is fearful that the man will recognise her.

Which of the following best represents the process that should follow this disclosure?

A. Following the PTPH, no further pre-trial case management hearings may be held. The next hearing that takes place will be the trial itself.

B. Following the PTPH, the court may conduct a further pre-trial case management hearing on the basis that such a hearing is required to set ground rules for the conduct of the questioning of a witness or defendant.

C. Following the PTPH, the court may conduct a further pre-trial case management hearing without any restrictions.

D. Following the PTPH, the court may conduct a further pre-trial case management hearing on the basis that it is necessary to conduct such a hearing in order to give directions for an effective trial.

E. Following the PTPH, the court must conduct a further pre-trial case management hearing given the new evidence that has come to light.

QUESTION 4

A man is charged with robbery, contrary to s 8 Theft Act 1968. During trial, the prosecution withholds information which might have weakened the prosecution case. This action was taken because the prosecution considered that public interest immunity should attach to the relevant material. Neither the trial judge nor the defence were informed about this.

Which of the following best describes the conduct of the prosecution in this case?

A. The prosecution was incorrect in its conduct. The prosecution was required to apply to the trial judge for a ruling that the evidence was protected by public interest immunity. There would be no obligation for the prosecution to inform the defence of this application.

B. The prosecution was correct in its conduct. It is for the prosecution to determine whether evidence is protected by public interest immunity and neither the trial judge nor the defence is entitled to know about it.

C. The prosecution was incorrect in its conduct. The prosecution was required to apply to the trial judge for a ruling that the evidence was protected by public interest immunity. There would also be an obligation for the prosecution to inform the defence of this application.

D. The prosecution was incorrect in its conduct. Whilst there was no requirement to inform the judge of the withheld material, there was an obligation for the prosecution to inform the defence of the withheld material.

E. The prosecution was correct in its conduct. It is for the prosecution to determine whether evidence is protected by public interest immunity and neither the trial judge nor the defence is entitled to know about it. Ideally, the prosecution would have recorded the withheld information on a schedule of sensitive material.

QUESTION 5

A man is charged with inflicting malicious wounding, contrary to s 20 Offences Against the Person Act 1861, in the Crown Court. The prosecution's case is that the man became intoxicated and attacked the victim without provocation by hitting him over the head with a glass bottle, causing cuts to the head. The man accepts that he struck the victim with the bottle but claims that he did so in self-defence, having been threatened earlier in the evening by the victim. The attack was witnessed by a woman, who is due to give evidence at trial. The prosecution has reviewed its unused material and discovers that the man has a previous conviction for battery, committed whilst intoxicated. The prosecution also discovers that the victim has three previous convictions for violence. Finally, the prosecution has evidence from the woman, in the form of a second witness statement, which suggests that the victim was heard to threaten the man with a knife.

Which of the following best describes the new disclosure obligations of the prosecution?

A. The prosecution must disclose the previous convictions of the victim and the second witness statement of the woman. The prosecution does not have to disclose the previous convictions of the man.

B. The prosecution must disclose the previous convictions of the man, the previous convictions of the victim and the second witness statement of the woman.

C. The prosecution must disclose the previous convictions of the victim. The prosecution does not have to disclose the previous convictions of the man or the second witness statement of the woman.

D. The prosecution must disclose the previous convictions of the man and the second witness statement of the woman. The prosecution does not have to disclose the previous convictions of the victim.

E. The prosecution is not obliged to disclose any of the unused material.

■ ANSWERS TO QUESTIONS

Answers to 'What do you know already?' questions at the start of the chapter

1) Active case management involves the early identification of the real issues, the early identification of the needs of witnesses, achieving certainty as to what must be done, by whom and when, in particular by the early setting of a timetable for the progress of the case, monitoring the progress of the case and compliance with directions, ensuring that evidence, whether disputed or not, is presented in the shortest and clearest way, discouraging delay, dealing with as many aspects of the case as possible on the same occasion, and avoiding unnecessary hearings, encouraging the participants to co-operate in the progression of the case and making use of technology. Active case management is vital to further the overriding objective (that criminal cases be dealt with justly).
2) Standard directions from the magistrates' court would include the disclosure of further evidence (if required), providing the details, and securing the attendance, of witnesses, any special measures applications or applications to adduce expert evidence. The directions will ensure, in summary, that the prosecution and defence comply with their obligations to ensure an effective trial.
3) The court may hold further pre-trial hearings if it is necessary to conduct such a hearing in order to give directions for an effective trial, or such a hearing is required to set ground rules for the conduct of the questioning of a witness or defendant.
4) False. The prosecution is under a duty to disclose evidence which might be reasonably considered capable of undermining the case for the prosecution, or positively advancing the case for the defendant. There is no duty to disclose any evidence which is neutral to both parties, nor is there a duty to disclose evidence which negatively affects the defence.

Answers to end-of-chapter SQE1-style questions

Question 1

The correct answer was E. This is because the man is under an obligation to disclose the details of any witnesses he intends to call other than himself (including the name, address and date of birth of the witness). However, the man is under no obligation to give a defence statement in the magistrates' court. If the man does decide to give a witness statement, he must do so not more than 14 days following the initial disclosure of the prosecution. All other options are wrong as they either suggest that a defence statement is mandatory (options A and C) or stipulate the wrong time period (options B and D).

Question 2

The correct answer was C. This is because the prosecution's duty is to disclose any evidence which might reasonably be considered capable of undermining the case for the prosecution or of assisting the case for the defendant. The evidence in this case would potentially strengthen the prosecution's case due to the eyewitness testimony being offered. As such, given that the evidence is not detrimental to the prosecution, nor does it bolster the case for the defence, the evidence does not pass the disclosure test and need not be disclosed (option A is therefore wrong). Option B is incorrect because the prosecution should only disclose information which satisfies the disclosure test; the prosecution should not unnecessarily disclose any other information. Option D is incorrect for the same reason as option B and it makes no difference that the case is being tried in the Crown Court. Option E is incorrect as whilst the prosecution is not under a duty to disclose, the reliability of the witness is not the reason for their lack of obligation to disclose.

Question 3

The correct answer was B. This is because the court *may* conduct a further pre-trial hearing if it is either necessary to conduct such a hearing in order to give directions for an effective trial or the hearing is required to set ground rules for the conduct of the questioning of a witness or defendant. In this case, the witness is an elderly woman who has demonstrated fear towards the man (and for allegedly good reasons). This would suggest that the woman is potentially a vulnerable witness and as such a ground rules hearing should be held to determine how to manage the evidence of this witness. Option D, whilst correct in law, is not the single best answer, for the reasons provided above. Option A is generally correct, in that no further pre-trial hearings should be held following the PTPH; however, there are exceptions to this rule (as detailed above). Option C is incorrect because the court is only permitted to hold further pre-trial hearings in the two circumstances listed above. Option E is wrong because it is not sufficiently precise to be the best answer.

Question 4

The correct answer was A. This is because the prosecution must apply to the trial judge for a ruling that the evidence is subject to public interest immunity. This is not a decision that can be made by the prosecution alone (therefore options B and E are wrong). Given the potentially sensitive material involved, the defence should not ordinarily be informed as to the withheld material (thus options C and D are wrong).

Question 5

The correct answer was A. This is because the prosecution is obliged to disclose any evidence which might reasonably be considered capable of undermining the case for the prosecution or of assisting the case for the defendant. The previous convictions for the victim could be capable of both undermining the prosecution's case and assisting the case for the defendant on the basis that it goes towards proving the man's story that he acted in self-defence. If the victim has a history of violence, the defence can argue that this history resulted in threatened violence to the man also. The previous convictions of the man would not undermine the prosecution's case, nor would it assist the defendant. Rather, those previous convictions would potentially assist the prosecution's case and, as such, would not satisfy the disclosure test. The second statement of the woman could potentially undermine the prosecution's case and assist the case of the defendant in that it goes towards proving the man's story that he acted in self-defence. For these reasons, all other options are incorrect.

■ KEY CASES, RULES, STATUTES AND INSTRUMENTS

The SQE1 Assessment Specification does not require you to know any case names, or statutory materials, for the topic of case management and pre-trial hearings.

6

Principles and procedures to admit and exclude evidence

■ MAKE SURE YOU KNOW

This chapter will cover the principles relating to admitting and excluding evidence in criminal proceedings. For the purposes of SQE1, you are required to know:

- visual identification evidence and Turnbull guideline
- inferences from silence
- hearsay evidence
- confession evidence
- bad character evidence
- exclusion of evidence.

The SQE1 Assessment Specification has identified that candidates are required to know and be able to use:

- *R v Turnbull* [1977] QB 224
- ss 34, 35, 36, 37 and 38 Criminal Justice and Public Order Act (CJPOA) 1994
- ss 76 and 78 Police and Criminal Evidence Act (PACE) 1984
- ss 100(1) and 101(1) Criminal Justice Act (CJA) 2003.

■ SQE ASSESSMENT ADVICE

As you work through this chapter, remember to pay particular attention in your revision to:

- the differing rules, procedures and requirements for the admission and exclusion of evidence in criminal cases
- the different gateways for which bad character evidence may be admitted
- the circumstances in which hearsay evidence may be adduced
- methods of excluding evidence, and when the different provisions apply.

■ WHAT DO YOU KNOW ALREADY?

Have a go at these questions before reading this chapter. If you find some difficult or cannot remember the answers, make a note to look more closely at that area during your revision.

1) What is the definition of 'bad character' under the Criminal Justice Act 2003, and what will not amount to bad character under those provisions?

   [Bad character evidence, page 152]

2) Fill in the blank: The evidence of a witness who is unavailable to attend the trial to give live oral evidence, because they are out of the country, may be admitted into evidence as hearsay where ________________.

   [Hearsay evidence, page 141]

3) True or false? Confessions are only admissible as evidence if they were made to a person in authority who is investigating an alleged offence.

   [Confession evidence, page 147]

4) What are the two main legal provisions for challenging any evidence which the prosecution intends to rely on?

   [Exclusion of evidence, page 163]

INTRODUCTION TO EVIDENCE

Evidence is used to prove, or disprove, a fact/matter in issue (ie a contested fact between the parties) and can take many forms (which we will see throughout this chapter).

VISUAL IDENTIFICATION EVIDENCE AND TURNBULL GUIDELINE

Where the issue in the case is one of identity, the prosecution will usually rely on **visual identification evidence** to prove that the defendant is the one who committed the alleged offence (eg a witness claims to have seen the defendant commit the offence).

Key term: visual identification evidence

Visual identification evidence encompasses any evidence which purports that a witness has positively identified a suspect (eg ID parades, witness statements and dock identification).

In criminal proceedings, a witness may visually identify a suspect at two distinct stages:

- pre-trial identification
- dock identification at trial.

Pre-trial identification

In many cases, witnesses may purport to positively identify a suspect who later becomes a defendant. Such evidence may stem from, for example, witness statements with a description of the suspect, or carrying out identification procedures (see **Chapter 1**).

It is not uncommon for visual identification evidence to be accompanied by other evidence which the prosecution will argue shows the defendant's guilt. Nevertheless, it may be the case that pre-trial identification evidence is the only form of evidence that the prosecution relies on (as witnesses may be unable to remember facts at trial, for example).

Dock identification

Where a witness positively identifies *for the first time* an accused who is sitting in the dock at trial, this is known as 'dock identification'.

It is important to note that at trial, the prosecution is *not* permitted to invite a witness to identify the defendant through dock identification if that particular witness has not previously identified the defendant at an identity procedure unless:

- it was impractical or unnecessary for the witness to carry out an ID procedure or
- there are exceptional circumstances.

If a witness, without invitation from the prosecution, makes a dock identification, then the judge may need to warn the jury against giving the dock indication any weight.

Turnbull guideline

Where there is a dispute between the prosecution and defence as to visual identification evidence, a **Turnbull direction** may be given.

Key term: Turnbull direction

R v Turnbull [1977] QB 224 established guidelines for judges in trials where identification evidence is disputed. A direction given to the jury which follows the guidance from Turnbull is thus known as a Turnbull direction.

Importantly, whilst it is common to refer to a Turnbull direction being given to a jury, the Turnbull guidelines apply equally to cases in the magistrates' court.

When identification is a matter in issue, the task falls to the judge to determine the quality of the evidence. The quality of the evidence will determine the course of conduct to be taken by the judge.

Assessing the quality of the evidence

In assessing the quality of the evidence, consideration should be given by the judge to the following circumstances:

- the length of time a witness had the defendant under observation
- whether the observation was impeded by anything (eg can the witness see the defendant entirely or is it a partial identification due to some obstruction to their line of sight?)

- the conditions of the identification (eg the distance, the lighting, the weather)
- whether the defendant was known to the witness previously
- the length of time which had elapsed between the witness's original observation and further identification to the police
- whether or not there are any significant discrepancies between a witness's description of the defendant and the actual appearance of the defendant
- whether any significant discrepancies have been provided to the defence.

Once the judge has identified what they consider the quality of the identification evidence to be, the judge will then consider what actions should be taken.

Actions to be taken by the judge following the assessment of the quality of the evidence

A distinction is often drawn between three different circumstances involving the quality of evidence. These circumstances dictate the actions that the judge should take and are detailed in **Table 6.2**.

Table 6.2: Turnbull guidelines

<table>
<tr><th>Circumstance</th><th>Explanation and appropriate course of conduct</th></tr>
<tr><td>Identification is of good quality</td><td rowspan="2">Where a case depends wholly or substantially on whether an identification of the defendant is correct, a Turnbull direction should be given to the jury to warn the jury of the need for caution before convicting after relying on identification evidence

A Turnbull direction should be given whether the evidence is good or poor (but supported by other prosecution evidence). In both circumstances, the judge should direct the jury to:
• the fact that even convincing witnesses can be mistaken, and that there may be a number of witnesses called who could be mistaken
• the requirement to examine the circumstances closely in which each identification was made by each witness</td></tr>
<tr><td>Identification is of poor quality, but supported by other prosecution evidence (eg in a case of theft, the stolen property being found in the defendant's house)</td></tr>
</table>

Table 6.2: (continued)

Circumstance	Explanation and appropriate course of conduct
Identification is of poor quality, and unsupported	The judge should invite submissions from the advocates and, if appropriate, withdraw the case from the jury at the conclusion of the prosecution's case The judge will direct the jury to acquit the defendant in this case

Use **Table 6.2** and **Practice example 6.2** to consolidate your understanding.

Exam warning

It is important to remember that a Turnbull direction is not needed in every instance. It is only required when the prosecution's case depends *wholly or substantially* on visual identification evidence. Do not allow an MCQ to catch you out on this.

Practice example 6.2

Mark is charged with burglary, contrary to s 9 Theft Act 1968, and is being tried in the Crown Court. The prosecution alleges that Mark stole items of expensive stationery from his employer's premises. The police searched Mark's office and home and could not find the items in question, but Mark cannot provide an alibi. The prosecution is relying substantially on a witness, James, who purports to have seen Mark take the items. James picked out Mark in an ID procedure. Whilst giving evidence, James states that he saw someone of Mark's height and hair colour, and wearing similar garments to what Mark wears, take the items from the stationery cupboard. In cross-examination, James admitted that his view of the person taking the items in question was obscured by frosted glass and the artificial lights were not turned on.

Will a Turnbull direction be necessary in this case?

It is likely that a Turnbull direction will be given in this instance. The reason for this is that the prosecution is relying substantially on James' visual identification evidence, and it appears that James' evidence is the only evidence which links Mark to the alleged offence. Had there been no previous identification by James, it would be likely that this case would be withdrawn from the jury due to the lack of evidence to support a conviction.

INFERENCES FROM SILENCE

There may be occasions during criminal proceedings when a suspect remains silent when being questioned at a particular time, or on a particular matter. Whilst an individual has a general right to remain silent, that individual's silence or failure to account may lead to **inferences** being drawn.

> **Key term: inferences**
>
> A court may draw any inferences that 'appear proper' from a defendant's silence. Such inferences may include whether the defendant was preventing self-incrimination, whether there is a case to answer, or the defendant had no explanation. The term 'adverse inferences' is often used to demonstrate that the court may draw a negative conclusion from the defendant's silence.

The SQE1 Assessment Specification has identified that candidates must know and be able to use a number of provisions from the Criminal Justice and Public Order Act (CJPOA) 1994:

- silence when being questioned or charged (CJPOA 1994, s 34)
- silence at trial (CJPOA 1994, s 35)
- silence in respect of objects, substances or marks (CJPOA 1994, s 36)
- silence as to their presence at a particular place (CJPOA 1994, s 37)
- statutory interpretation matters (CJPOA 1994, s 38).

We shall take each of these in turn.

Silence when questioned or charged (CJPOA 1994, s 34)

Where a defendant is arrested and questioned under caution, and they fail to answer a question, but later put forward a fact or account at trial that could have been given in response to that original question, inferences may be drawn.

Adverse inferences may only be drawn at trial where six conditions are met (known as the *Argent* factors):

- Criminal proceedings against a person for an offence have started.
- The alleged failure occurred before or on charge.
- The alleged failure occurred when the defendant was questioned by a constable.
- The constable's questioning was for the purpose of discovering how and who committed the alleged offence.
- The defendant relied on a fact as part of their defence that was not mentioned to a constable when questioned.

- It was reasonable, in the circumstances, for the defendant to have mentioned the fact to a constable when questioned before or on charge.

Failure to testify at trial (CJPOA 1994, s 35)

At the close of the prosecution's case, the defendant must choose whether to give evidence. The defendant is not obligated to give evidence; they have a right to refuse to give evidence. However, a failure to give evidence at trial may result in an adverse inference being drawn.

Revision tip

Whilst the provisions of the CJPOA 1994 will often overlap, it will be beneficial if you keep the provisions separate. For example, if a defendant remains silent at trial, no inferences can be drawn under s 34 (because they have not relied on a matter not previously mentioned). However, s 35 may permit inferences to be drawn in this circumstance.

The court is permitted to draw inferences if a defendant does not testify at their own trial at all, or chooses to give evidence, but refuses to answer a question put by an advocate 'without good cause'.

'Without good cause' has been interpreted by the case law as meaning that the defendant's silence can only sensibly be attributed to the defendant having no answer, or no answer that would stand up to cross-examination.

Please note, however, that where the defendant's physical or mental state would make it undesirable for them to give evidence, inferences may not be drawn. It is important to note, however, that the court *must* also satisfy itself that at the conclusion of the evidence:

- the defendant was given the opportunity to testify, and
- the defendant understood the court's ability to draw inferences from their failure to testify or their refusal, without good reason, to answer a question put to them.

The court will do so by asking the defendant's advocate questions in the presence of the jury relating to the defendant's choice not to give evidence.

Failure to account for objects or presence at a particular place (CJPOA 1994, ss 36 and 37)

Under s 36 CJPOA 1994, if, on arrest, a suspect is asked to account for a particular object, substance, or mark and fails or refuses to give an explanation, inferences may be drawn from that failure. The object, substance or mark is something which is found on their person, in or on their clothing, otherwise in their possession, or in any place they are at the time of their arrest (eg a suspected stolen item, a packet of suspected drugs or an injury).

Under s 37 CJPOA 1994, if, on arrest at a place at or about the time the alleged offence was committed, a suspect is asked by a constable to account for their presence at the particular place, but fails or refuses to do so, inferences may be drawn from that failure.

Exam warning

Be aware that whilst s 34 imposes a restriction on the drawing of adverse inferences (ie only where the defendant later relies on a matter at trial), no such restriction exists for ss 36 and 37. The mere failure to account is, in and of itself, a reason to draw adverse inferences.

It is important to note that inferences may *only* be drawn under ss 36 and 37 CJPOA 1994 if when the defendant is arrested, a constable reasonably believes that the object, substance, mark or presence at a particular place relates to the defendant's participation in an offence, and a **special warning** has been issued.

Key term: special warning

A 'special warning' must be given to the suspect in ordinary language. In particular, they must be told:

- what offence is being investigated
- what fact they are being asked to account for
- that this fact may be due to them taking part in the commission of the offence
- that a court may draw such inferences as appear proper if they fail or refuse to account for this fact
- that a record is being made of the interview and it may be given in evidence if they are brought to trial.

Interpretation (CJPOA 1994, s 38)

Section 38 provides some crucial interpretation to the provisions covered above. Section 38 also provides that a defendant cannot be convicted of an offence solely on an inference which has been drawn. In other words, additional evidence is needed to satisfy the court of the defendant's guilt.

Please also note that inferences cannot be drawn under ss 34, 36 or 37 where the defendant was at an authorised place of detention (ie a police station) at the time of the failure to account for a particular fact, and had not been allowed an *opportunity* to consult a solicitor prior to being questioned or charged.

Exam warning

The restriction on drawing inferences only extends to the *opportunity* to consult a solicitor. If the defendant is offered the opportunity and declines, adverse inferences may still be drawn where appropriate. Do not allow an MCQ to catch you out on this.

To consolidate your understanding of the drawing of inferences, use **Figure 6.2**.

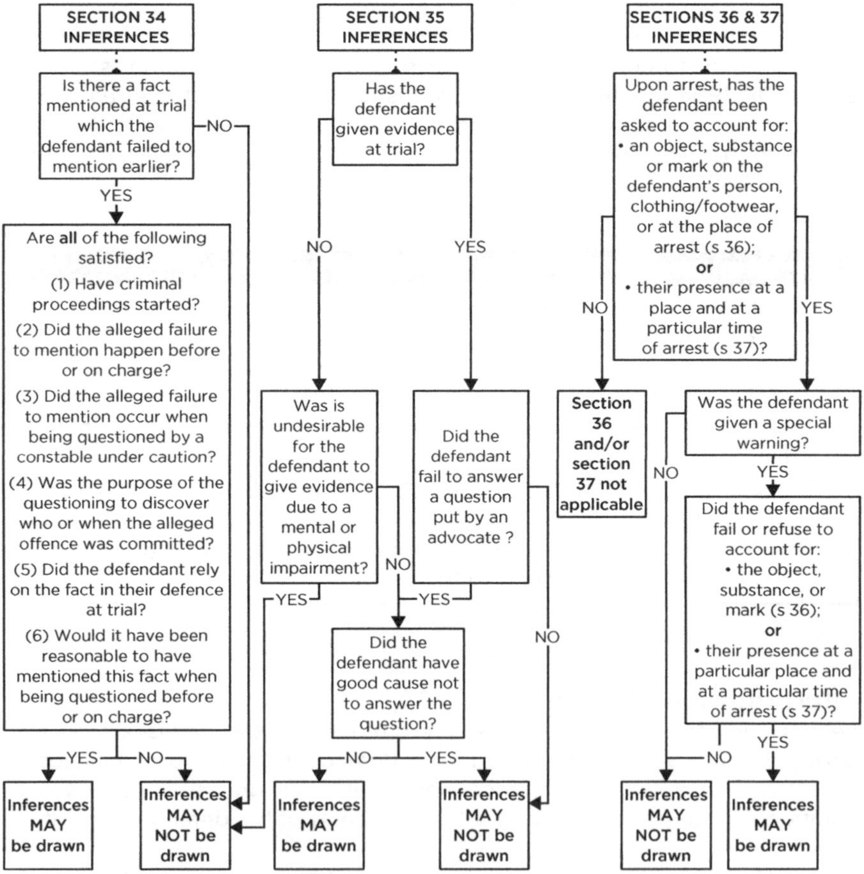

Figure 6.2: Process for drawing adverse inferences

HEARSAY EVIDENCE

In circumstances where a witness is unable to give evidence in court, an application may be made to adduce their evidence as **hearsay**.

> **Key term: hearsay**
>
> Hearsay evidence is where evidence is presented to the court not by the person who originally made the evidence out of court. For example, an advocate may read out a witness statement instead of the person who made the statement attending and giving live evidence. By way of another example, a witness may give evidence of what they were told by another person.

Ultimately, due to the limited ability to test hearsay evidence, it is vital to remember that, as a starting point, hearsay is generally *inadmissible* in criminal proceedings. Therefore, when considering whether an application could be made to adduce evidence as hearsay, it is important to consider what forms of evidence are capable of being adduced as hearsay, and the grounds hearsay evidence may be admitted on.

Definition

We will now look at whether the evidence in question is capable of being considered as hearsay. Whilst there is no concrete definition, statute provides that evidence may be admitted as hearsay in criminal proceedings if the evidence:

- is a statement (made by a person)
- is not made in oral evidence, and
- is tendered to prove a matter stated.

Let us look at each of these in turn.

A statement made by a person

Firstly, we must establish whether the evidence being sought to be adduced as hearsay is a statement.

A statement is a representation of any fact or opinion made by a person by whatever means and includes a representation made in a sketch, photofit or other pictorial form.

With the above in mind, a statement, in addition to representing a fact or opinion, must:

- be made by a person (ie not a computer)
- be made by whatever means (eg orally, in writing, by conduct, etc).

Not made in oral evidence

Hearsay is commonly referred to when dealing with statements made 'out of court'. This is the second requirement for evidence to be classed as hearsay (eg a witness at trial repeating what had been told to them by another person out of court).

Prove a matter stated

The statement must also have been made to prove a **matter stated**.

Key term: matter stated

The person who makes a statement must make it with the intention to either:

- cause someone to believe that what is being represented in the statement is true, or
- cause someone or something to operate on the basis that what is being represented in the statement is true.

There may be more than one intention as to why a statement was made, therefore it is important to exercise caution. If this is the case, the statement is not necessarily excluded from falling within the definition of hearsay.

Exam warning

You may be required to work out if a statement is capable of being hearsay. Ensure you pay particular attention to *who* made the statement and the *purpose* of the statement (ie why it was made). Candidates often overlook the purpose of why a statement was made, forgetting that a statement will only be considered as hearsay if it was made for one of the purposes prescribed above.

Grounds for admitting hearsay evidence

The admissibility provisions for hearsay evidence are *strict*. Evidence which amounts to hearsay will *only* be admitted if:

- a statutory provision applies
- a common law principle preserved by statute applies
- all parties to the proceedings agree to its admissibility, or
- the court is satisfied that it would be in the interests of justice to admit the evidence.

We shall briefly deal with each below. The Court of Appeal has formulated a seven-step approach that ought to be adopted when seeking to admit a statement as hearsay:

- Step 1 – Is the court satisfied that the prosecution has adduced all relevant evidence, and disclosed all relevant unused material to enable the court to assess the extent to which the hearsay evidence is demonstrably reliable and, if not, the extent to which it can be safely assessed and tested? If not, should the court simply refuse the application, or do the interests of justice require directions for a proper disclosure process?

- Step 2- Is there a specific statutory justification (or 'gateway') permitting the admission of hearsay evidence (CJA 2003, ss 116–118)?
- Step 3 - What material is there which can help to test or assess the hearsay?
- Step 4 - Is there a specific 'interests of justice' test at the admissibility stage?
- Step 5 - If there is no other justification or gateway, should the evidence nevertheless be considered for admission on the grounds that admission is, despite the difficulties, in the interests of justice (CJA 2003, s 114(1)(d))?
- Step 6 - Even if admissible, ought the evidence to be ruled inadmissible (Police and Criminal Evidence Act 1984 (PACE), s 78 and/or CJA 2003, s 126)?
- Step 7 - If the evidence is admitted, then should the case subsequently be stopped under CJA 2003, s 125?

A statutory provision applies

The main statutory provision for hearsay evidence is the Criminal Justice Act (CJA) 2003. Candidates must be aware of the CJA 2003 for the purposes of bad character evidence (see **Bad character evidence, page 152**) but are not required to know such for hearsay evidence (though, of course, the principles within the CJA 2003 must be understood).

A qualifying statement may be admitted as hearsay under one of the provisions of the CJA 2003. Generally, evidence may be admissible as hearsay if the witness who originally made the statement is unavailable (CJA 2003, s 116), or if the statement is a business document (CJA 2003, s 117). Other statutory gateways exist to admit hearsay outside of the CJA 2003. For example, a statement from a witness that is not in dispute may be read out in court without requiring the witness to attend in person or may be the subject of an agreed fact/admission. We shall focus solely on the two gateways in the CJA 2003.

Unavailable witnesses

If a witness is unavailable to attend court in person, then their evidence may be admitted as hearsay. This provision only applies to 'first-hand' hearsay, as opposed to 'multiple' hearsay. First-hand hearsay refers to information that has only passed through one other person. Multiple hearsay refers to information that has passed through two or more people.

Hearsay evidence may be admissible under s 116 if:

- oral evidence of the person making the statement would have been admissible had they attended in person
- the person who made the statement is identified to the court's satisfaction (ie the court knows who they are), and
- any of the reasons listed in **Table 6.3** exist.

Table 6.3: Reasons for unavailability

Reason for unavailability	Explanation and examples
Witness is dead	The court will move immediately to consider whether it is in the interests of justice to admit their evidence
Witness is unfit due to a bodily or mental condition	Investigations must be carried out to decide if the condition is satisfied. This condition is satisfied if the witness *could* be brought to court, but if they were to attend, their bodily or mental condition would render their attendance pointless
Witness is outside the UK and it is not reasonably practicable to secure their attendance	The witness's evidence may be admitted as hearsay. The court will consider any steps taken to secure the attendance of the witness, or the reason for the witness being abroad. The prosecution will need to provide compelling reasons to satisfy this condition and the courts will consider the level of contact before the trial started
Witness cannot be found despite reasonably practicable steps being taken	All reasonably practicable steps must have been taken to locate a witness who is lost, and this not only includes looking for the witness, but keeping track of the witness to satisfy this condition. Regular contact should be maintained between the witness and the party calling the witness
Witness is in fear of giving evidence	Widely construed, a witness's evidence may be adduced as hearsay if they are in fear of giving evidence. Any evidence of fear must relate to the relevant time, and may come from, for example: • being in fear as a result of witness intimidation • fear of injury or financial loss This condition is not easily satisfied, however, as the courts deploy special measures (discussed in **Chapter 7**) to mitigate the impact of fear on a witness's ability to give evidence. It is important to remember that every effort must have been made to get the witness to court before this condition is satisfied. There are additional statutory factors in s 116(4) that you should consult when considering whether the court will admit a hearsay statement on the fear gateway

Business documents

Statements contained in business documents may be admissible as hearsay evidence if the statement:

- would have been admissible as evidence of a matter stated in oral evidence
- was created or received by a person who at the time was acting in their occupation or as a holder of an unpaid or paid office, and
- was supplied by someone who had personal knowledge of the matters stated.

Additionally, if the evidence is multiple hearsay, then each person passing the statement must have done so when acting in their employment or as a holder of an unpaid or paid office.

In addition, and generally speaking, the following must apply for a document to be admitted as hearsay:

- the original witness is unavailable
- it is unreasonable to expect the witness to remember the matters referred to.

Common law principles

Section 118 CJA 2003 preserves a number of common law exceptions to the rule against hearsay. The SQE1 Assessment Specification has not identified that candidates need to be aware of any of the common law exceptions. However, if such exceptions were assessable, it is likely that the only relevant exception would be that of **res gestae.**

Key term: res gestae

Res gestae is a principle whereby if a statement is made as a result of a close and intimate connection with the event in issue, and it is made contemporaneously with that event, then it may be admitted as hearsay evidence.

Res gestae is justified on the basis that the spontaneous reaction to an event would have dominated the thoughts of the victim, making it unlikely that the reaction would have been concocted (see **Practice example 6.3**).

Practice example 6.3

James is charged with assaulting Mark, inflicting grievous bodily harm, contrary to s 20 Offences Against the Person Act 1861. The prosecution alleges that James spontaneously entered Mark's house and punched Mark in the head, causing him to fall to the ground; he then kicked Mark whilst he lay on the floor; Mark suffered a number of broken ribs as a result. James then fled the property. Seconds after James hit Mark, Mark dialled 999 and spoke to a police operator (the call was recorded). Mark told the operator '... It was James. James hit me. I need help' and then the phone line was cut. Mark lost consciousness and woke up later in hospital. He could not, however, remember who attacked him, and the only evidence the prosecution has to identify James is the 999 call.

Can the recorded 999 call be admitted as hearsay?

The 999 call could be admitted as hearsay evidence under the res gestae principle, as Mark's statement of '... It was James. James hit me. I need help' was made almost instantaneously after the alleged assault occurred. It is therefore unlikely that Mark could have concocted the statement due to the spontaneity of the event.

There is a large body of case law on the topic of res gestae and you are strongly advised to consult a specialist evidence textbook on this issue.

All parties to the proceedings agree to its admissibility

Hearsay evidence is admissible where all parties to the proceedings agree to the evidence being admitted.

Interests of justice

The final circumstance where hearsay may be admitted is where it is in the interests of justice to do so (this is a catch-all provision in case the evidence is not admitted under any other provision). Where the court is considering whether it is in the interests of justice to admit a statement as hearsay, it *must* consider:

- how much probative value is in the statement or how valuable it is for assisting the court to understand other matters in the case
- whether any other evidence has been, or can be, given on the matter to which the hearsay evidence relates
- how important the matter is in which the hearsay evidence relates to in the context of the case as a whole
- the circumstances in which the statement was made
- how reliable the evidence and maker of the statement appear to be
- whether oral evidence on the matter stated can be given, and if not, why not
- how difficult it would be to challenge the statement
- the extent to which that difficulty would prejudice the party facing it.

This provision should be treated with caution, and should not be used to circumvent any constraints of any other provision. It is important to note that even if evidence may be admissible under s 114 CJA 2003, the court retains the discretionary exclusionary power under s 126 CJA 2003.

Challenging admissibility

If a party wishes to challenge the admissibility of hearsay, there are three main options available to them:

- First, the party may argue that the relevant criteria for the admission of hearsay are not made out.

- Second, the party may seek to exclude the evidence pursuant to the court's statutory power under s 126 CJA 2003.
- Third, the party may seek to exclude the evidence pursuant to s 78 PACE 1984.

We shall consider each in turn.

Criteria not made out

The first objection that should be made is to argue that the strict criteria for admitting hearsay are not made out. For example, in a case where the prosecution seeks to admit a hearsay statement on the basis that the victim is in fear, the defence may argue that the criteria for the fear gateway are not made out. The defence may suggest that there are other options available to the court, rather than admitting the evidence as hearsay (eg special measures for the witness allegedly in fear).

CJA 2003, s 126

By s 126 CJA 2003, the court may refuse to admit hearsay evidence if the court is satisfied that the case for excluding the statement substantially outweighs the case for admitting it. In making that assessment, the court must take into account:

- the danger that to admit it would result in undue waste of time, and
- the value of the evidence.

PACE 1984, s 78

The exclusion of evidence pursuant to s 78 PACE 1984 is considered in full below. It is common for a s 78 argument to made in addition to the above two arguments. In summary, this objection would be made on the basis that the admission of hearsay would have such an adverse effect on the fairness of the proceedings that it ought not be admitted.

Importantly, however, s 78 only applies to prosecution evidence. This means that the prosecution cannot seek to rely on s 78 to exclude defence hearsay.

CONFESSION EVIDENCE

During the course of an investigation, a defendant may make a number of statements in respect of the investigation. The law traditionally draws a distinction between so-called **exculpatory statements** and **inculpatory statements.**

Key term: exculpatory statements

Statements which are exculpatory will seek to demonstrate a suspect's innocence of committing a particular offence. Such statements may be entirely or partly exculpatory, may relate to other co-defendants and may not necessarily be conclusive.

Key term: inculpatory statements

Conversely, where a suspect makes a statement which demonstrates their guilt, this would be considered inculpatory. Again, statements may be entirely or partly inculpatory, and may inculpate (or implicate) a co-defendant.

These inculpatory statements may amount, in law, to a **confession**.

Key term: confession

A confession is essentially an inculpatory statement which adversely affects the person who makes it, either wholly or partly. A confession can be admitted in evidence with damaging consequences, which is why there are additional criteria which need to be satisfied before an inculpatory statement can be considered a confession.

Definition

A confession includes any statement which is:

- wholly or partly adverse to the person who made it
- made to a person in authority or not, and
- made in words or otherwise.

Let us consider each aspect in turn.

Revision tip

The main statutory provision for confession evidence is the Police and Criminal Evidence Act (PACE) 1984. The SQE1 Assessment Specification has identified ss 76 and 78 of PACE 1984 as legal authorities that candidates must know and be able to use. Keep this in mind as we progress through this section.

Wholly or partly adverse to the maker

A statement constituting a confession may be wholly adverse (for example, it admits the suspect's guilt in respect of all elements of the offence) or it may be partly adverse, which may come from a **mixed statement**.

Key term: mixed statement

A mixed statement is where there are elements of the statement which seem to both exculpate and inculpate the maker. For example, 'I hit them, but only because I felt that they were going to hit me'. It follows that the inculpatory elements of the mixed statement may constitute a confession. Generally speaking, mixed statements are admissible as evidence providing that the requirements of s 76 PACE 1984 are complied with. See **Admissibility**, below, for further discussion.

Made to a person in authority or someone else

A statement which constitutes a confession does not necessarily have to be made to a person in authority. Usually, a statement would be made to a police officer, who would be considered as a person in authority, and these are the statements which are widely challenged. However, under s 82(1) PACE 1984, a confession may be a statement made to someone else, for example, a friend.

Made in words or otherwise

Generally, a confession may be made by a suspect in an interview, which would have been recorded. A statement constituting a confession may, in addition to oral or written admissions, be made through conduct (for example, nodding the head, a thumbs-up, or in sign language). We can see this in **Practice example 6.4**.

Practice example 6.4

James has been arrested on suspicion of the theft of a watch, contrary to s 1 Theft Act 1968. At interview, and when being questioned, James gave a 'no comment' interview when asked about the particulars of the offence. Released pending charge, James returned home and asked his best friend, Mark, to come over. When Mark arrived, he asked James about the alleged theft. James told Mark that he did take the watch, but only because it was his originally.

Does James' statement to Mark constitute a confession?

The statement which James made to Mark is likely to constitute a confession. It was a mixed statement which was partly inculpatory (admitting that he took the watch) thus proving *some* of the elements of the offence, but partly exculpatory (because he claims that the watch belonged to him and not someone else thus the elements of 'property belonging to another' and 'dishonesty' may not be currently made out). The statement was not made to a person in authority, but to Mark, and was made verbally. With this in mind, James' statement to Mark will likely satisfy s 82(1) PACE 1984 and be considered a confession.

Admissibility

Once the prosecution has identified a statement which constitutes a confession, the statement has to be admitted into evidence.

Exam warning

You may think that a confession made out of court would constitute hearsay, thus rendering it generally inadmissible. This is a common mistake made by candidates (see CJA 2003, s 118(1)5). However, s 76 PACE 1984 provides a separate framework to allow confessions to be adduced as evidence.

General admissibility

Section 76(1) PACE 1984 permits a confession made by a defendant providing that it is relevant to a matter in issue, and it is not excluded by any statutory provision (see **Challenging admissibility**, below). It is important to note that the prosecution will *only* have to prove that the confession is admissible if the defence represents that it is inadmissible under s 76(2) PACE 1984, or the court, on its own motion, requires proof of admissibility.

If the prosecution is required to demonstrate that the confession is admissible, it must satisfy the court so that it is sure that the confession was not, or may not have been, obtained by oppression or obtained unreliably due to police actions.

These shall be discussed in more detail under **Challenging admissibility**, below.

A defendant admitting a confession of a co-defendant

Naturally, a defendant may seek to adduce the confession of their co-defendant in circumstances where such confession does not implicate themselves. Section 76A PACE 1984 provides that a defendant may adduce a confession of a co-defendant only if it was not obtained by the excluded methods set out in s 76(2)(a) and (b) PACE 1984 (see below, **Challenging admissibility**). The only difference, however, is that if a defendant is seeking to introduce a confession of a co-defendant and the admissibility is challenged, the party seeking to introduce it must satisfy the court on the balance of probabilities that the confession is admissible.

Challenging admissibility

If a party wishes to challenge the admissibility of a confession, they may represent that it should be excluded due to it being obtained:

- by oppression
- unreliably, or
- if the confession is admitted, it would have an adverse effect on the fairness of the proceedings (see **Exclusion of evidence, page 161**).

Once admissibility is challenged, a **voir dire** will then take place to determine whether the confession will be introduced to the arbiter of fact as evidence.

Key term: voir dire

A voir dire is a hearing which takes place before the magistrates, or judge (and in the latter, in the absence of the jury), to determine whether a piece of evidence, usually a confession, is to be admitted. The prosecution and defence may call witnesses, who are subject to cross-examination, and the judge will decide whether the evidence will be admitted.

Our primary focus will relate to the exclusion of a confession due to it being obtained either through oppression or in consequence of something said or done which may render a confession unreliable. Evidence which is excluded on the grounds of having an adverse effect on the fairness of proceedings is discussed under **Exclusion of evidence** (see **page 161**).

Confession obtained by oppression (PACE 1984, s 76(2)(a))

If it appears to the court that the confession being challenged was, or may have been, obtained by **oppression,** then the court *shall not* allow it to be admitted. This is so even if the court thinks that the confession is true or genuine.

Key term: oppression

Oppression includes being tortured, or treated in an inhumane or degrading way, or the use or threat of violence. If a confession is obtained as a result of oppression, it *must* be excluded.

Unreliable confession (PACE 1984, s 76(2)(b))

A confession which was obtained as a consequence of anything said or done which, in the circumstances, would render it unreliable, shall be excluded. Such instances include:

- breaches of PACE Codes (see **Chapter 1**) (eg failing to appoint an appropriate adult or misrepresenting the strength of the police case)
- the suspect's vulnerabilities (eg taking advantage of a suspect's learning difficulty)
- the suspect's emotional state (eg demanding a confession when the suspect is clearly distressed for whatever reason).

It is important to note that the question which the court must ask itself is whether *any* confession obtained in these circumstances would be reliable, not just the one in question.

Revision tip

Do not forget to pay particular attention to excluding confessions as a result of a breach of a PACE code. A breach of a PACE code will not automatically lead to having the confession excluded, and even where a confession is excluded, any further evidence obtained in light of a confession ruled inadmissible is not necessarily automatically excluded.

Adverse effect (PACE 1984, s 78)

In our final section, **Exclusion of evidence,** we shall discuss s 78 in greater detail. In summary, a confession may be excluded from evidence if the court considers that the admission of the confession would have such an adverse effect on the fairness of proceedings that it ought not to be admitted. See **Practice example 6.5** for application of this principle.

Exam warning

If you are presented with an MCQ on exclusion of confession evidence, remember to pay close attention to the wording of the answers relating to exclusionary powers:

- If a confession was obtained by oppression, or in an unreliable manner, the court *must* exclude it (ie it has no choice).
- If admitting a confession would, however, adversely affect the fairness of proceedings, the court can exercise its discretion and *may* exclude it.

Practice example 6.5

James is being tried in the Crown Court for assault occasioning actual bodily harm, contrary to s 47 Offences Against the Person Act 1861. The prosecution intends to introduce a confession which James allegedly made. James' solicitor asks James about this alleged confession, and James explained that he only made it as a result of what PC Thomas said to him, before the interview. PC Thomas told James that if he admitted to committing the offence, PC Thomas would 'make the charge go away'. In a tape-recorded interview, James admitted that he committed the assault.

How can James' solicitor challenge the admissibility of this confession?

James' solicitor would 'represent' that this confession was obtained unreliably. The judge would then hold a voir dire, and the prosecution would likely call PC Thomas to give evidence; PC Thomas would also be cross-examined by James' advocate. The court would consider whether in these particular circumstances a confession in general (not this specific confession) would be considered unreliable. It is for the prosecution to satisfy the court so that it is sure that the confession was not unreliably obtained.

BAD CHARACTER EVIDENCE

The evidence of one's character can be used in proceedings. The SQE1 Assessment Specification states that candidates must know the law relating to both defendant and non-defendant bad character evidence. The former is covered by s 101(1) CJA 2003 and the latter by s 100(1) CJA 2003. We shall deal with each in turn. The relevance of a defendant's good character is considered in **Chapter 7**.

Definition of bad character

First, we must define what **bad character** means.

Key term: bad character

Bad character is evidence of, or of a disposition towards, misconduct on the part of the defendant. 'Misconduct' is concerned with the commission of an offence or other reprehensible behaviour. It does not include evidence which:

- has to do with the alleged facts of the offence with which the defendant is charged (eg racist abuse directed towards the victim during the commission of the offence)
- is evidence of misconduct in connection with the investigation or prosecution of that offence (eg attempting to conceal a weapon used in the commission of the offence).

This definition is applicable to both defendant and non-defendant bad character evidence. Examples of evidence of bad character (ie misconduct) could include previous convictions or membership of a violent gang.

The seven gateways: s 101(1) Criminal Justice Act 2003

Evidence of a defendant's bad character is admissible under s 101 CJA 2003.

Bad character will *only* be admitted, on application by the prosecution or a co-defendant, if it satisfies one of the seven 'gateways' in s 101(1)(a)–(g) CJA 2003. These gateways are as follows:

(a) All parties agree to the evidence being admitted.

(b) The evidence is adduced by the defendant themselves, or is given in answer to a question asked by them in cross-examination and intended to elicit it.

(c) The evidence is important explanatory evidence.

(d) The evidence is relevant to an important matter in issue between the defendant and prosecution.

(e) The evidence has substantial probative value in relation to an important matter in issue between the defendant and a co-defendant.

(f) The evidence is required to correct a false impression given by the defendant.

(g) The defendant has made an attack on another person's character.

We shall briefly consider each gateway in turn.

All parties agree (CJA 2003, s 101(1)(a))

If both the prosecution and defence agree to the defendant's bad character evidence being admitted, then it may be admitted under this gateway. If there are multiple defendants being tried, then the co-accused(s) must also agree, as each defendant may have differing interests.

Adduced by the defendant themselves (CJA 2003, s 101(1)(b))

A defendant may wish to bring their own bad character to the court's attention if, for example, they wish to make it clear that they have not been convicted of an offence which is the same, or similar to, the one which they are being tried for. Another reason may be that the defendant will attempt to downplay their previous convictions or reprehensible behaviour and control that information before the prosecution have the opportunity to do so.

Important explanatory evidence (CJA 2003, s 101(1)(c))

Bad character evidence may be admitted if it will assist the court in understanding the case as a whole. Evidence is classed as explanatory if:

- without it, the court would find it difficult or impossible to properly understand the other evidence in the case, and
- the value of the evidence for understanding the case as a whole is substantial.

Relevant to an important matter in issue between the defence and prosecution (CJA 2003, s 101(1)(d))

If the defendant's bad character is relevant to a matter in issue between the prosecution and defence, it may be admitted. This is *by far* the most important gateway under s 101(1). The key focus under s 101(1)(d) is whether the evidence shows a particular **propensity** on the part of the defendant.

Key term: propensity

Propensity refers to a likelihood to do something. For the purposes of s 101(1)(d), propensity may refer to:

- propensity to commit offences of the kind with which the defendant is charged (ie an offence of the same description, eg assault occasioning actual bodily harm, or an offence of the same category, eg theft)
- propensity to be untruthful (ie the manner in which previous offences were committed demonstrates a propensity to be untruthful, eg fraud by false representation).

To establish whether bad character evidence will be admitted for the purpose of demonstrating propensity to commit offences of the kind alleged, the court will turn to the *Hanson* factors, and consider:

- whether the history of previous convictions establishes a propensity to commit offences of the kind with which the defendant is charged
- if so, whether the propensity makes it more likely that the defendant committed the alleged offence
- the number of previous convictions: although there are no minimum events necessary to demonstrate propensity, the fewer the previous convictions, the weaker the evidence of propensity is

- the strength of the prosecution case: if there is little or no other evidence, it would likely be unjust to admit previous convictions
- the individual circumstances of each conviction rather than the name of the offence.

Substantial probative value in relation to a matter between the defendant and co-defendant (CJA 2003, s 101(1)(e))

The defence may make an application to adduce the bad character of a co-defendant, to demonstrate that a co-defendant has the propensity to be untruthful or a propensity to commit offences of the kind with which they have both been charged.

Correct a false impression given by the defendant (CJA 2003, s 101(1)(f))

If the defendant expressly or impliedly purports that they are of absolute good character before proceedings or during testimony, evidence of the defendant's bad character may be adduced to correct this false impression.

The defendant has attacked another person's character (CJA 2003, s 101(1)(g))

This gateway is exclusively available to the prosecution: Where a defendant asserts that someone involved in the proceedings has committed an offence or has behaved in a reprehensible way, the defendant's bad character may be adduced. Such an imputation on the part of the defendant may have been made before charge when interviewed under caution, on being charged or advised that a prosecution will take place or during questioning at trial.

Procedure for admitting defendant bad character evidence

A rigid framework exists in Part 21 Criminal Procedure Rules 2025 for introducing evidence of a *defendant's* bad character. We shall consider each part of that procedure here.

Notice

If the prosecution or a co-defendant wishes to introduce evidence of a defendant's bad character, they must draft and serve a notice. The notice, which essentially puts all parties on notice that the evidence will be admitted unless opposed, must include the following three key details:

- the facts of the misconduct relied upon (for example, previous convictions)
- an explanation as to how those facts will be proved, and
- a statement as to why the evidence is admissible.

Table 6.4 details the relevant time limits for serving the notice.

Table 6.4: Time limits for serving notice to introduce bad character evidence

Prosecution drafts and serves the notice	Co-defendant drafts and serves the notice
Not more than: • 20 business days after a not-guilty plea in the magistrates' court, or • ten business days after a not-guilty plea in the Crown Court	Not more than: • ten business days after the prosecution discloses material on which the notice is based And in any event: • as soon as reasonably practicable

The procedure is different for a defendant who wishes to adduce their own bad character. They must:

- give notice either orally or in writing
- as soon as reasonably practicable and, in any event, before the evidence is introduced
- if in the Crown Court, give notice of any desired direction to be given to the jury at the same time notice is given of the defendant's intention to introduce their bad character.

Objecting against the prosecution or co-defendant's notice

If a party wishes to object to the notice of having bad character evidence of a defendant admitted, they must draft an application. An application challenges the notice, and results in the court determining the outcome. Along with the application being served on the court officer and all parties not more than ten business days after the initial notice was served, the application must state:

- which facts identified in the notice the defendant objects to
- which, if any, facts of the misconduct the party instead admits to
- why the evidence is inadmissible
- why it would be unfair to admit the evidence
- any additional objections to the notice.

Determining the application

The court may hear the application in public or in private, without a hearing, or adjourn the application. It is not, however, permitted to determine the application without the party who made the application being present, unless it had reasonable opportunity to respond. When the outcome is determined, the court must announce the reason to admit, or refuse to admit, the evidence as bad character.

Court's powers to exclude defendant bad character evidence

The general power to exclude bad character evidence is provided to the court under s 101(3) CJA 2003. If the arbiter of law takes the view that the bad character evidence of a defendant, if admitted, would have 'such an adverse effect on the fairness of proceedings that the court ought not to admit it', the court *must* exclude it. This power arises when:

- The prosecution applies under s 101(1)(d) or (g) to admit the defendant's bad character evidence.
- The defence makes an application to exclude the evidence or, if the defendant is unrepresented, such an application to exclude is prompted by the court.

If an application is made to exclude the bad character evidence in the form of previous convictions to demonstrate propensity, s 101(4) CJA 2003 requires the court to consider both the length of time which has passed relating to those previous convictions and the facts which formed the subject of those previous convictions.

Essentially, the more time that has passed since the occurrence of the bad character evidence wishing to be adduced, or the less similarity there is between the facts relating to the bad character wishing to be adduced, the less likely the evidence will be adduced (see **Practice example 6.6**).

Practice example 6.6

Mark is charged with theft, contrary to s 1 Theft Act 1968. It is alleged that he stole £200 from a till in a bookshop. Mark has two previous convictions from four years ago when he was convicted of the same offence as the one which he is currently charged with, but he stole several boxes of expensive biscuits. The prosecution serves notice under s 101(1)(d) CJA 2003 to adduce these previous convictions as evidence of propensity to commit offences of the same or similar nature, and the defence makes an application to exclude under s 101(3) CJA 2003.

What is the likelihood of the prosecution successfully adducing evidence of Mark's bad character?

In Mark's case, it is unlikely that the prosecution would be successful in adducing his bad character. Applying the considerations under s 101(4) CJA 2003, the fact that these previous offences occurred four years ago, and the particulars of those offences are relatively dissimilar to the facts of the instant case, the court is likely to conclude that adducing Mark's bad character would have an adverse effect on the fairness of the current proceedings. Therefore, the defence's application is likely to succeed.

The three gateways: s 100(1) CJA 2003

Now that we are aware of how evidence of a defendant's bad character can be admitted, we can turn to consider how a party can introduce the bad character of a **non-defendant**.

Key term: non-defendant

Whilst there is no express statutory definition, the term is self-explanatory. Section 100 of the CJA 2003 applies to 'a person other than the defendant'. Accordingly, any witness (prosecution or defence) or complainant who has relevant bad character is susceptible to having it introduced. Even individuals who are not called to give evidence are susceptible to having their bad character admitted into evidence if it is relevant and passes through the necessary gateway(s).

Much like the bad character of a defendant, there are statutory 'gateways' that must be satisfied before a party can introduce a non-defendant's bad character. These are contained within s 100 of the CJA 2003. In summary, a non-defendant's bad character is admissible if, *and only if*:

(a) it is important explanatory evidence, or

(b) it is of substantial probative value, or

(c) all parties agree.

Revision tip

Should an MCQ ask you about the appropriateness of applying to admit non-defendant bad character evidence, keep in your mind that any such attack may open up a defendant's bad character under gateway (g) (see **page 153**). The defence has to be careful not to expose their own bad character by an attack on a prosecution witness. This may impact on your assessment of the single best answer.

In respect of gateways (a) and (b), evidence of the bad character of a non-defendant must not be given without leave of the court (meaning that the evidence cannot be admitted in any way, eg in cross-examination, unless the court has first given permission for the evidence to be admitted).

Each will be considered in turn.

Important explanatory evidence (CJA 2003, s 100(1)(a))

This gateway mirrors that of defendant bad character. If a non-defendant's bad character is important explanatory evidence, then it is admissible. This gateway was designed to reflect gateway (c) for defendant bad character evidence (see **page 154**).

For example, the evidence of a non-defendant's bad character may amount to important explanatory evidence if it is capable of explaining their motive (or hidden agenda) for giving evidence in the present case.

Substantial probative value (CJA 2003, s 100(1)(b))

Under this gateway, the court will consider how far the non-defendant's bad character goes to proving a matter in issue (eg credibility and reliability).

When determining admissibility under this gateway, the trial judge must address the following two questions:

- Is the issue to which the bad character evidence relates one of substantial importance in the context of the case overall?
- If so, does the bad character evidence have *substantial* probative value in relation to a matter in issue in the proceedings?

Revision tip

This two-stage test is fundamental to understanding gateway (b). When answering any MCQ on the admission of non-defendant bad character under gateway (b), consider these two questions in sequence (see **Practice example 6.7** for an example of their use).

In assessing the probative value of evidence for the purposes of gateway (b), the court must have regard to a number of factors. These are detailed in **Table 6.5**.

Table 6.5: Factors relevant to assessing probative value

Factor	Explanation
The nature and number of the events, or other things, to which the evidence relates	This is self-explanatory: the more circumstances of misconduct alleged, the more probative weight it will have. A single incident of misconduct will be more difficult to admit than a string of incidents.
When those events or things are alleged to have happened or existed	The more recent the alleged misconduct, the more probative the evidence will be. Old incidents of misconduct, or those carried out when an adult non-defendant was a youth, will have less probative value.

Table 6.5: (continued)

Factor	Explanation
Where: (i) the evidence is evidence of a person's misconduct, and (ii) it is suggested that the evidence has probative value by reason of similarity between that misconduct and other alleged misconduct, the nature and extent of the similarities and the dissimilarities between each of the alleged instances of misconduct.	In essence, the court must consider the similarities and differences between the bad character sought to be admitted and the alleged misconduct that the bad character is being used to prove (eg previous convictions for dishonesty-related offences being used to prove a propensity to lie).
Where: (i) the evidence is evidence of a person's misconduct, (ii) it is suggested that the person is also responsible for the misconduct charged, and (iii) the identity of the person responsible for the misconduct charged is disputed, the extent to which the evidence shows or tends to show that the same person was responsible each time.	Where, for example, the defendant denies committing the offence and alleges that another person must have committed the offence, the court must assess whether the bad character of the non-defendant shows that they were responsible for the offence.
Any other factor the court considers relevant.	The statute is clear that the list of factors is not exhaustive.

Practice example 6.7 applies gateway (b) to a common scenario.

Practice example 6.7

Mark is being called as a witness for the prosecution. Mark's evidence is that he saw James assault Samantha, causing her actual bodily harm. James advises his legal team that Mark has a vendetta against him and has numerous previous convictions for dishonesty-related offences. The prosecution discloses Mark's criminal record which shows he does have a large number of theft-related offences.

How should the defence approach admitting Mark's previous convictions for dishonesty?

The first question to be asked by James' legal team is what their purpose of admitting Mark's previous convictions would be. In this case, it would be Mark's credibility. If that is the case, James' legal team must satisfy the judge of two matters:

First, is creditworthiness a matter in issue of substantial importance in the context of the case as a whole? The simple fact that Mark has convictions for dishonesty-related offences does not entitle James' legal team to attack his credibility. The convictions must be a matter in issue of substantial importance to the case as a whole. If James alleges that Mark has a vendetta against him, and is prone to lie, this would be a matter in issue (whether Mark actually saw James commit the offence) of substantial importance to the case as a whole.

If the first hurdle is surpassed, the second issue is whether the bad character evidence sought to be relied upon is of substantial probative value in relation to that issue. This question essentially asks whether a fair-minded tribunal would regard Mark's previous convictions as affecting the worth of his evidence. Dishonesty-related offences are probative to the issue of truth telling, coupled with Mark's alleged vendetta against James. In light of that, the second limb is also likely satisfied and Mark's convictions will likely be admitted as relevant.

All parties agree (CJA 2003, s 100(1)(c))

If there is no objection from the prosecution or defence in admitting a non-defendant's bad character, then the evidence can be admitted. Remember, if there are co-defendants, *all* must be consulted and agree the evidence for this gateway to be relied upon.

Exam warning

Be careful when answering an MCQ on bad character, and make sure you are clear about whose bad character is being admitted. Do not get confused between the gateways which apply to defendants (CJA 2003, s 101) and those of non-defendants (CJA 2003, s 100). There are some subtle differences between the wording of the gateways. These differences will probably be reflected in the wording of the possible answers to a question.

Procedure for admitting non-defendant bad character evidence

Part 21 of the Criminal Procedure Rules 2025 sets out the requirements that a party must comply with to adduce the bad character of a non-defendant. This can be broken down into three stages:

- serving notice

- objections
- determining the application.

Notice

First, the party wishing to adduce the evidence must serve an application on the court officer and each other party. The application sets out the reasons why the party wishes to introduce the bad character of a non-defendant, and must be done:

- as soon as is reasonably practicable, and in any event
- not more than ten business days after the prosecutor discloses material on which the application is based (if the prosecutor is not the applicant).

Objecting to the introduction of a non-defendant's bad character

Should a party object to a non-defendant's bad character being admitted, they must serve notice on the court officer and each party not more than ten business days after service of the initial application. In addition, the notice of objection must explain:

- which, if any, facts of the misconduct set out in the application are disputed
- what, if any, facts of the misconduct that party admits instead
- why the evidence is not admissible
- any other objection to the application.

Determining the application

The court has the power to determine an application with a hearing in public or private, or without a hearing. It is important to remember, however, that the court cannot determine the outcome of the application unless each party, other than the applicant, is present, or has had at least ten business days to serve notice of objection.

In any event, the court may adjourn an application, and in limited circumstances, discharge or vary a determination.

Court's powers to exclude non-defendant bad character evidence

Unlike with defendant bad character, there is no specific power to exclude non-defendant bad character once the court has determined the outcome of an application (as the court will have been satisfied that the criteria for the relevant gateway has been met). The only option, practically speaking, is to invite the court to exercise its case management powers (eg through the restriction in the manner or length of cross-examination) or refer to the general rules of admissibility (see the final two sections of **Figure 6.3**). Remember, for any evidence to be admissible, it must be relevant. Also remember that the general exclusion of evidence under s 78 PACE 1984 applies to prosecution evidence, but not to defendant evidence (below).

EXCLUSION OF EVIDENCE

Whilst some methods of challenging the admissibility of specific types of evidence have been discussed in this chapter, we now turn to consider s 78 PACE 1984, which has been identified in the SQE1 Assessment Specification. Candidates may also be required to be aware of the common law power to exclude evidence; however, this is not expressly identified in the SQE1 Assessment Specification. Therefore, the common law power to exclude will not be considered here.

Use **Figure 6.3** along with the text below to grasp the law relating to exclusion of evidence.

Section 76: Confession evidence	• Who may rely on it: defence/co-defence • Power of exclusion: *shall* exclude • Test: may have been obtained through oppression/anything said or done rendering confession unreliable
Section 78: Any prosecution evidence	• Who may rely on it: defence/co-defence • Power of exclusion: *may* exclude • Test: the admission of evidence would have such an adverse effect on the fairness of proceedings
Common law (prejudicial effect outweighs probative value): Any prosecution evidence	• Who may rely on it: defence/co-defence • Power to exclude: *may* exclude • Test: the prejudicial effect on the arbiter of fact's mind outweighs any probative value of the evidence
Common law (relevance): Any evidence	• Who may rely on it: prosecution/defence/co-defence • Power of exclusion: *may* exclude • Test: the evidence will not be admitted if it is not relevant to a matter in issue

Figure 6.3: Exclusion of evidence

As the SQE1 Assessment Specification has identified that candidates need to be familiar with s 78 PACE 1984, we shall focus our attention here.

Scope and application of s 78 PACE 1984 and the right to a fair trial

Under s 78 PACE 1984, *any* evidence which the prosecution *proposes* to rely on *may not* be allowed if the court is persuaded that in all of the circumstances, including how the evidence was obtained, admitting certain evidence would have an adverse effect on the fairness of the proceedings. Even evidence which is capable of being excluded under a specific provision (eg confessions under s 76 PACE 1984 - see above, **Confession evidence**) may be excluded under the discretionary power of s 78 PACE 1984.

Reference to the 'fairness of proceedings' is inextricably linked to the right to a fair trial that each defendant possesses. Section 78 is designed to provide the court with this broad discretion to exclude evidence where its admission would otherwise lead to an unfair trial (see **Practice example 6.8**).

Exam warning

Be aware, the above provisions relating to the exclusion of evidence apply *only* to the exclusion of prosecution evidence by the defence. The prosecution may *only* seek to have defence evidence excluded on the common law basis of relevance (ie showing that the evidence is irrelevant to the matters in issue). It is common for MCQs to ask you about the prosecution attempting to exclude evidence; do not make the mistake that s 78 applies equally to the prosecution.

Practice example 6.8

Mark, a police officer, is being tried for misconduct in public office (an offence which you are *not* required to know about for SQE1). The prosecution argues that he should have responded to a distress call sooner after a colleague was shot by a drug dealer. The prosecution has obtained closed-circuit television (CCTV) footage which they say shows Mark purposefully loitering behind a building just after acknowledging the call - evidence that they say demonstrates his misconduct. The CCTV footage, however, is of poor quality, and the face of the individual is not clear. The defence now challenges the admissibility of the CCTV footage.

What is the likelihood of the evidence being excluded?

It is likely that the evidence would be excluded under s 78 PACE 1984. As the identity of the individual cannot be established due to the poor quality of the footage, it might be prejudicial for the prosecution to suggest to the jury that it is Mark in the image. On this basis, admitting the evidence may have such an adverse effect on the fairness of the proceedings that it ought not to be admitted. The judge would likely rule that the footage, and any reference to it, should be excluded.

KEY POINT CHECKLIST

This chapter has covered the following key knowledge points. You can use these to structure your revision, ensuring you recall the key details for each point, as covered in this chapter.

- A Turnbull direction is not always required – only where the prosecution's case is wholly or substantially built on contested visual identification evidence.
- Adverse inferences may be drawn for the defendant's failure to answer questions during investigation or trial, or from their failure to account for any objects or their presence at a particular place. Such inferences cannot solely be relied upon, however, to prove the defendant's guilt.
- Hearsay is generally inadmissible in criminal proceedings, unless the party wishing to rely on hearsay can satisfy one of the many exceptions.
- A confession is a statement which wholly or partially inculpates the defendant. The defendant may seek to have any confession excluded on the grounds of oppression or unreliability.
- A defendant's bad character may be admitted in criminal proceedings through one of seven gateways under s 101(1) CJA 2003. A non-defendant's bad character may be admitted through one of three gateways under s 100(1) CJA 2003.
- Whilst each form of evidence has its own specific provisions for exclusion, the courts retain a general right to exclude evidence under s 78 PACE 1984.

KEY TERMS AND CONCEPTS

- visual identification evidence (**page 133**)
- Turnbull direction (**page 134**)
- inferences (**page 137**)
- special warning (**page 139**)
- hearsay (**page 141**)
- matter stated (**page 142**)
- res gestae (**page 145**)
- exculpatory statements (**page 147**)
- inculpatory statements (**page 148**)
- confession (**page 148**)
- mixed statement (**page 148**)
- voir dire (**page 150**)
- oppression (**page 151**)
- bad character (**page 153**)
- propensity (**page 154**)
- non-defendant (**page 158**)

SQE1-STYLE QUESTIONS

QUESTION 1

A man is being tried for murder. His defence is one of mistaken identity and argues that he was not at the scene of the alleged offence at the material time. The prosecution's only witness who can place the man at the scene of the alleged offence at the material time made a sworn statement to that effect, and was willing to attend court despite being somewhat scared initially. At the start of the trial, the prosecution discovers that this witness, after getting the trial dates confused due to inaccurate information given by the prosecution, is on a ten-day transatlantic voyage with poor, intermittent communication. The prosecution makes an application to admit the witness's statement as hearsay due to its importance.

Which of the following best describes the course of action the prosecution should take?

A. The prosecution should make an application to admit the statement as hearsay on the grounds that the witness is outside the UK and it is not reasonably practicable to secure their attendance.

B. The prosecution should make an application to admit the statement as hearsay on the grounds that it is in the interests of justice to do so.

C. The prosecution should make an application to admit the statement as hearsay on the grounds that there is evidence that the witness was in fear of giving evidence.

D. The prosecution should make an application to admit the statement as hearsay on the grounds that the witness cannot be contacted despite all efforts being made.

E. The prosecution should make an application to admit the statement as hearsay on the grounds that the statement is a document made in relation to criminal proceedings and is thus capable of being admitted as hearsay.

QUESTION 2

A woman is charged with murder and her trial is due to start. The prosecution has complied with their duty of continuing disclosure and the defence has reviewed the evidence. Before the prosecution opens the case, the defence explains that they have some new evidence in respect of a prosecution witness's medical records. It was discovered that they were obtained unlawfully, but the defence argues that they are pivotal to the case. The prosecution objects and argues that allowing this evidence to be admitted would have an adverse effect on the proceedings, and that as it bears little relevance to the matters in issue, there is no probative value to the evidence.

Which of the following best describes the option open to the court for excluding the evidence?

A. The court must exclude the evidence under the common law principle of relevance, as the prosecution contends that the medical records are of little relevance to the matters in issue.

B. The court may exclude the evidence under s 78 PACE 1984 because it was obtained unlawfully and introducing it would have such an adverse effect on the fairness of the proceedings that it ought to be excluded.

C. The court may exclude the evidence under s 78 PACE 1984 because the prosecution argues that the medical records bear little relevance to the matters in issue, and if it were adduced, it would have such an adverse effect on the fairness of the proceedings that it ought to be excluded.

D. The court may exclude the evidence under the common law principle of relevance, as the prosecution contends that medical records are of little relevance to the matters in issue.

E. The court must exclude the evidence under s 76 PACE 1984 because it was unfairly obtained and introducing it would have such an adverse effect on the fairness of the proceedings that it ought to be excluded.

QUESTION 3

A man is charged with unlawful act manslaughter. The man pleaded not guilty and is about to stand trial. The prosecution has disclosed the evidence which it intends to rely on, and included in this is a confession which was entirely inculpatory in a police interview. Despite this, the man pursued a not-guilty plea. In conference, the man tells his solicitor that he only made this confession because a police officer in the case said aggressively, 'It would be much better for you if you admitted that it was you. The judge will go easy on you if you do'. The trial is just about to start, and the solicitor informs defence counsel.

Which of the following best describes what will likely happen in light of the man's conversation with his solicitor?

A. Defence counsel will advise the prosecutor that they intend to challenge the admissibility of the confession as it was obtained in consequence of something said or done that makes the confession unreliable. A voir dire will take place and the prosecution must satisfy the court, on the balance of probabilities, that the confession is admissible. If it fails to do so, the court may exclude the confession.

B. Defence counsel will advise the prosecutor that they intend to challenge the admissibility of the confession as it was obtained in consequence of something said or done that makes the confession unreliable. A voir dire will take place and the prosecution must satisfy the court, on the balance of probabilities, that the confession is admissible. If it fails to do so, the court shall exclude the confession.

C. Defence counsel will advise the prosecutor that they intend to challenge the admissibility of the confession as it was obtained through oppression. A voir dire will take place and the prosecution must satisfy the court, so that it is sure, that the confession is admissible. If it fails to do so, the court shall exclude the confession.

D. Defence counsel will advise the prosecutor that they intend to challenge the admissibility of the confession as it was obtained in consequence of something said or done that makes the confession unreliable. A voir dire will take place and the prosecution must satisfy the court, so that it is sure, that the confession is admissible. If it fails to do so, the court shall exclude the confession.

E. Defence counsel will advise the prosecutor that they intend to challenge the admissibility of the confession as it was obtained in consequence of something said or done that makes the confession unreliable. A voir dire will take place and the prosecution must satisfy the court, so that it is sure, that the confession is admissible. If it fails to do so, the court may exclude the confession.

QUESTION 4

A man is charged with causing grievous bodily harm with intent, contrary to s 18 Offences Against the Person Act 1861. The man has pleaded not guilty. During the course of disclosure, and before the trial in the Crown Court, the prosecution serves notice of their intention to rely on the man's bad character as evidence. The prosecution contends that his previous convictions for battery four years earlier demonstrate evidence of propensity to commit violent offences. The defence intends to object to the admission of this evidence.

Which of the following best describes the steps which the defence needs to take to object to the prosecution's notice?

A. The defence must make an application to the court to determine the objection and serve the application on the court officer and the prosecution not more than 20 business days after being served with the prosecution notice.

B. The defence should initially make an application to have the bad character evidence excluded, in the first instance, under s 78 PACE 1984; the court must exclude the evidence if admitting it would have an adverse effect on the fairness of the proceedings.

C. The defence must make an application to the court to determine the objection and serve the application on the court officer and the prosecution not more than 14 business days after being served with the prosecution notice.

D. The defence must make an application to the court to determine the objection and serve the application on the court officer and the prosecution not more than ten business days after being served with the prosecution notice.

E. The defence should initially make an application to have the bad character evidence excluded under s 78 PACE 1984; the court may exclude the evidence if admitting it would have an adverse effect on the fairness of the proceedings.

■ ANSWERS TO QUESTIONS

Answers to 'What do you know already?' questions at the start of the chapter

1) Bad character is defined as evidence of, or of a disposition towards, misconduct on the part of a person (defendant or non-defendant). This does not include evidence which has to do with the alleged facts of the offence with which the defendant is charged, or is evidence of misconduct in connection with the investigation or prosecution of that offence.
2) The evidence of a witness who is unavailable to attend the trial to give live oral evidence, because they are out of the country, may be admitted into evidence as hearsay where oral evidence of the person making the statement would have been admissible had they attended in person, the person who made the statement is identified to the court's satisfaction (ie the court knows who they are) and it is not reasonably practicable to secure their attendance.
3) False. A confession is admissible even if it has been made to someone who is not in a position of authority or investigating an alleged offence. A confession may be admissible irrespective of who it was made to.
4) Prosecution evidence, including confessions, may be excluded under s 76 PACE 1984 and s 78 PACE 1984.

Answers to end-of-chapter SQE1-style questions

Question 1

The correct answer was B. This is because out of the options available, an application made on the grounds that it would be in the interests of justice to admit the statement as hearsay is the most likely to succeed in the circumstances. Option A is wrong because, although the witness is outside the UK and transiting the Atlantic Ocean (not reasonably practical to secure their attendance), this was caused by poor prosecution information and it was not the fault of the witness. Option C is wrong because the witness was not in fear to the extent that they are not willing to attend court, nor is their fear the primary reason for the application. Option D is wrong because it is not a strong argument to make for admitting the evidence as hearsay. Whilst there are communication issues, these are temporary and the witness's location is known. Option E is wrong because whilst the evidence is capable of being admitted as hearsay, the option does not reflect one of the provisions which *permit* the evidence to be admitted as hearsay.

Question 2

The correct answer was D. This is because the only way the prosecution can object to defence evidence being admitted is based on the principle of relevance. Option A is wrong because the power to exclude irrelevant evidence is at the discretion of the trial judge; there is nothing *compelling* the court to exclude. Option E is wrong as s 76 PACE 1984 only applies to confession evidence; this question deals with non-confession evidence. Option B is also wrong because s 78 PACE 1984 only applies to evidence which the prosecution proposes to rely on, and, even if the defence evidence was obtained unlawfully, it may still be relied upon. Option C is wrong because the prosecution cannot rely on s 78 PACE 1984 at all.

Question 3

The correct answer was D. This is because the defence must inform the prosecution that they challenge the admissibility of a confession, and 'represent' to the prosecution that it was obtained unlawfully. A voir dire will then take place and the prosecution needs to satisfy the court beyond reasonable doubt, not on the balance of probabilities, that the confession is admissible. If the prosecution cannot do this, the court must exclude the confession. Options A and B are wrong because the standard of proof for the prosecution in a voir dire is not on the balance of probabilities. Option C is wrong because this confession was not obtained through oppression. Option E is wrong because the exclusion power under s 76 PACE 1994 is mandatory, not discretionary; the court *must* exclude the evidence.

Question 4

The correct answer was D. This is because this answer sets out what the defence needs to do first to object to the prosecution's notice, and includes the correct time period prescribed by law. Options A and C are wrong because they include incorrect timescales for responding to the prosecution's notice. Option B is wrong because, initially, the defence should object using the procedure specifically in place to deal with excluding bad character; s 78 PACE 1984 is an alternative option if s 101(3) CJA 2003 fails. Option E is also wrong for the same reason as option B and s 78 PACE 1984 exclusions are discretionary.

■ KEY CASES, RULES, STATUTES AND INSTRUMENTS

The SQE1 Assessment Specification has identified that you need to know and be able to use:

- ss 34, 35, 36, 37 and 38 CJPOA 1994
- ss 76 and 78 PACE 1984
- ss 100(1) and 101(1) CJA 2003
- *R v Turnbull* [1977] QB 224.

The SQE1 Assessment Specification does not require you to know any other case names, or statutory materials, for the topic of evidence.

7

Trial procedure in the magistrates' court and Crown Court

MAKE SURE YOU KNOW

This chapter will cover the trial procedure in the magistrates' court and Crown Court. For the purposes of SQE1, you are required to know:

- burden and standard of proof
- stages of a criminal trial, including submission of no case to answer
- modes of address and court room etiquette
- difference between leading and non-leading questions
- competence and compellability
- special measures
- relevance of defendant's good character
- solicitor's duty to the court
- preliminary considerations for the use of the Welsh language in criminal proceedings.

SQE ASSESSMENT ADVICE

As you work through this chapter, remember to pay particular attention in your revision to:

- the distinctions between the burden of proof and standard of proof, and when they apply
- the differences in trial procedure between the magistrates' court and the Crown Court
- the differences between leading and non-leading questions, and the rules relating to such
- the circumstances where an individual will be competent and compellable to give evidence
- any special measures that may be in place to assist a witness in providing evidence.

WHAT DO YOU KNOW ALREADY?

Have a go at these questions before reading this chapter. If you find some difficult or cannot remember the answers, make a note to look more closely at that area during your revision.

1) True or false? Whilst the defence are not permitted to ask leading questions in examination-in-chief, the prosecution is permitted.

   [Difference between leading and non-leading questions, page 190]

2) You arrive at the Crown Court and notice that the trial judge listed in your case is 'The Honourable Mrs Justice Stevenson'. How do you refer to Stevenson J in court?

   [What do I call a judge?, page 175]

3) Andrew is a 13-year-old boy and is being called to give evidence in the Crown Court. Will special measures be available to Andrew and, if so, which measures will likely be used?

   [Special measures, page 180]

4) What is the test to be applied when determining whether or not there is a case to answer? (Remember, you do not need to know the case name but you must know the principle behind the case.)

   [Submissions of no case to answer, page 188]

INTRODUCTION TO TRIAL PROCEDURE

In the circumstances where a defendant pleads not guilty to an allegation, a trial must be conducted to determine whether the defendant is guilty or not. In **Chapters 3** and **4**, we discussed trial venue. By way of reminder, the location of a defendant's trial is dependent on the classification of the offence and the plea of the defendant.

In addition, special rules apply that dictate which court a case must be heard in. In this chapter, we now focus on the trial procedure, with particular focus on the stages of a criminal trial.

BURDEN AND STANDARD OF PROOF

In criminal proceedings, there are particular matters in issue that need to be proved by a particular party. For any matter that requires proof, we must understand the burden and the standard of proof.

Burden of proof

Let us begin with a consideration of the **burden of proof**.

> **Key term: burden of proof**
>
> The burden of proof is the term given for the responsibility or obligation to prove, or disprove, a particular matter which is in dispute. The burden of proof may be a legal or evidential burden.

The law draws a distinction between the legal and evidential burden of proof:

- legal burden: the burden to prove a matter (or fact) in issue between the parties
- evidential burden: the burden to make an issue 'live' (ie make an issue one that can be considered by the arbiter of fact).

Table 7.1 highlights some examples of matters that need to be proved, and identifies who bears the burden to prove such matters.

Table 7.1 Examples of where parties possess the burden of proof

Prosecution bears the burden to:	Defence bears the burden to:
• Prove a defendant's guilt (legal burden) • Disprove any relevant defences (eg that a defendant was not acting in self-defence) (legal burden) • Prove a confession was obtained reliably/not through oppression (if the prosecution seeks to introduce a confession) (legal burden)	• Raise sufficient evidence to make an issue live (eg raise sufficient evidence to demonstrate that the defendant may have acted in self-defence) (evidential burden) • Prove any matters that the law reverses on to them (see below)

As you will see from the above, the prosecution will generally bear the legal burden of proof. There are rare exceptions, however, where the defendant will bear a reversed legal burden. For the purposes of SQE1, the only circumstance where a reverse burden of proof exists is in respect of the partial defence to murder of diminished responsibility. Unlike self-defence, for example, it is for the defendant to prove the defence of diminished responsibility (see ***Revise SQE: Criminal Law*** for more detail).

Exam warning

It is a common mistake amongst candidates to confuse the operation of legal and evidential burdens. Remember simply this: Whilst the defence may bear the evidential burden of making an issue 'live' (eg self-defence), the prosecution will continue to possess the legal burden of disproving any issue raised by the defence (eg that the defendant did not act in self-defence).

The burden of proof may be discharged by either party in a number of ways. A party may discharge the burden by calling evidence, or cross-examining a witness for the opposing side. For example, should the defence advocate cross-examine the complainant and allege that they were the aggressor, and put to the complainant that the defendant was acting in self-defence, they will likely have discharged the evidential burden of making the issue live.

Standard of proof

In order for a party to succeed in discharging the burden of proof on a particular issue, they must satisfy the arbiter of fact to the correct standard. This is known as the **standard of proof**.

Key term: standard of proof

The standard of proof is the term given for the degree or level required to satisfy the arbiter of fact that a matter has been proved (ie a party is said to have discharged their burden to prove a matter when the arbiter of fact is satisfied that it has been proved). The standard of proof differs in degree depending on which party bears the burden of proof.

There are two standards of proof which apply in criminal proceedings, illustrated in **Figure 7.1.**

Beyond reasonable doubt/so that you are sure	• Known as the 'criminal standard' • The arbiter of fact must be 'sure' that the matter has been proved • Higher standard of proof (applies only when the prosecution bears a burden of proof)
Balance of probabilities	• Known as the 'civil standard' • The arbiter of fact must be satisfied that it is 'more likely than not' that the matter has been proved • Lower standard of proof (applies anytime when the defence bears a burden of proof)

Figure 7.1: Standards of proof

Now use **Practice example 7.1** to apply your understanding.

Practice example 7.1

James is charged with murder, having picked up a heavy vase and thrown it at Mark, causing a fractured skull and ultimately his death. James, however, argues that he was acting in self-defence as he perceived Mark to be an immediate threat to his safety. Alternatively, James argues the defence of diminished responsibility on the basis that he suffers from schizophrenia, which substantially impaired his ability to form rational judgement.

What are the relevant burdens and standards of proof in this instance?

The prosecution bears the burden to satisfy the jury that James unlawfully and maliciously wounded Mark with intent, and must discharge this burden beyond reasonable doubt (or make the jury sure that all of the elements of the offence are present). In addition, as James has raised self-defence, the prosecution must, in order to prove their case, demonstrate that James did not act in self-defence and thus, in effect, disprove his defence. The legal burden of proof is thus on the prosecution.

The burden of proof applicable to James is more complicated. In respect of self-defence, James possesses an evidential burden to raise sufficient evidence to make the issue of self-defence live; it is not for James to *prove* self-defence. This burden must be satisfied on the balance of probabilities. However, in respect of the defence of diminished responsibility, James will bear a legal burden to prove this defence (ie prove all of the elements of the defence). Whilst James possesses this reverse legal burden, the standard of proof is the civil standard (balance of probabilities).

MODE OF ADDRESS AND COURT ROOM ETIQUETTE

A rather simple, but not to be underestimated, piece of knowledge concerns so-called **mode of address**.

Key term: mode of address

Mode of address refers to the name used to describe a particular individual in the criminal process. The main parties you must be familiar with are the names of the judges, and the names of fellow lawyers in the trial.

What do I call a judge?

Knowing the correct name for a judge is vital in both the magistrates' court and Crown Court. **Table 7.2** provides an overview of the key terms you need to be aware of for SQE1.

Table 7.2: What do I call a judge?

Type of judge	Court found in	Mode of address in person	Mode of address in correspondence
Lay magistrates	Magistrates' court	'Sir' or 'Madam', or collectively, 'Your Worships'	'Mr/Ms/Mrs [full name] JP'

Table 7.2: (continued)

Type of judge	Court found in	Mode of address in person	Mode of address in correspondence
District Judge (magistrates' courts) (including Deputy District Judges)	Magistrates' court	'Judge'	'District Judge (magistrates' courts) [surname]'
Circuit Judges, Deputy Circuit Judges, and Recorders	Crown Court	'Your Honour'	'His/Her Honour Judge [surname] [King's Counsel]'
High Court Judge	Crown Court	'My Lord' or 'My Lady'	'The Honourable Mr/Ms/ Mrs Justice [surname]'

What do I call a fellow advocate?

The answer to this question depends on whether the advocate to whom you are referring is a solicitor or a barrister:

- solicitor: 'My friend' (eg 'My friend for the prosecution')
- barrister: 'My learned friend' (eg 'My learned friend for the defence').

Court room etiquette

Table 7.3 provides some of the fundamental examples of court room etiquette.

Table 7.3: Court room etiquette

Example of etiquette and explanation
Bowing Upon entry and exit from a courtroom, all persons should bow. Whilst it may appear that you are bowing to the judge, you are in fact bowing to the Royal Coat of Arms which sits behind the judge.
Standing and sitting All parties should stand upon the entry and exit of a judge in court. This will usually be signalled by the court usher calling 'Court rise'. No two advocates should be on their feet at the same time unless they are both being addressed by the judge. If one advocate stands, to make an objection for example, the other advocate should take their seat. When questioning a witness, an advocate should be on their feet (though this will not apply in the Youth Court or where the witness appears by live link).

Table 7.3: (continued)

Seating location In the Crown Court, the defence should always sit closest to the jury. Ordinarily, this means that the prosecution would sit closest to the witness box.
Dressing the judge By convention, a judge is never permitted to be left alone in a courtroom. At least one advocate must remain in court at all times whilst the judge is present. This is known as 'dressing the judge'. The judge will quite often, however, excuse the advocate, at which point they are permitted to leave.
Entering and exiting court An advocate should not enter or leave court when the judge is addressing the defendant directly. This may be when giving warnings/directions, when passing sentencing remarks etc. An advocate should wait until the judge has finished addressing the defendant. The same rule applies whilst a jury is being sworn, or returning their verdict.
Turning your back on the judge An advocate should never turn their back on the judge unless permitted to do so (eg to take instructions from the defendant in the dock). Traditionally, advocates would walk backwards out of court so as to not turn their back. This convention of walking backwards has largely faded away.
Walking across the well of the court An advocate should never walk across the well of the court (the open space between the judge's bench and the advocates' bench). An advocate should walk around the well of the court.

COMPETENCE AND COMPELLABILITY

The rules relating to competence and compellability are vital for determining whether a witness *can* give evidence, and whether they can be *forced* to give evidence. We shall consider each term in turn.

Competence

First, we must identify whether the witness is **competent** to give evidence.

Key term: competent (competence)

A witness is said to be competent if they are able to be called to give evidence for either the prosecution or defence. As a general rule, all persons are competent to give evidence. This is so regardless of the age or mental infirmity of an individual.

The general rule is of paramount importance. However, that rule is subject to a number of exceptions. An individual is not considered as being competent if it appears to the court that they are unable to:

- understand questions put to them as a witness, and
- give answers to them which can be understood.

This is known as the 'intelligible testimony' test and is a test of understanding, not one of credibility or reliability. The exception will most likely apply to children and those with a mental impairment.

Exam warning

Remember that the presumption is in favour of competence; the competence of a witness should only be investigated where the judge has any reason to doubt that competence. The age of a child or the disability of an individual will not be determinative; a judgement call must be made based upon the specific circumstances of that witness. For example, whilst the age of a child is not determinative, the younger the child, and the longer the delay in court proceedings, the more likely the child will be unable to understand questions and give answers which can be understood.

Any objection to the competence of a witness should be made before the witness gives evidence and, if in the Crown Court, in the absence of the jury. The burden is on the party calling the witness to prove their competence on the balance of probabilities. Expert evidence may be called to prove such competence, and an intermediary may be required to assist a witness in giving their evidence.

In addition, special rules apply to defendants and co-defendants (**Table 7.4**).

Table 7.4: Competence of defendants

Witness	Competent for the prosecution?	Competent for the defence?
Defendant	No	Yes
Co-defendant	No, unless they have pleaded guilty, have been acquitted, have severed their trial so as to be tried separately or the Attorney General has filed a *nolle prosequi* (ie a formal notice abandoning the prosecution)	Yes

Compellability

Once a witness is deemed to be competent, they are free to give evidence. There will be instances, however, where a witness does not wish to give evidence voluntarily. In this situation, you must consider whether the witness is **compellable**.

Key term: compellable (compellability)

A witness is said to be compellable if, being competent, they may be compelled by the court to give evidence under a legal obligation. As a general rule, all persons are compellable to give evidence.

There are exceptions to the general rule of compellability:

- First, the defendant is not compellable in their own defence. This means that the defendant is not obligated to provide evidence in their own defence. However, remember that adverse inferences may be drawn where a defendant does not testify in their own defence (see **Chapter 6**).
- Second, whilst a defendant is competent to give evidence for a co-defendant, they are not compellable to do so.

A special exception also exists in respect of the defendant's spouse.

Compellability of the spouse of the defendant

In line with the general rule, the **spouse of a defendant** is competent to give evidence. Their compellability, however, is slightly more complex.

Key term: spouse of a defendant

Reference to spouse includes married couples (both heterosexual and homosexual) and civil partners. The term (and exception) does not apply to cohabitees, former spouses, future spouses and polygamous spouses (the latter not being a recognised marriage in English law).

The rules depend on the party intending to call the spouse to give evidence. **Table 7.5** provides the rules relating to this, and see also **Practice example 7.2**.

Table 7.5: Compellability of a spouse

Party calling the spouse	Generally compellable?	Exception
Prosecution	No	A spouse can be compellable for the prosecution where the defendant is charged with a **specified offence**
Defence (ie spouse)	Yes	Unless the spouse is a co-defendant
Co-defendant	No	Same exceptions as apply to the prosecution

Key term: specified offence

A 'specified offence' includes:

(a) an assault on, or injury or threat of injury to, the spouse or a person who was at the material time under the age of 16 (ie 15 and younger)
(b) a sexual offence alleged to have been committed in respect of a person who was at the material time under the age of 16
(c) attempting or conspiring to commit, or aiding, abetting, counselling, procuring or inciting the commission of, an offence falling within paragraph (a) or (b) above.

An individual therefore has a general right to refuse to give evidence against their defendant spouse *unless* the defendant is charged with a specified offence.

Practice example 7.2

James is charged with assaulting Mark (aged 21), contrary to s 47 Offences Against the Person Act 1861. Samantha, James' ex-wife, and Katie, James' current wife, were present at the scene of the alleged assault, and at the material time. The prosecution is compiling its witness list and seeks advice as to who it can call to give evidence.

Which witnesses are compellable to give evidence for the prosecution?

Mark is competent and compellable for the prosecution as he is the complainant in this case. Samantha is the former spouse of James, the defendant, and Katie is the current spouse of James. Katie may attempt to rely on the rule that a spouse cannot be compelled to give evidence against her spouse, James. However, the spousal exception does not apply where James is charged with a 'specified offence'. The assault against Mark would not satisfy the definition of a 'specified offence'. As such, Katie would not be compellable for the prosecution; she could refuse to give evidence against James. Samantha, however, can be compelled to give evidence against James because the spousal exception only applies to current, and not former, spouses/civil partners. As such, Samantha can be compelled to give evidence against James.

A practical factor to bear in mind is that whilst an individual may be compellable in theory, it may not be the best idea to compel them in practice. For example, a spouse who is compellable against their partner is likely to become a hostile witness.

SPECIAL MEASURES

For many witnesses the experience of giving evidence in court can be quite stressful. For this reason, a witness may be permitted to give evidence assisted by one or a number of **special measures**.

Key term: special measures

Special measures assist vulnerable or intimidated witnesses in giving evidence, by reducing the stress associated with giving evidence, and are designed to improve the quality of the evidence of a witness (also referred to as 'achieving best evidence').

Special measures are available to both prosecution and defence witnesses, but are limited for defendants.

Exam warning

There is a difference between a 'defendant' and a 'defence witness'. Do not confuse the two as the rules relating to special measures differ, namely:

- defendant = special measures restricted
- defence witness = no restrictions on special measures.

In order to qualify for special measures, in either the magistrates' court or Crown Court, a two-stage test needs to be considered:

(a) Is the witness eligible for special measures on the grounds of vulnerability or intimidation?

(b) Would any of the special measures available (or any combination of them) be likely to improve the quality of evidence given by the witness?

If the court is satisfied on both of these:

- The court shall then determine which of those measures (or combination of them) would be likely to maximise so far as practicable the quality of such evidence.
- The court shall give a direction providing for the measure(s) to apply.

The trial judge is required by law to warn the jury that any special measures used in the trial must not prejudice the defendant (ie they cannot be viewed negatively against the defendant).

We shall consider each stage of the test in turn, before then considering the special measures available.

Eligibility for special measures

First, the witness must be eligible for assistance. Eligibility is divided into so-called 'vulnerable' and 'intimidated' witnesses.

Vulnerable witnesses

A witness is considered as being vulnerable if:

- they are under the age of 18 (ie 17 or younger) at the time of the hearing, or

- the court considers that the quality of evidence given by the witness is likely to be diminished because the witness suffers from a mental disorder or otherwise has a significant impairment of intelligence and social functioning, or that the witness has a physical disability or is suffering from a physical disorder.

Intimidated witnesses

A witness is considered as being intimidated if the court is satisfied that the quality of evidence will be diminished by reason of fear or distress as a result of giving evidence. In making this determination, the court *must* consider a number of statutory factors. These include, for example:
- the witness's age and maturity
- the witness's ability to understand the consequences of giving evidence in court rather than via video-recorded statement
- any views expressed by the witness, as well as any other factors the court considers relevant.

A special rule applies to a witness who is a complainant in a sexual offence, an offence under the Modern Slavery Act 2015 (slavery, servitude, forced/compulsory labour or human trafficking), or any offence where it is alleged that the behaviour of the accused amounted to domestic abuse. The same rule applies to a witness in certain cases involving guns or knives. In these cases, the witness is automatically eligible for assistance unless the witness has informed the court that they do not wish to be eligible.

Improvement to the quality of the evidence

Where the court has determined that a witness is eligible for special measures, they must then consider whether, in their opinion, the measures would be likely to improve the quality of the evidence given by the witness. In making this decision, the court must consider any views expressed by the witness and whether any measure(s) would inhibit the evidence of the witness from being effectively tested.

Special measures available

There are various provisions available for vulnerable or intimidated witnesses. These measures are briefly discussed in **Table 7.6.** Please note that the court may direct for any one or a combination of measures to apply for a witness.

Table 7.6: Range of special measures

Special measure	Explanation
Screening witness from defendant	A witness may be prevented, by means of a screen or other arrangement, from seeing the defendant. The focus is preventing the *witness* from seeing the defendant, not preventing the defendant from seeing the witness

Table 7.6: (continued)

Special measure	Explanation
Evidence by live link	A witness may provide evidence via live television link whereby, although absent from the court, they are able to provide evidence as though they were in court. A 'specified person', eg a parent, may accompany the witness
Evidence given in private	A witness may provide evidence in circumstances where specified persons are excluded from the court. The defendant cannot be excluded from the court under this measure NB this measure is only available in sexual offence cases or a case where there are reasonable grounds to believe that any person, other than the defendant, has sought, or will seek, to intimidate the witness
Removal of wigs and gowns	A witness may provide evidence in the Crown Court with advocates being required to dispense with the wearing of wigs and gowns. NB wigs and gowns are not worn in the magistrates' court; therefore, this measure is not applicable in the magistrates' court
Video-recorded evidence-in-chief	A video recording of a witness may be admitted as their evidence-in-chief. Any part of the recording should be excluded if the court believes that, in the interests of justice, it should not be admitted
Video-recorded cross-examination or re-examination	Where examination-in-chief has already been conducted by way of video recording, the court may direct that cross-examination and re-examination also are conducted by video recording. Such recording is done in the absence of the defendant
Examination of witness through intermediary	A witness may be examined through an interpreter or other intermediary, who will assist the witness by communicating questions asked and answers given. Please note, this measure is not available to 'intimidated' witnesses
Aids to communication	A witness may be provided with a device to enable questions and answers to be communicated in overcoming a disability, eg a sign board Please note, this measure is not available to 'intimidated' witnesses

Measures to assist a defendant

Please note that the above measures that we have discussed do not apply to defendants. The only measure available to a defendant is the use of a live link when giving evidence. A defendant may give evidence by live link, but only where:

- they suffer from a mental disorder or otherwise have a significant impairment of intelligence and social function
- they are for that reason unable to participate effectively in the proceedings as a witness giving oral evidence in court, and
- use of a live link would enable them to participate more effectively.

Special measures presumptions

Special rules apply in respect of children and complainants in sexual offence cases who give evidence in the Crown Court.

- Complainants in sexual offence cases: A presumption exists in favour of complainants in sexual offences permitting them to give evidence via pre-recorded examination-in-chief.
- Child witnesses: Evidence-in-chief *must* be admitted as video-recorded evidence (ie not live evidence). Any evidence not given by video recording (ie cross-examination) *must* be conducted by live link. This is known as the 'primary rule'.

The 'primary rule' does not apply where:

- the witness informs the court that the rule should not apply, and the court is satisfied that to do so will not diminish the quality of the child's evidence, or
- the court is satisfied that compliance with the rule would not be likely to maximise the quality of the witness's evidence (ie the special measure would not help the witness).

STAGES OF A CRIMINAL TRIAL, INCLUDING SUBMISSION OF NO CASE TO ANSWER

The process adopted in a criminal trial is broadly similar in both the magistrates' court and the Crown Court. Both involve the provision of opening and closing speeches, the introduction of evidence by both parties and the ability to make a submission of no case to answer.

We will briefly consider the stages of a criminal trial in the magistrates' court (summary trial) and Crown Court (trial on indictment) in turn. Submissions of no case to answer are explicitly referenced in the SQE1 Assessment Specification. We will consider such submissions separately at the end of this section. We considered the voir dire procedure in **Chapter 6**.

Stages of a summary trial

The following provides a brief overview of the stages of a criminal trial in the magistrates' court. Proceeding on the basis that the defendant has pleaded not guilty:

(a) *Prosecution opening*: The prosecutor may summarise the prosecution case, concisely identifying the relevant law, outlining the facts and indicating the matters likely to be in dispute. The prosecution should remind the magistrates of the burden and standard of proof. The defendant does not have the right to make an opening speech but may be invited, at the discretion of the court, to concisely identify what they consider to be the issue.

(b) *Prosecution's case*: Next, the prosecution will present the evidence that it relies upon to prove the defendant's guilt. This will include evidence from the alleged victim of the offence, any other witnesses to the offence and any other relevant evidence. All witnesses testifying in court must swear an oath or make a solemn affirmation to tell the truth. The prosecutor will conduct **examination-in-chief** for their own witnesses, before then making the witness available for **cross-examination** by the defence. The prosecutor will then be permitted to conduct **re-examination** of the witness. Where a witness is not attending court, their witness statement will be read out or (more uncommon in the magistrates' court) will form the basis of an agreed fact. The transcript of the defendant's police interview, or the audio of that interview, will also be presented to the court (unless the defendant remained silent or provided 'no comment' answers). The prosecution will present any admissible exhibits as part of its case including, for example, 999 calls, CCTV footage etc. Once all evidence has been admitted, the prosecution will then close its case.

Key term: examination-in-chief

Examination-in-chief allows the calling party (ie the prosecution or defence) to elicit relevant information from the witness. Examination-in-chief is designed to allow the witness to tell their side of the story in a controlled manner.

Key term: cross-examination

Cross-examination is undertaken by the opposing party. The purpose of cross-examination is to test the evidence-in-chief of the witness, question its reliability and to discredit the witness.

Key term: re-examination

Re-examination occurs following cross-examination and allows the calling party to reaffirm or clarify any matters arising out of cross-examination. No new evidence may be introduced during re-examination; only matters arising out of cross-examination may be questioned.

(c) *Submission of no case to answer*: At the close of the prosecution's case, the defendant may make a submission of no case to answer (see **Submissions of no case to answer, page 188**). If the submission is successful, the defendant will be acquitted. If the submission is unsuccessful, the trial continues. We will continue our process as if the submission is unsuccessful.

(d) *Right of the defendant to give evidence*: The magistrates' legal adviser will then explain to the defendant that they have the right to give evidence, and the potential effect of not doing so at all, or of refusing to answer a question whilst doing so.

(e) *Defendant's case*: The defendant will then have the opportunity to present evidence to the court. The same process as with the prosecution's case will be followed. If the defendant chooses to testify, they must be called first, if there are any other defence witnesses to be called.

(f) *Any further evidence*: At the close of the case for the defence, either party may introduce further evidence which has subsequently become admissible (eg evidence admitted in rebuttal of other evidence already introduced).

(g) *Prosecution closing speech*: The prosecution may then make a closing speech (or 'final representations'). Such representations can *only* be made where the defendant is legally represented, or, whether represented or not, the defendant has introduced evidence other than their own.

(h) *Defence closing speech*: The defence may then make any final representations in support of their defence. Unlike the prosecution, there are no restrictions on the defendant's ability to make a closing speech.

(i) *Legal directions:* The magistrates' legal adviser will then provide any necessary legal directions to the magistrates before they retire. If the trial is presided over by a District Judge, they will remind and direct themselves of the relevant law in open court.

(j) *Retirement of magistrates and delivery of verdict*: The magistrates will 'retire' to consider their verdict. The magistrates will then return to open court to deliver their verdict. If the court convicts the defendant, it *must* give sufficient reasons to explain its decision. The court will then proceed to sentencing or adjourn for pre-sentence reports. If the court acquits the defendant, it *may* give an explanation of its decision. The defendant is discharged from the court upon a not-guilty verdict.

Stages of a trial on indictment

The process in the Crown Court is very similar to that in the magistrates' court. For the sake of brevity, we shall only consider those stages in the process that are different to the magistrates' court.

Proceeding on the basis that the defendant has pleaded not guilty:

(a) *Empanelling the jury*: A jury of 12 will be empanelled and sworn in. The court will inform the jury of the charge(s) faced by the defendant and explain to the jury that it is their duty, after hearing the evidence, to decide whether the defendant is guilty or not guilty of each offence (often referred to as placing the defendant 'in the charge' of the jury).

(b) *Prosecution opening.*

(c) *Prosecution's case.*

(d) *Submission of no case to answer* (see below).

(e) *Intention to give evidence*: Unlike in the magistrates' court, before the start of the defence's case, the Crown Court is obliged to ask the defendant whether they intend to give evidence. If the answer is 'no', then the court must satisfy itself that the right to give evidence, and the consequences of not doing so, have been explained to the defendant.

(f) *Defence opening*: The defence is *only* permitted to make an opening speech in the Crown Court if they intend to call at least one witness other than themselves to give evidence. As discussed above, no right to give an opening speech exists in the magistrates' court.

(g) *Defendant's case.*

(h) *Any further evidence.*

(i) *Prosecution closing speech*: The prosecution's right to make a closing speech is restricted in the same way as in the magistrates' court. However, the Crown Court possesses a discretion to allow the prosecution to make a closing speech if 'the court so permits'.

(j) *Defence closing speech.*

(k) *Summing up by the judge*: The judge will then sum up the case for the jury. The judge will provide a summary of the case presented by both the prosecution and defence and provide any directions on any matters of law for the jury (including the defendant's character - see below). The judge will often provide a **route to verdict** for the jury to use in their deliberations.

Key term: route to verdict

A route to verdict is a sequential list of written questions used to provide the jury with a logical route to verdict. The questions should be fact-based and confined to the issue(s) in question. Exemplar routes to verdict can be found in the Crown Court Compendium, a resource used by judges in creating their directions to juries.

(l) *Retirement of jury and delivery of verdict*: Once the judge has summarised the evidence, the jury will then retire to the jury room to consider its verdict. The jury may be recalled if they have questions they wish to ask the judge or if the judge wishes to give the jury further directions. Questions from the jury to the judge must usually be heard in open court and in the presence of counsel, who may make submissions as to the appropriate response to the jury's question. The jury must generally return a unanimous verdict (ie all 12 must agree). If the jury are unable to return a unanimous verdict, the trial judge may permit the jury to return a **majority verdict**.

Key term: majority verdict

The jury may be permitted to return a majority verdict if they have deliberated for at least two hours and ten minutes. The number of jurors required to form a majority verdict depends on the number of jurors remaining (should any of them have been dismissed during the trial) at the point the verdict is delivered:
- 12 jurors: 11–1 or 10–2
- 11 jurors: 10–1
- 10 jurors: 9–1.

A majority verdict may not be returned where there are only nine jurors.

If the verdict is guilty, the foreman of the jury must inform the court how many jurors were in the majority, and how many were in the minority. The judge will then thank and discharge the jury before proceeding to sentence the defendant (or adjourn the case for pre-sentence reports). If the verdict is not guilty, the defendant will be acquitted and discharged (the jury should not be invited to say how many were in the majority or minority). If the jury cannot reach a majority verdict (referred to as a 'hung jury'), the judge will discharge the jury; the prosecution will likely request a retrial before a new jury.

Submissions of no case to answer

As discussed above, at the close of the prosecution's case, the defence is permitted to make a **submission of no case to answer**.

Key term: submission of no case to answer

A submission of no case to answer is a submission made by the defence to persuade the judge to stop the case. This submission will be made because of the weakness of the prosecution's evidence. Such submission can be made in both summary trials and trials on indictment. In trials on indictment, the submission will be made in the absence of the jury.

Timing of a submission

Colloquially referred to as a 'half-time' submission, the defence can make a submission of no case to answer following the close of the prosecution case. This applies in every case, subject to some exceptions that are outside the scope of the SQE1 Assessment Specification.

Right to make representations

Following the submissions made by the defence, the prosecution must be afforded the opportunity to respond to the submission of no case to answer.

Test to be applied

The test for submissions of no case to answer comes from the case of *R v Galbraith* [1981] 2 All ER 1060.

The principles from *Galbraith* can be broken down into three separate scenarios (see **Practice example 7.3** for assistance with applying the test):

(a) If there is no evidence that the crime alleged has been committed by the defendant, there is no difficulty. The judge will of course stop the case. The difficulty arises where there is *some* evidence, but it is of a tenuous character.

(b) Where the judge comes to the conclusion that the prosecution's evidence, *taken at its highest*, is such that a properly directed jury could not properly convict on it, the judge must stop the case.

(c) Where the strength or weakness of the prosecution's case is generally a matter for the jury to consider (eg the reliability of a witness), the judge should allow the matter to be tried by the jury if there is evidence on which a jury could properly come to the conclusion that the defendant is guilty.

Practice example 7.3

James is charged with aggravated burglary, contrary to s 10 Theft Act 1968. The prosecution's case is that James unlawfully entered Mark's house, using a crowbar to gain entry. Whilst in the house, the prosecution's case is that James threatened Mark with the crowbar in order to steal an expensive laptop. James was arrested several days later at his home, and after an extensive search of James' house, the police could not find either the crowbar or the laptop, or evidence of the presence of either within James' house. The prosecution relies solely on the testimony of Mark, who it is later revealed has a reputation for being untruthful and holds a vendetta against James. During cross-examination, James' advocate unpicks Mark's testimony, and clearly demonstrates that Mark's evidence has significant gaps and inconsistencies. The defence advocate also gets Mark to admit to his personal feud with James. Once the prosecution closes its case, James' advocate makes a submission of no case to answer.

What will the judge consider when deciding whether there is a case for James to answer?

The judge will look at the prosecution evidence as a whole (in this case, simply Mark's testimony, including the cross-examination, as the prosecution relies on nothing more), and consider whether a properly directed jury could convict on Mark's evidence alone, taken at its highest. In this instance, it is likely that a judge may agree with a submission of no case to answer, as even at its highest, Mark's evidence has significant gaps and inconsistencies along with evidence of a personal vendetta against James; this, combined with no further evidence, would not likely satisfy a jury so that they are sure of James' guilt. Given Mark's vendetta and the inconsistencies in his testimony, it is likely that the defence will argue that Mark has invented this robbery and that no such robbery took place.

As discussed above, where the submission of no case to answer is successful, the defendant will be formally acquitted and discharged. Where the submission is unsuccessful, the trial continues to the defence's case.

DIFFERENCE BETWEEN LEADING AND NON-LEADING QUESTIONS

As part of your understanding of the stages of a criminal trial, it is also pertinent that you are aware of the different ways of asking a question. In particular, SQE1 expects you to understand the difference between a **leading question** and a **non-leading question**.

Key term: leading question

A leading question is one that suggests the answer. A leading question is often one where the answer can only be 'yes' or 'no'. For example, 'You saw James sitting in the park, didn't you?'

Key term: non-leading question

A non-leading question is an open question, which does not suggest the answer. A witness is permitted to speak freely in terms of the answer provided. For example, 'Where was James when you saw him?' (assuming the witness has already stated that they have seen James).

For our purposes, we shall first discuss the rules relating to leading and non-leading questions, and then give some examples of how to distinguish the two.

Rules relating to leading and non-leading questions

The rules differ dependent on whether the witness is being questioned under examination-in-chief or cross-examination.

- *Examination-in-chief/re-examination*: Leading questions cannot generally be asked in examination-in-chief. Any evidence elicited by such questions is inadmissible; advocates will be asked to rephrase the question. Leading questions may be asked in examination-in-chief where such evidence is not in dispute (such as introductory matters relating to the witness's name, occupation, etc), or where the witness has been treated as hostile (ie not desirous of telling the truth to the court). Given that an advocate may lead on issues not in dispute, it is important to identify from the outset what evidence is disputed and what is not. For the most part, therefore, non-leading questions must be used.
- *Cross-examination*: Leading questions are permitted (and are expected) in cross-examination. However, an actual question must be asked; a tactic adopted by many advocates is to make a statement disguised as a question. There must be a question to be answered.

Distinguishing leading and non-leading questions

Differentiating a leading from a non-leading question is not always a simple task. It is pertinent, therefore, that you can spot the difference and understand how to spot the difference.

A simple technique to adopt is to look at the structure of the sentence. Take the following two examples:

- 'Mark was waving a knife at you, wasn't he?'
- 'What was Mark doing?'

The former involves a statement ('Mark was waving a knife at you'), with a tagline that transforms it into a question ('wasn't he?'). This is a leading question: The question provides the answer and merely requires the witness to agree with it. The latter example is an open question, not suggesting the answer, which allows the witness to speak freely about the evidence they wish to provide. **Table 7.7** provides you with some tools to work out whether a question is leading or not.

Table 7.7: Distinguishing leading and non-leading questions

In a leading question, look out for ...	In a non-leading question, look out for ...
A statement coupled with a tagline. Popular taglines include 'that's right, isn't it?' or 'isn't that so?'	'Open'-worded questions allowing the witness to provide their answer freely
Questions that restrict the answer of the witness to 'yes', 'no' or some other suggested answer	Look out for questions which begin with 'who', 'what', 'where', 'when' and 'how'. These are generally non-leading

THE RELEVANCE OF A DEFENDANT'S GOOD CHARACTER

In **Chapter 6**, we considered the law relating to defendant and non-defendant bad character. As discussed in that chapter, unless certain stringent criteria are met, magistrates or a jury are not informed of an individual's bad character. The rules, however, are different when it concerns so-called 'good character'.

Generally, the good character of a non-defendant is inadmissible. There are limited circumstances where the good character of a non-defendant (eg the complainant in a case) is admissible. However, this is outside the scope of the SQE1 Assessment Specification; our focus is on the good character of defendants.

Meaning of 'good character'

The appellate authorities have defined 'good character' in two primary ways. These descriptors are outlined in **Table 7.8**.

Table 7.8: Meaning of good character

Absolute good character	Effective good character
The defendant has no previous convictions, cautions or reprimands, nor is there any other reprehensible conduct alleged, admitted, or proven.	The defendant has previous convictions, cautions or reprimands recorded against them. However, these are old, minor, and have no relevance to the present charge.

Whether a defendant is of 'effective good character' is a matter of law for the judge. It is for the judge to make a judgment, by assessing all the circumstances of the offence(s) and the offender, to the extent known, and then deciding what fairness to all dictates

Admitting a defendant's good character

Where a defendant is of good character (absolute or effective), the defence will want that fact adducing into evidence. This may be done in a variety of ways, including by way of agreed fact with the prosecution, through asking a question of the Officer in the Case, and through asking the defendant during examination-in-chief.

It is often the case that where a defendant is of good character, character witnesses will be called in their favour also (eg to comment on their personal and professional experiences with the defendant).

Good character directions

Where a defendant is of good character, there will need to be a good character direction. In the magistrates' court, this direction is provided by the legal advisor to the lay magistrates (or the district judge will direct themselves on character), and in the Crown Court, the judge will direct the jury on good character.

The good character limbs

Directions on character can involve one or both of the following 'limbs':

- Propensity limb: This is a direction that the defendant's good character is relevant in the assessment as to whether the defendant is less likely to have committed the offence charged.
- Credibility limb: This is a direction that the defendant's good character is relevant in the assessment as to whether the evidence he has given at trial, or during a police interview, is more likely to have been truthful.

It is for the arbiters of fact to decide what weight they give to the evidence of good character, taking into account everything they have heard about the defendant.

Exam warning

Importantly, good character is *not* a defence to the charge and, as explained above, relevance and weight given to good character is entirely a matter for the arbiters of fact (magistrates or jury). An MCQ may seek to trick you when it comes to the relevance of a defendant's good character.

Giving a good character direction

In light of these limbs, the following summary reflects the legal position relating to good character directions:

- Where a defendant is of 'absolute good character' *and* has given evidence or has made pre-trial statements (eg in police interview), they are entitled to *both* good character limbs.

- Where a defendant is of 'absolute good character' but has not given evidence or has not made pre-trial statements, they are entitled to a good character direction on their likelihood of having committed the offence(s), but are *not* entitled to a direction on credibility.
- Where a defendant is decided to be of 'effective good character' and has given evidence or has made pre-trial statements, they are entitled to both good character limbs, but the direction may be modified as necessary to reflect other matters to ensure that the arbiters of fact are not misled.
- Where a defendant is decided to be of 'effective good character' but has not given evidence or has not made pre-trial statements, they are entitled to a good character direction on their likelihood of having committed the offence(s) (modified as necessary), but are *not* entitled to a direction on credibility.
- Where a defendant has adduced previous convictions or cautions which are of a different category to the offences alleged, they are not entitled to either limb of the good character direction, but the judge had a wide discretion as to whether a good character direction should be given, and in what terms.
- Where a defendant (D1) is of absolute or effective good character, and is tried alongside another defendant (D2) who is not of good character, D1 is still entitled to a good character direction. The judge should, in this case, consider what to say about D2. In most cases, a warning against speculation is appropriate.

It is important to note that where a defendant does not give evidence, but relies on statements made pre-trial in police interview, the direction should include reference to the fact that the account was not given under oath or affirmation, and has not been tested in cross-examination.

Practice example 7.4

James is before the magistrates' court for trial in respect of two offences of shop theft. James has no previous convictions, nor cautions, and the prosecution has not sought to rely on any other reprehensible behaviour. James provided a prepared statement in police interview where he simply stated that he was not at the store on that date and this is a case of mistaken identity. James does not give evidence at trial.

Is James entitled to a good character direction?

James is of absolute good character, and is therefore entitled to a good character direction in terms of his propensity (likelihood) to commit the offences alleged. In respect of his credibility, he is entitled to a good character direction in respect of his account in interview. However, the direction should include a caveat that this account was not given under

oath or affirmation, and has not been tested in cross-examination. Furthermore, as per Chapter 6, a separate direction on s 35 inferences will likely be required.

SOLICITOR'S DUTY TO THE COURT

Revise SQE: Ethics and Professional Conduct discusses in full a solicitor's duty to the court and their client. Chapter 5 of that text specifically concerns ethics and professional conduct in the context of criminal practice.

A vital point to note is that a solicitor is an officer of the court and must conduct themselves in accordance with the overriding objective (see **Chapter 5**).

The *SRA Code of Conduct* describes the principles and standards of professionalism expected of solicitors.

USE OF THE WELSH LANGUAGE IN CRIMINAL PROCEEDINGS

The Criminal Practice Directions 2023, as amended in 2025, deal with the use of the Welsh language in criminal proceedings.

The following provides a summary of the preliminary considerations that SQE candidates must have to the Welsh language in criminal proceedings:

- English and Welsh languages should be treated equally. The fact that an individual is bilingual and is competent in English does not affect or limit their right to use the Welsh language.
- In any legal proceedings in Wales, the Welsh language may be spoken by any party, witness or other person who desires to use it.
- In any legal proceedings in England, legal representatives must inform the court when Welsh may be used by any witness or party, or in any document, to ensure appropriate listing arrangements.
- If a defendant in a court in England asks to give/call evidence in Welsh, the case should not be transferred to Wales before consultation with the Presiding Judge. Where such a transfer is considered appropriate, the Welsh Language Unit should be contacted to discuss specific case requirements. Consulting the Welsh language liaison judge would also be advisable.
- If at the time of sending or lodging appeal to the Crown Court, it is known that Welsh might be used in the case, the court should be informed immediately, or as soon as it becomes known thereafter.
- When each witness is called, the court officer administering the oath/affirmation shall inform the witness that they may be sworn/affirm in

Welsh/English. If Welsh is chosen, the witness should not be asked to repeat it in English.
- The law does not permit juror selection methods enabling discovery of whether a juror speaks Welsh, or to secure a bilingual jury, to try a case in which the Welsh language may be used.
- Should Welsh be used by any party or witness in a trial, an interpreter will be required to provide simultaneous translation from Welsh to English for the court.

■ KEY POINT CHECKLIST

This chapter has covered the following key knowledge points. You can use these to structure your revision, ensuring you recall the key details for each point, as covered in this chapter.

- The prosecution will always bear the burden of proof to satisfy the arbiter of fact of a defendant's guilt, and they must do so beyond reasonable doubt, or so that the arbiter of fact is sure.
- The mode of address will vary according to the type of judge one is appearing before. Understanding the type/rank of judge will determine the appropriate mode of address.
- All witnesses are generally competent and compellable to give evidence. Some exceptions exist for the defendant and their spouse.
- Special measures permit a vulnerable or intimidated witness to provide evidence through the use of some measure which is likely to increase the quality of the evidence.
- The stages of the criminal trial are broadly similar in the magistrates' court and Crown Court and involve opening and closing speeches, the presentation of evidence by the prosecution and defence, submissions of no case to answer and the return of a verdict based upon the evidence.
- A leading question is one which suggests the answer and is not permitted in examination-in-chief unless the evidence is not in dispute.
- A solicitor is an officer of the court and, whilst they must act in their client's best interests, they must also not mislead the court. The solicitor must conduct themselves in accordance with the overriding objective.

■ KEY TERMS AND CONCEPTS

- burden of proof (**page 172**)
- standard of proof (**page 174**)
- mode of address (**page 174**)
- competent (competence) (**page 177**)
- compellable (compellability) (**page 179**)
- spouse of a defendant (**page 179**)
- specified offence (**page 180**)
- special measures (**page 181**)
- examination-in-chief (**page 185**)
- cross-examination (**page 185**)
- re-examination (**page 186**)

- route to verdict (**page 187**)
- majority verdict (**page 188**)
- submission of no case to answer (**page 188**)
- leading question (**page 190**)
- non-leading question (**page 190**)

■ SQE1-STYLE QUESTIONS

QUESTION 1

A woman is being tried in the Crown Court for assault occasioning actual bodily harm, contrary to s 47 Offences Against the Person Act 1861. It is alleged that the woman saw her ex-husband in the street, shouted him over and then punched him in the head several times, resulting in severe bruising and a broken nose. The woman told the police at interview that she was acting in self-defence and will be running the same defence at trial.

Which of the following best describes the approach to the issues surrounding the burdens and standards of proof?

A. The defence bears the legal burden to raise and prove the issue of self-defence, and the prosecution bears the legal burden to prove that the woman committed the assault. The prosecution will discharge its legal burden if it satisfies the jury of the woman's guilt to the criminal standard, beyond reasonable doubt (or so that the jury is sure).

B. The defence bears the evidential burden to raise the issue of self-defence, and the prosecution bears the legal burden to prove that the woman committed the assault and disprove the issue of self-defence. The prosecution will discharge its legal burden if it satisfies the jury of the woman's guilt to the criminal standard, on balance of probabilities (or so that the jury is more sure than not).

C. The defence bears the legal burden to raise the issue of self-defence, and the prosecution bears the evidential burden to prove that the woman committed the assault and disprove the issue of self-defence. The prosecution will discharge its burden if it satisfies the jury of the woman's guilt to the criminal standard, beyond reasonable doubt (or so that the jury is sure).

D. The defence bears the evidential burden to raise the issue of self-defence, and the prosecution bears the legal burden to prove that the woman committed the assault and disprove the issue of self-defence. The prosecution will discharge its burden if it satisfies the jury of the woman's guilt to the civil standard, beyond reasonable doubt (or so that the jury is sure).

E. The defence bears the evidential burden to raise the issue of self-defence, and the prosecution bears the legal burden to prove that the woman committed the assault and disprove the issue of self-defence. The prosecution will discharge its burden if it satisfies the jury of the woman's guilt to the criminal standard, beyond reasonable doubt (or so that the jury is sure).

QUESTION 2

A man is charged with murder in the Crown Court. The prosecution calls a woman who claims to have witnessed the man running away from the scene of the crime. The defence claims that the man has an alibi and was not in the vicinity of the crime at the time in question. During examination-in-chief, the prosecutor asks the woman, 'You saw the defendant running from the alleyway, that's right, isn't it?'

Which of the following best describes the legal position of the prosecutor's question?

A. The evidence elicited from the prosecutor's question is admissible as the prosecution is entitled to ask non-leading questions during examination-in-chief.

B. The evidence elicited from the prosecutor's question is inadmissible as the prosecution is not entitled to ask leading questions during examination-in-chief. The prosecutor will be required to rephrase the question.

C. The evidence elicited from the prosecutor's question is admissible as the prosecution is entitled to ask leading questions during examination-in-chief where the evidence is not disputed.

D. The evidence elicited from the prosecutor's question is admissible as the prosecution is entitled to ask leading questions during examination-in-chief.

E. The evidence elicited from the prosecutor's question is inadmissible as the prosecution is not entitled to ask leading questions during examination-in-chief. The prosecutor will now not be entitled to ask a similar question.

QUESTION 3

A woman is charged with wounding with intent, contrary to s 18 Offences Against the Person Act 1861. The allegation is that the woman threw a wine glass at a 16-year-old girl, causing serious cuts to the face. The prosecution wishes to call the woman's husband to testify that he witnessed the crime being committed. The husband refuses to do so.

Which of the following best describes the legal position of the husband?

A. The husband is both a competent and compellable witness for the prosecution.

B. The husband is not a competent or compellable witness for the prosecution due to the fact that he is married to the accused.

C. The husband is a competent witness for the prosecution but is not compellable.

D. The husband is a competent and compellable witness for the prosecution because the offence charged against the woman is a specified offence.
E. The husband is not a competent witness for the prosecution due to the fact that he is a co-defendant.

QUESTION 4

A man is charged with theft, contrary to s 1 Theft Act 1968. The man elected trial in the Crown Court. The man is legally unrepresented and appears on his own behalf. The man does not intend to call any witnesses other than himself.

Which of the following most accurately describes the law relating to opening and closing speeches?

A. The prosecution may make both an opening and closing speech. The defence may only make a closing speech.
B. The prosecution may only make an opening speech. The defence may make both an opening and a closing speech.
C. The prosecution may make both an opening and closing speech. The defence may also make both an opening and a closing speech.
D. The prosecution may only make a closing speech. The defence may only make an opening speech.
E. The prosecution may only make an opening speech. The defence may only make a closing speech.

QUESTION 5

A man is charged in the magistrates' court with assault by beating. The man enters a plea of not guilty and is acquitted after summary trial.

How should the magistrates announce their decision?

A. The magistrates have a duty to give sufficient reasons to explain their decision.
B. The magistrates may give an explanation for their decision, but they are not required to do so.
C. The magistrates are required to state their reasons in the form of a judgement to explain their decision.
D. The magistrates are obliged to give adequate reasons to explain their decision under the Human Rights Act 1998.
E. The magistrates are only required to provide reasons to explain their decision if the man requests it.

QUESTION 6

A woman is charged with robbery, contrary to s 8 Theft Act 1968 in the Crown Court. During the trial, one of the jurors is discharged due to ill health, leaving only 11 jurors on the jury. The jury has now retired to consider its verdict. After three hours, the judge is considering giving the majority verdict direction to the jury.

Which of the following most accurately describes the law relating to majority verdicts?

A. The judge can direct the jury that they can accept a verdict upon which at least ten of them are agreed.

B. Because there are only 11 jurors, the judge cannot give a majority verdict direction at all.

C. The judge can direct the jury that they can accept a verdict upon which at least eight of them are agreed.

D. The judge must wait a minimum of four hours and ten minutes before giving a majority verdict decision.

E. The judge can direct the jury that they can accept a verdict upon which at least nine of them are agreed.

■ ANSWERS TO QUESTIONS

Answers to 'What do you know already?' questions at the start of the chapter

1) False. No party may ask leading questions during examination-in-chief unless the evidence to be elicited is not disputed or the witness has been treated as hostile.
2) Stephenson J would be referred to as 'My Lady'/'Your Ladyship' as she is a High Court judge sitting in the Crown Court.
3) As Andrew is under the age of 18, he is eligible for special measures. The prosecution would have to demonstrate that Andrew's quality of evidence would likely be improved by any special measures granted. If eligible, the primary rule is that Andrew's evidence-in-chief would be admitted by video recording and any further examination would be conducted by live link.
4) Where the judge comes to the conclusion that the prosecution evidence, taken at its highest, is such that a jury properly directed could not properly convict upon it, it is the judge's duty, upon a submission being made, to stop the case. Where the strength or weakness of the prosecution's case is generally a matter for the jury to consider (eg the reliability of a witness), the judge should allow the matter to be tried by the jury if there

is evidence on which a jury could properly come to the conclusion that the defendant is guilty. This is known as the *Galbraith* test.

Answers to end-of-chapter SQE1-style questions

Question 1

The correct answer was E. This is because the defence bears the evidential burden to make the issue of self-defence live. The prosecution then has the legal burden to prove that the woman committed the offence to the criminal standard (beyond reasonable doubt or so that the jury is sure), and disprove the issue of self-defence. Option A is wrong because the defence does not have a legal burden to satisfy the defence of self-defence. Option B is wrong because the criminal standard of proof is not on the balance of probabilities. Option C is wrong because the burden placed on the defence in this instance is an evidential, not legal, burden, and the prosecution bears the legal burden to prove the woman's guilt; this is not an evidential burden. Option D is wrong because the prosecution must prove their case to the criminal standard - beyond reasonable doubt or so that the jury is sure.

Question 2

The correct answer was B. The prosecutor has asked a leading question, the suggested answer to which is disputed by the defence. The evidence is therefore inadmissible (options A, C and D are wrong) and the prosecutor will be required to rephrase the question (option E is therefore also wrong).

Question 3

The correct answer was C. Whilst the husband is a competent witness for the prosecution (therefore options B and E are wrong), the husband is not compellable (option A is therefore wrong). An individual is only compellable where their spouse is charged with a specified offence. Whilst this is an offence of violence, it has not taken place against someone *under* the age of 16 (therefore option D is wrong).

Question 4

The correct answer was E. The permissibility of speeches is dependent on whether a defendant is legally represented or intends to call witnesses other than himself. In this case, the man is neither represented nor calling any other witness. As such, the prosecution is only permitted to make an opening speech, and the defence is only permitted to make a closing speech. All other options are therefore wrong.

Question 5

The correct answer was B. As the man has been acquitted, the magistrates are under no obligation to provide an explanation for their decision; it is at their own discretion as to whether such explanation is provided. Magistrates only possess an obligation to provide reasons to explain their decision where they convict the defendant. All other options are therefore incorrect.

Question 6

The correct answer was A. In a situation where only 11 jurors remain on a jury, a majority verdict can consist of no fewer than ten jurors (options C and E are therefore incorrect). Option B is incorrect because a majority verdict is available, so long as there are a minimum of ten jurors (if there are only nine jurors, the verdict must be unanimous). Option D is incorrect because a majority verdict may be offered after the jury have deliberated for at least two hours and ten minutes, not four hours and ten minutes.

KEY CASES, RULES, STATUTES AND INSTRUMENTS

The SQE1 Assessment Specification does not require you to know any case names, or statutory materials, for the topic of trial procedure in the magistrates' court and Crown Court.

8

Sentencing

MAKE SURE YOU KNOW

This chapter will cover the concept of sentencing following criminal proceedings. For the purposes of the SQE1, you are required to know:

- the role of the sentencing guidelines
- determining seriousness, aggravating and mitigating facts
- concurrent and consecutive sentences
- mitigation
- types of sentences, including custodial, suspended and community orders
- Newton hearings.

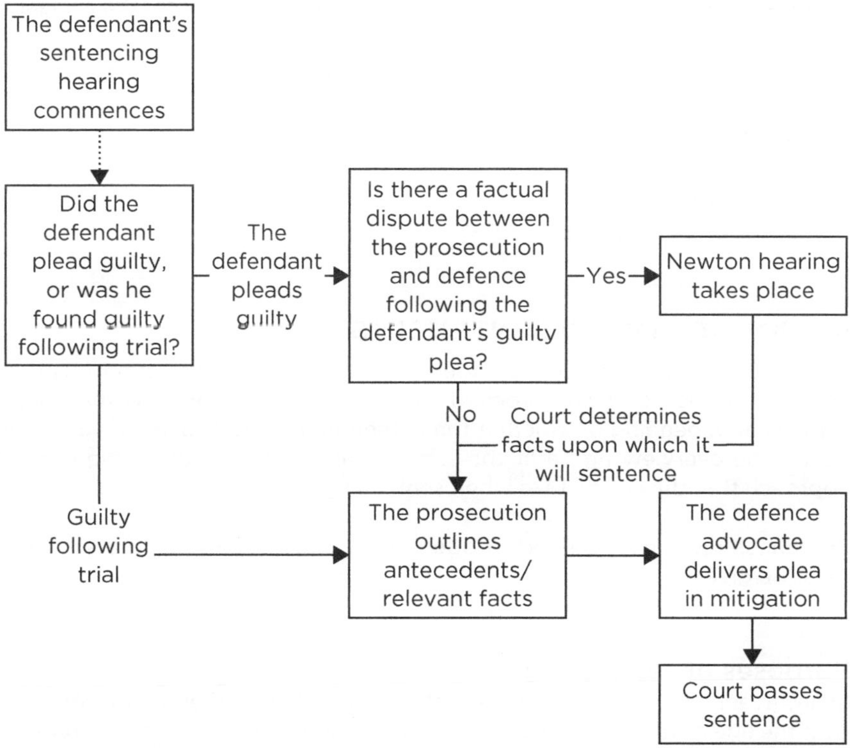

Overview of sentencing

■ SQE ASSESSMENT ADVICE

As you work through this chapter, remember to pay particular attention in your revision to:

- the importance of the sentencing guidelines and how they are used
- the principles of totality, and its relationship with concurrent and consecutive sentences
- the procedure to be followed in sentencing, and when certain hearings apply
- when particular sentences can and cannot be imposed.

■ WHAT DO YOU KNOW ALREADY?

Have a go at these questions before reading this chapter. If you find some difficult or cannot remember the answers, make a note to look more closely at that area during your revision.

1) True or false? Some serious offences carry a mandatory life sentence. If it is true, how many can you name relevant to SQE1?

   [Custodial sentences, page 215]

2) True or false? The courts must follow the sentencing guidelines at all times, and any deviation from them will give rise to a successful appeal against sentence.

   [Role of the sentencing guidelines, page 205]

3) Fill in the blank: A Newton hearing is best described as ______.

   [Newton hearings, page 222]

4) What are the two categories of the general types of sentence a court can impose?

   [Types of sentences, page 214]

INTRODUCTION TO SENTENCING

Once a defendant has either pleaded guilty to, or has been found guilty of, an offence, the court will proceed to sentencing. The process may differ somewhat depending on whether the defendant *pleaded* guilty or was *found* guilty. The **overview figure** at the start of this chapter outlines the general approach that the courts take when sentencing.

Sentences must be declared in open court and reasons for the sentence must be given.

Purposes of sentencing

In any event, when a court passes sentence on an adult offender (ie someone over the age of 18), and unless there is a mandatory life sentence requirement, it must have regard to the **purposes of sentencing**.

Key term: purposes of sentencing

The court must have regard to the following purposes of sentencing:

- the punishment of offenders
- the reduction of crime (including its reduction by deterrence)
- the reform and rehabilitation of offenders
- the protection of the public (including the victims of crime)
- the making of reparation by offenders to those affected by their criminal conduct.

Exam warning

You may get an MCQ on the general principles of sentencing and what factors the court must take into account when passing sentence. Remember to check what offence the offender has pleaded guilty to/ been found guilty of and whether a mandatory sentence requirement applies. If this is the case, the five factors listed above do not apply.

THE ROLE OF THE SENTENCING GUIDELINES

As previously mentioned, some offences carry mandatory life sentences. In such circumstances, the sentencing judge is bound by that mandatory requirement and cannot depart from it. For most, if not all, other offences, however, the sentencing guidelines assist the court in determining the most appropriate sentence.

What are the sentencing guidelines?

Developed by the Sentencing Council, the sentencing guidelines ('the guidelines') assist the court to categorise the seriousness of the offence. The sentencing guidelines can be accessed on the Sentencing Council's website: www.sentencingcouncil.org.uk/.

There are several types of guidelines, which apply at different stages of criminal litigation. These are detailed in **Table 8.1**.

Table 8.1: Types of sentencing guidelines

Guideline type and explanation
Overreaching guidelines These guidelines offer general guidance on approaches to sentencing and are used in conjunction with the offence-specific guidelines
These guidelines include the General Guideline: Overreaching Principles; Imposition of Community and Custodial Sentences; and Sentencing Children and Young People (for the latter, see **Chapter 10**)

Table 8.1: (continued)

Guideline type and explanation
Magistrates' court guidelines The sentencing guidelines for magistrates' courts provide offence-specific guidelines for offences which are tried summarily. In addition, there is explanatory material which assists the magistrates' courts when dealing with offenders
Guidelines specific to offences for Crown Court use The sentencing guidelines for Crown Court provide offence-specific guidelines for offences tried on indictment or offences committed to the Crown Court for sentence

Must the court always follow the sentencing guidelines?

Generally speaking, every court, when passing sentence, *must* follow the guidelines which are relevant to the offender's case, and any additional relevant sentencing guidelines. The court may *only* depart from the guidelines if it is satisfied that it is in the interests of justice to do so.

Any departure from the guidelines may give rise to an appeal against sentence; appeals are considered in more detail in **Chapter 9**.

Revision tip

To get yourself comfortable with the guidelines, take a look at the relevant guidelines for the specific criminal offences which you are required to know about, detailed in the ***Revise SQE: Criminal Law*** guide in this series. This will not only allow you to enhance your knowledge of the principles of sentencing, but will aid your revision of the substantive criminal law for SQE1.

Reading the sentencing guidelines

In order to get to grips with sentencing, it is important that you understand the structure of a sentencing guideline. Generally, the offence-specific guidelines will follow the same process (or 'steps'). We shall briefly consider the steps here before we proceed with particular aspects of that process.

- Step 1 – Determining the offence category: The court should begin the process by determining the 'offence category'; they do so by considering the 'culpability' and 'harm' of the case. Generally, there are three levels of culpability ('higher', 'medium' and 'lower') and three levels of harm (phrased as categories 1, 2 or 3). 'Harm' and 'culpability' are explored below: see **Determining seriousness.**
- Step 2 – **Starting point** and **category range**: Having categorised the offence based on culpability and harm, the court must then determine the starting point and category range for each offence.

Key term: starting point

Depending on how the offence is categorised in terms of culpability and harm, a starting point is provided (see **Starting point: harm and culpability,** below). This is what the sentence would be after trial before any additional aggravating factors or mitigating factors are applied which may impact the severity of the offence (see **Aggravating factors** and **Mitigation,** below).

Key term: category range

The category range advises the court what form a sentence may take if the court applies aggravating or mitigating factors. The more serious the court deems the offence, the further up the range the sentence may be placed; conversely, the less serious the offence, the sentence may fall further down the range.

- Step 3 – Consider any other factors which indicate a reduction, such as assistance to the prosecution: Assistance given or offered to the investigator or prosecutor should be considered as mitigation (see below, **Mitigation**).
- Step 4 – Reduction for guilty pleas: The court must consider what reduction, if any, can be afforded for an early guilty plea (see below, **Mitigation**).
- Step 5 – Dangerousness: The court must consider whether to impose an extended sentence in line with the dangerous offender provisions (see **Chapter 10** in the context of youth offenders; the dangerous offender provisions for adults are not listed on the SQE1 Assessment Specification).
- Step 6 – Totality principle: The court must consider the proportionality of multiple sentences (see below, **Concurrent and consecutive sentences**).
- Step 7 – Compensation and ancillary orders (not listed on the SQE1 Assessment Specification).
- Step 8 – Reasons: The court is obliged to give reasons for, and explain the effect of, the sentence. This includes the effect of non-compliance with the sentence.
- Step 9 – Consideration for time spent on bail (tagged curfew) (not listed on the SQE1 Assessment Specification).

Take the opportunity to review the offence-specific guidelines for the offences covered in SQE1. Now, we shall proceed to deal with the remainder of the SQE1 sentencing syllabus.

DETERMINING SERIOUSNESS

Once the relevant guideline has been identified for an offence, the court will then refer to it in order to determine the seriousness of the offence.

Starting point: harm and culpability

Where a court is considering the seriousness of any offence, it must consider:

- the offender's culpability in committing the offence
- any harm which the offence caused, was intended to cause, or might foreseeably have caused.

Ultimately, the seriousness of an offence will determine whether a custodial or non-custodial sentence is appropriate (see **Types of sentences**, below).

Culpability

The first factor which the court will examine is that of the offender's **culpability**.

Key term: culpability

Culpability refers to the blameworthiness of the offender, and the role they played in the commission of the offence. It is assessed by reference to the level of intention and/or premeditation and the extent and sophistication of planning.

Whilst each offence may have specific, non-exhaustive examples which differentiate higher and lower levels of culpability, **Figure 8.1** demonstrates the four levels of general culpability.

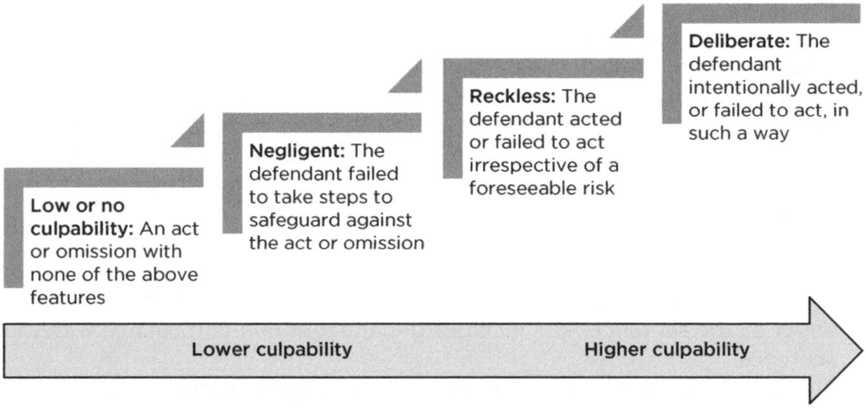

Figure 8.1: Assessing culpability in sentencing

In addition to the above, where some level of culpability is required for an offence, the court will have regard to the following when assessing culpability:

- high levels of planning/the offender played a leading role (suggests higher culpability)
- evidence of some planning/the offender played a significant role
- little or no planning/the offender played a minor role (suggests lower culpability).

Harm

Having assessed culpability, the court will then move on to assess the level of **harm** involved.

Key term: harm

The concept of harm is not confined to just physical harm which the offender actually caused. The court may also consider the level of harm which was *intended* to be caused, and harm which might *foreseeably* have been caused.

Figure 8.2 illustrates the four general levels of harm identified by the guidelines and is supported by **Practice example 8.1**.

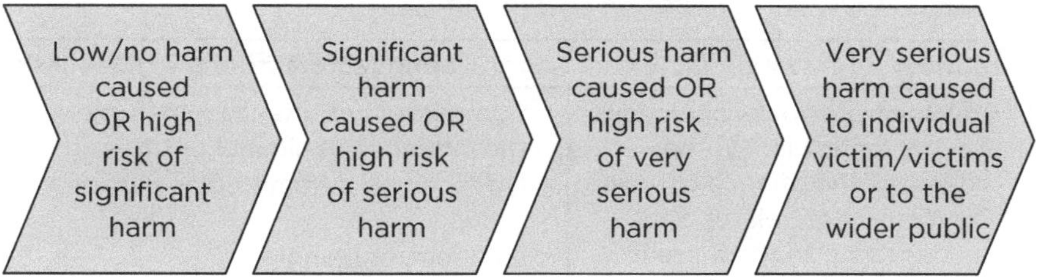

Figure 8.2: Assessing harm in sentencing

Practice example 8.1

James was convicted following trial on indictment of assaulting Mark, inflicting grievous bodily harm, contrary to s 20 Offences Against the Person Act 1861. After Mark had told James that he was awful at his job, James started planning Mark's assault through learning Mark's route home, identifying ambush points, procuring a blunt instrument and noting down what his plans were. James followed Mark home several weeks later and hit him over the head with a blunt instrument, causing a severe head injury, resulting in grievous bodily harm. Mark subsequently cannot carry out his job and requires extensive psychological intervention. Before the judge passes sentence, James asks you for your advice.

What advice may you give to James about his culpability and the level of harm caused?

James has demonstrated higher levels of culpability due to the evidence of high-level planning, and that he played a leading role in the commission of Mark's assault. Therefore, it would be necessary to advise James that he may receive a harsher sentence due to a higher level of culpability. Harm is also at a higher level here, as Mark has not only suffered physical injury, but he cannot continue his job and he requires ongoing medical treatment.

Aggravating factors

Relevant to the sentencing of an offence may be generic or specific **aggravating factors**.

Key term: aggravating factors

Aggravating factors are facts that may make the offence more serious, providing a justification for the court to pass a more severe sentence.

Aggravating factors have either a statutory source, or they arise from the sentencing guidelines. **Table 8.2** highlights some, but not all, examples of both types of aggravating factors.

Table 8.2: Aggravating factors in sentencing

Statutory aggravating factors	Aggravating factors from the guidelines
• Relevant previous convictions having regard to: (a) the nature of the offence to which the conviction relates and its relevance to the current offence; and (b) the time that has elapsed since the conviction • Offence committed whilst on bail • Hostility based on specified characteristics of the victim, for example, race, religion, disability, etc • Assaults on emergency workers	• Commission of offence whilst under the influence of alcohol or drugs • Offence was committed as part of a group • Evidence of planning • High level of profit from the offence • Location of the offence (eg in an isolated place) • Attempting to conceal evidence • Presence of others during the commission of the offence (ie children) • The offence involved the use of a weapon • Offences taken into consideration

Where the court takes an aggravating factor into account, it must state so in open court.

Offences taken into consideration

You will see in **Table 8.2** that the sentencing guidelines provide that **offences taken into consideration** (TICs) are a potentially aggravating factor.

Key term: offences taken into consideration

TICs are offences which the offender has not been convicted of, but has admitted to committing in addition to the offence which they are being sentenced for, and which the offender can ask the court to take into consideration when passing sentence.

Whilst TICs may be seen as a mitigating factor (through assisting the police and not wasting time), the court may impose a greater sentence which reflects the overall criminality of the offender. TICs should not be accepted where:

- the TIC is likely to result in a sentence which is greater than the convicted offence
- it is in the public interest that a separate prosecution should be sought for the TIC(s), or
- the offender would avoid a less severe consequence (for example, a prohibition or ancillary order) which would have been appropriate to impose on conviction.

In addition to aggravating factors, the court must take account of any facts that may reduce the seriousness of the offence or reflect personal mitigation. Mitigating factors are discussed fully in our next section.

MITIGATION

Part of the sentencing process is bringing mitigating factors to the court's attention, aiming to persuade the court to reduce the sentence from the original starting point, and to 'soften the blow' of any aggravating factors. This will usually take place during a **plea in mitigation**.

Key term: plea in mitigation

Shortly before the court passes sentence, the judge or magistrates will hear a plea in mitigation from the defence advocate. This is where the defence advocate, in line with the law and relevant guidelines, attempts to reduce the severity of the sentence imposed. Any factors advanced by the advocate must have a factual basis, and the solicitor must not mislead the court in any regard.

Mitigating factors

The court may take any relevant matters into account when passing sentence. In addition, the court can exercise its discretion as to the weight it decides to attach to the mitigating factors. There are usually two basic forms of mitigation which may be relied upon:

- mitigating factors relating to the offence
- personal mitigation relating to the offender.

Mitigating factors relating to the offence

Mitigating factors relating to the offence will usually coincide with evidence of lower culpability and harm (as discussed above). The defence advocate will bring these to the court's attention when attempting to categorise the offence. The defence advocate may also attempt to minimise the impact or weight placed on aggravating factors.

Mitigating factors relating to the offender

These are factors which are specific to the offender. Mitigating factors include, but are not limited to:

- no previous/relevant previous convictions
- good/exemplary character or conduct
- genuine remorse
- co-operation with the relevant authorities
- sole or primary carer for a dependent relative
- early guilty plea (see more detail below)
- determination to treat behaviour which may fuel offending
- assistance given (or offered) to the prosecutor or investigator.

In addition to the submissions made by the defence advocate, a **pre-sentence report** (PSR) may be obtained and used in support of a plea in mitigation.

Key term: pre-sentence report

Compiled by the Probation Service, the PSR usually details, inter alia, the nature of the offence, the cause of the offending behaviour, personal mitigation, assessment of the likelihood of reoffending and a suggested appropriate sentence. It is important to note, also, that a defence advocate is not obliged to agree with the PSR when recommending a sentence.

Reduction for early guilty pleas

The court is required by law to have regard to any early guilty plea as this may result in a more lenient sentence. In particular, the court must consider:

- the stage of proceedings at which a guilty plea was given
- the circumstances in which that guilty plea was given.

The appropriate discount that can be applied, as detailed in the Reduction in Sentence for a Guilty Plea Guideline, is demonstrated in **Figure 8.3**.

Plea indicated **at** the first stage of the proceedings	→	Plea indicated **after** the first stage of proceedings	→	Plea indicated during the course of the trial
• **Maximum reduction of one-third**		• **Maximum reduction of one-quarter**		• **Sliding scale: one-tenth on first day of trial; can be reduced to zero**

Figure 8.3: Early guilty pleas

The 'first stage' will normally be the first hearing at which a plea or indication of plea is sought and recorded by the court. If a guilty plea is entered *after*, the maximum discount is subject to a sliding scale. The amount of reduction decreases as the proceedings progress (maximum of one-tenth on the first day of trial) and may eventually reach zero. It is important to note, however, that these reductions only apply to sentences which are punitive; there is no reduction in, for example, rehabilitation or ancillary orders. Furthermore, a one-third reduction is still available if it was unreasonable to expect the defendant to indicate a guilty plea sooner than was done.

CONCURRENT AND CONSECUTIVE SENTENCES

Many offenders may have been charged with, and convicted of/pleaded guilty to, multiple offences. In such cases, the court will need to determine whether the offender will serve the sentences at the same time (concurrently) or one after another (consecutively). **Table 8.3** demonstrates the circumstances when, according to the Sentencing Council, it is more appropriate to impose a concurrent sentence or consecutive sentence.

Table 8.3: Concurrent and consecutive sentences

Consecutive sentence appropriate where:	Concurrent sentence appropriate where:
Offences arise under unrelated facts or incidents, for example: • An offender commits a theft on one occasion, and assaults a different victim at another time • An attempt to pervert the course of justice relating to another offence charged • A Bail Act offence **Similar offences, but where concurrent sentences would not reflect overall criminality, for example:** • Repeated thefts involving attacks on several different shopping assistants • Repeated domestic abuse over a period of time against the same victim **One or more offences qualifies for a statutory minimum sentence, and concurrent sentences would undermine this:** • It is important to note that consecutive sentences should not be imposed to evade a statutory maximum	**Offences arise out of the same incident or facts, for example:** • A single incident of dangerous driving where multiple victims were injured • Fraud or relevant forgery • Robbery using a weapon, but the weapon offence is ancillary to the robbery and not distinctively independent **Series of offences of the same or similar kind, for example:** • Small and repetitive thefts from the same person over a period of time

Totality principle

The court is, in any event, required to have regard to the **totality principle**.

Key term: totality principle

When the court is sentencing an offender for multiple offences, the court must assess the overall criminality of the offender and pass a sentence which is just and proportionate in the circumstances.

From this, the concept of totality has two limbs:

- Firstly, where sentencing for more than one offence, the sentence should be reflective of all of the offending behaviour; the sentence must be one which is just and proportionate.
- Secondly, it is necessary to address both the offending behaviour and the factors specific to the offender.

With the above in mind, the courts will then consider whether sentences should run consecutively or concurrently. The court will:

- consider the category for each individual offence in accordance with the relevant guidelines
- after doing so, assess whether the offences call for concurrent or consecutive sentences.

TYPES OF SENTENCES

We now turn to consider the types and range of sentences which are available to the sentencing court. The sentence which an offender receives will fall into one of two categories; **non-custodial sentences** or **custodial sentences**.

Key term: non-custodial sentences

Any sentence which a court passes that does not involve a term of imprisonment will be considered a non-custodial sentence. These can include, for example, fines, discharge or community orders.

Key term: custodial sentences

Custodial sentences involve imposing a term of imprisonment on the offender and are usually handed down when all other forms of sentencing are inappropriate.

Whilst there are a range of sentences (both custodial and non-custodial) available to the courts, the SQE1 Assessment Specification specifically identifies that you need to be particularly familiar with custodial sentences, suspended sentences and community orders.

These shall now be discussed in more depth, in turn.

Custodial sentences

The court may decide to impose a term of imprisonment for an offender. When the court is determining whether a custodial sentence should be imposed, it must have regard to the **custody threshold**.

> **Key term: custody threshold**
>
> The courts must have regard to the custody threshold when considering whether to impose a custodial sentence. The custody threshold provides that the court must not pass a custodial sentence unless the offence is of sufficient severity and where an appropriate non-custodial sentence cannot be justified, essentially implying that custody is a measure of last resort.

Even with the custody threshold in mind, the courts are provided with guidance on imposing custodial sentences by the Sentencing Council. The guidance provides that:

- The custody threshold test reserves a custodial sentence for only the most serious offences and offenders.
- Even if the custody threshold is passed, a custodial sentence should not be deemed inevitable; if a community order could restrict an offender's liberty sufficiently whilst addressing any rehabilitation requirements, then a custodial sentence should not be imposed.
- If a custodial sentence would have an impact on any dependants of an offender who is on the cusp of meeting the custody threshold, to an extent which would make a custodial sentence disproportionate to the aims of sentencing, then custody should not be imposed.

Whilst community orders are discussed in more detail later on in this chapter, some community and rehabilitation orders can only be imposed *with the consent of the offender.* These include alcohol treatment requirements (ATRs), drug rehabilitation requirements (DRR) or mental health treatment requirements (MHTR). If an offender fails to express a willingness to comply with such an order, a court would still be able to impose a custodial sentence.

Determining the length of a custodial sentence

Where the court is of the view that the custody threshold has been met, and a custodial sentence is the only appropriate option, it shall then determine the length of the term of imprisonment. Generally, the following provisions apply for determining the length of a custodial sentence:

- The custodial sentence must be for the shortest term which, in the opinion of the court, is commensurate with the severity of the offence/ combination of offences and does not exceed the permitted maximum.
- Where an offender is convicted on indictment (see **Chapter 3**) of a statutory offence punishable by imprisonment, but there is no limit on a maximum term and there is no mandatory life sentence, the maximum

custodial sentence is two years. Otherwise, the Crown Court is generally not restricted in its sentencing powers, except by any statutory maximum.

In addition to the above, it is worth remembering that the magistrates' courts have limited sentencing powers in terms of imposing custodial sentences. **Table 8.4** provides an overview of the sentencing powers of the magistrates' courts.

Table 8.4: Sentencing in the magistrates' courts

Number of offences	Maximum length of custodial sentence
Single summary only offence (see **Chapter 3)**	Six months (unless statute provides a lower term)
Two or more summary only offences	Aggregate must not exceed six months
Single either way offence (see **Chapter 3**)	12 months' imprisonment
Two or more either way offences	Aggregate must not exceed 12 months

Release following a custodial sentence

When an offender has spent 40% of their custodial sentence in prison, generally they must be released on licence into the community (subject to exceptions). The offender would then be required to comply with both 'standard' and 'prescribed' conditions, and the licence would be in place until the sentence expires. This licence may be revoked, resulting in the offender being returned to custody for the remainder of the sentence. See revise4law.co.uk for full details. As of 11 May 2026, offenders who receive a custodial sentence shorter than two years are no longer subject to post-sentence supervision (PSS) following the expiration of their licence. This change in the law is retrospective in effect, applying to all offenders.

Mandatory life sentences

An offender who has been convicted of, or has pleaded guilty to, murder is subject to a mandatory life sentence. Whilst this is deemed a sentence for life, an offender is generally eligible for early release after a specified minimum period of detention.

Suspended sentences

In some circumstances, the court may suspend a custodial sentence. This is known as a **suspended sentence**.

Key term: suspended sentence

A suspended sentence is where a term of imprisonment has been imposed on an offender, but it does not take effect immediately and the offender is not sent to prison. Instead, the offender may return to the community, having to comply with specified conditions (known as 'community requirements'). Committing an 'activation event' (another offence, or breaching the community requirements) has consequences which shall be discussed later in this chapter.

Importantly, the court is not permitted to pass both a suspended sentence order and a community order at the same time (for the same offence or for different offences appearing before the court at the same time).

Determining whether to suspended a sentence

If the term of imprisonment is of a length that is capable of being suspended (see below for offenders convicted before and after 22 March 2026), the court must consider whether it is appropriate to suspend that custodial term. In doing so, the court will have regard to the Sentencing Council guideline on the *Imposition of community and custodial sentences*. In that guideline, the court must weigh the relevant factors below to consider whether it is possible to suspend the sentence. **Table 8.5** illustrates the factors that the court must consider.

Table 8.5: Factors to consider for suspended sentences

Factors indicating that it *may* be appropriate to suspend a custodial sentence	**Factors indicating that it *may not* be appropriate to suspend a custodial sentence**
• Realistic prospect of rehabilitation in the community • Offender does not present high risk of reoffending or harm • Strong personal mitigation • Immediate custody will result in significant harmful impact upon others, including any dependent children or where the offender is pregnant or postnatal (has given birth in the previous 12 months)	• Offender presents a risk to any person • The seriousness of the offence means that appropriate punishment can only be achieved by immediate custody • History of poor compliance with court orders *and* unlikely to comply in the future

These factors must be weighed in the balance; one factor may bear more weight than another in a given case. The factors are case and fact specific.

Operational and supervision period

If the court considers that a sentence of imprisonment can be suspended, it must then specify the 'operational period' of the order. The operational period is the overall length of the suspended sentence order; this is a period whereby if the offender reoffends within it, the suspended sentence may take effect. The operational period must be for a minimum of six months; the maximum period depends on whether the offender was convicted before or after 22 March 2026 (see below).

When a court imposes a suspended sentence order, it has the discretion to decide whether to also impose community requirements to that order. The court is not obligated to impose community requirements; the suspended sentence can be a 'stand-alone' order. Where the court does impose any community requirement, however, it must also impose and specify a 'supervision period'. The supervision period is the length of time that the offender is subject to supervision from the Probation Service; it is within this period that the offender must complete their community requirements (eg unpaid work, curfew, programme requirement). A supervision period begins on the day on which the order is made and *must* last for a minimum of six months. Regardless of when the offender was convicted (before or after 22 March 2026), the supervision period *cannot* exceed two years, and *cannot* exceed the length of the operational period. Any breach of a community requirement within the supervision period can result in the suspended sentence being activated (see below).

Two different sentencing regimes

Having now considered the basic structure of suspended sentence orders, it is imperative that we consider the two different sentencing regimes relating to such orders.

The law relating to suspended sentence orders changed for any individual convicted *on or after* 22 March 2026. The new law features a presumption in favour of suspended sentence orders, and increased the length of potential suspended sentence orders. We will consider each in turn.

However, it is important to emphasise that this change in the law was not retrospective (ie it does not apply to any person convicted *before* 22 March 2026). This means that you must be aware of the legal position for defendants convicted *before* 22 March 2026 and *on or after* that date.

Revision tip

The new provisions only apply where a defendant has been *convicted* of an offence *on or after* 22 March 2026. It does not therefore apply to offences for which the offender is convicted *before* 22 March 2026, but sentenced *after*. Keep this date and the fact that it must be the *conviction* firmly in your mind for any future MCQ.

Offenders convicted before 22 March 2026

For offenders convicted before 22 March 2026:

- The minimum custodial sentence that can be suspended is 14 days (for offenders aged 21 and over) and 21 days (for offenders aged 18–20).
- The maximum custodial sentence that can be suspended is two years.
- The minimum operational and supervision period is six months.
- The maximum operational and supervision period is two years (though the supervision period cannot be longer than the operational period).

Unlike offenders convicted *on or after* 22 March 2026, there is *no* presumption in favour of suspended sentence orders under 12 months.

Offenders convicted on or after 22 March 2026

For offenders convicted on or after 22 March 2026:

- The minimum custodial sentence that can be suspended is 14 days (for offenders aged 21 and over) and 21 days (for offenders aged 18–20).
- The maximum custodial sentence that can be suspended is three years.
- The minimum operational and supervision period is six months.
- The maximum operational period is three years (but *only* where the sentence of imprisonment (individually or as part of two or more offences to be served consecutively) is over two years.
- The maximum supervision period is two years (though the supervision period cannot be longer than the operational period).

Exam warning

The new maximum operational period has the capability of catching candidates out. Pay close attention to all key figures and dates:

- If the sentence of imprisonment is two years or less, the maximum operational period remains two years.
- If the sentence of imprisonment is more than two years, the maximum operational period is three years (but only if the defendant was convicted *on or after* 22 March 2026).

Presumption of suspended sentence orders

For offenders convicted on or after 22 March 2026, there exists a presumption in favour of suspended sentence orders under 12 months. This means that if the court is intending to impose a custodial sentence of 12 months or less, it *must* suspend the sentence. Where, therefore, the sentence to be imposed is more than 12 months' imprisonment, the court retains the usual discretion to impose a suspended sentence order.

This presumption is subject to one exception, and eight exemptions.

Exception to the presumption

The court need not impose a suspended sentence order where it is of the opinion that there are exceptional circumstances which:

(a) relate to the offence (or the combination of the offence and one or more offences associated with it) or the offender, *and*

(b) justify not making the order.

This is a matter of judgement for the court, and the parties will be invited to make submissions in the normal course of events. This 'exception' is relevant where the presumption still applies. This is different, therefore, to the 'exemptions' (see below) where the presumption simply does not apply.

Exemptions to the presumption

There are several circumstances where the presumption in favour of a suspended sentence order does not apply. These circumstances apply equally between offenders aged 18–20 and those aged 21 and over. The exemptions are detailed in **Table 8.6**.

Table 8.6: Exemptions to the presumption of a suspended sentence

Exemptions
The defendant is in custody at the time of the sentence as a result of a custodial sentence, or being remanded in custody on other offences, or being committed to custody by an order of the court.
The defendant is detained in a hospital at the time of the sentence as a result of a hospital order.
Where the defendant is being sentenced for two or more offences on the same occasion and the term of any of those sentences is more than 12 months, or those sentences are to be served consecutively and the terms of those sentences are in aggregate more than 12 months.
Where the defendant is being sentenced for an offence which is or already has been subject to a supervision order (including a community order), *and* the court is re-sentencing that offender on that order.
Where the offence being sentenced was *committed* during the currency of a supervision order (including a community order and suspended sentence order).
The offence was committed in circumstances which 'constituted, or occurred in circumstances closely connected with, a breach by the offender of an order of a court'.
Where the court is of the opinion that making the order would put a particular individual at significant risk of physical or psychological harm.

Consequences for breaching requirements or reoffending

If an offender is brought before the court for either breaching any community requirements during the supervision period (by failing, without reasonable excuse, to comply with any requirement) or being *convicted* of an offence within the operational period, the court must take action on the breach. The court has a number of powers open to it; the court may:

- order that the suspended sentence takes immediate effect on the original term with no alterations (known as 'activation in full'),
- order that the suspended sentence takes immediate effect on a substituted, lesser term (known as 'activation in part'),
- order that the offender pays a fine not exceeding £2,500,
- (in a case where the suspended sentence order features one or more community requirements) amend the order by imposing more onerous

requirements, extending the supervision period, or extending the operational period, or
- (in a case where the suspended sentence order does not feature community requirements) amend the order by extending the operational period.

Exam warning

The consequences identified above only apply where the offender is *convicted* of a new offence committed *during the operational period* of the suspended sentence order; mere suspicion of commission is insufficient and an offence committed before the suspended sentence was imposed, or following its expiry, cannot bring about the consequences described above. Watch out for this in an MCQ. The court need not activate a suspended sentence (in full or in part) if it concludes that it would be unjust to do so.

Community orders

Instead of a custodial sentence, the courts may pass a community order. A community order is a non-custodial sentence, which requires the offender to complete one or more 'community order requirements', which include:
- an unpaid work requirement
- a rehabilitation activity requirement
- a curfew requirement
- a mental health treatment requirement
- a drug/alcohol rehabilitation requirement
- an electronic monitoring requirement.

When imposing a community order, at least one requirement must be for the purposes of punishment (eg unpaid work or a curfew). This is so unless the court also imposes a fine or concludes that there are exceptional circumstances relating to the offence or to the offender which would make it unjust in all the circumstances for the court to impose a requirement for the purpose of punishment in the particular case, *and* would make it unjust in all the circumstances for the court to impose a fine for the offence concerned.

When sentencing, the court must identify the community sentence band applicable to the offender (ie low, medium or high). This will affect, for example, the length of the community sentence, or the restrictions imposed. A community order can be imposed for a maximum period of three years.

Imposing a community order

The court must not pass a community order unless the offence is 'serious enough to warrant the making of such an order'. In addition, a community order may only be imposed if:

- the offence is punishable by imprisonment, and
- the offender is suitable for a particular type of community order.

A community order must include one of the requirements listed above and can be accompanied by a fine. It is important to remember, however, that a community order cannot be imposed at the same time as a custodial sentence.

Consequences for breaching a community order

In the initial instance of an offender breaching a community order, the supervising probation officer must provide the offender with a warning. If a warning has already been issued within the previous 12 months, the matter may be referred back to the court. The court may, if an offender over the age of 18 failed to comply without good reason:

- amend the terms of the order, and could add a requirement or extend the duration of an existing term, or
- revoke an order and then re-sentence, which could include custody if that was initially available
- fine the offender not more than £2,500
- impose a custodial sentence for the wilful and persistent non-compliance, even if the offence for which the community order was made did not cross the custody threshold.

NEWTON HEARINGS: APPLICABILITY AND PROCEDURE

Following a guilty plea, the court will proceed to sentence the defendant on the facts of the case which it is presented with. Usually, these will be agreed by the prosecution and defence. If, however, there is a factual dispute between the prosecution and defence, following *R v Newton* (1982) 77 Cr App R 13, the court may hold a **Newton hearing** (see **Practice example 8.2**).

Key term: Newton hearing

Formally known as a 'trial of issue', a Newton hearing is where:

- the judge listens to the evidence and comes to their own conclusion on what the issue is, or
- the judge hears no evidence but listens to submissions from the prosecution and defence. If this method is adopted and there is a substantial dispute on the facts, the judge *must* favour the facts advanced by the defence and sentence accordingly.

Applicability of Newton hearings

Where a defendant pleads guilty but disputes part of the prosecution case, they must submit a **basis of plea** for consideration by the prosecution.

Key term: basis of plea

A basis of plea must be in writing and must set out the basis upon which the defendant is pleading guilty. The basis of plea cannot be a defence to the charge; rather, it is an acceptance of the guilty plea but on facts different to those of the prosecution. For example, a defendant may accept punching the victim, but dispute how many times they punched them.

Where a defendant submits a basis of plea, it will be for the prosecution to review the basis and determine whether it accepts the defendant's basis, or not. If it accepts the defendant's basis, or cannot dispute that basis, the defendant will be sentenced on their version of events. Where, however, the prosecution does not accept the basis of plea, a Newton hearing may be required. A Newton hearing should generally only be necessary where the defendant's version of events would make a material difference to sentence. Reference to 'material difference' often means that the categorisation of the offence would be lessened if the defendant's basis were to be accepted. If the prosecution does not accept the basis, but the court does not consider it will make a material difference to sentence, the court will simply proceed to sentence on the defendant's basis.

Practice example 8.2

Mark is charged with assaulting James, occasioning actual bodily harm, contrary to s 47 Offences Against the Person Act 1861. The prosecution says that Mark caused severe bruising after punching James, who was intoxicated, and caused severe grazing and tarmac burns by dragging him across a road and some gravel. Mark pleads guilty to the charge and admits that he caused the severe bruising, but disputes that he dragged James and that he caused the severe grazing and tarmac burns. Mark submits a written basis of plea which says that the severe grazing and tarmac burns were caused by James falling down a steep hill.

What steps will the court take now?

First, the court will consider whether the defendant's version of events will make a material difference to sentence. In this case, it likely will. It is likely that the court will, through a Newton hearing, hear evidence to determine how James came about the severe tarmac burns and grazing, and then sentence on its finding. Alternatively, the court will not hold a Newton hearing and will accept Mark's account, and sentence accordingly. If the court finds or accepts that Mark did not cause the tarmac burns or grazing, it is likely that Mark's sentence would be less harsh due to lower harm being caused.

Newton hearing procedure

A Newton hearing follows a similar pattern to that of a trial:

- First, the prosecution will open the case, identifying clearly what the relevant issue is to be determined (eg how many punches the defendant threw) and will remind the court of the burden and standard of proof (the burden of proof is on the prosecution to disprove the defendant's version of events; this must be done to the criminal standard).
- Having opened the case, the prosecution will then call its evidence on the issue. This may be in the form of live evidence from witnesses (which will be examined-in-chief and cross-examined in the normal way), real evidence, such as CCTV, or agreed facts. Having called of its evidence, the prosecution will then close its case.
- The defence will then be required to call its evidence. In most cases, this will require the defendant to give evidence. The defendant will be examined-in-chief and cross-examined in the normal way. Having called all of its evidence, the defence will close their case.
- Both parties are then permitted to make closing speeches to the court.
- Having heard all the evidence and submissions, the judge will then determine whether the prosecution has successfully disproved the defendant's version of events. If the prosecution has succeeded, the defendant will be sentenced on the prosecution 'full facts'. Where the prosecution has not succeeded, the defendant will be sentenced on their version of events. The consequence of this is the impact on categorisation within the sentencing guidelines.

Effect of a Newton hearing on a defendant's credit for guilty plea

As discussed towards the start of this chapter, a defendant will be afforded a reduction in sentence for a guilty plea (on a sliding scale dependent on the timing of that plea). Where a defendant's version of events is accepted following a Newton hearing, their credit for guilty plea will generally be unaffected. Where, however, a defendant's version of events is rejected at a Newton hearing, the Sentencing Council proposes that any reduction should normally be halved. Where witnesses are called during such a hearing, it may be appropriate further to decrease the reduction.

■ KEY POINT CHECKLIST

This chapter has covered the following key knowledge points. You can use these to structure your revision, ensuring you recall the key details for each point, as covered in this chapter.

- The sentencing guidelines must be followed unless the court considers that it is in the interests of justice not to do so.
- A custodial sentence is not inevitable even if the custody threshold has been passed; custody is to be reserved for the most serious offenders.

- Suspended sentences may be imposed for a minimum period of 14 days, but a maximum period of two years. It may be a stand-alone order, or feature a number of community requirements.
- A community order cannot exceed three years in length and requires an offender to comply with any number of community order requirements.
- The sentence imposed should be announced in open court and reasons must be provided.
- If a court is sentencing for multiple offences, it must adhere to the totality principle and impose a sentence which is just and proportionate, reflecting overall criminality.

■ KEY TERMS AND CONCEPTS

- purposes of sentencing (**page 205**)
- starting point (**page 207**)
- category range (**page 207**)
- culpability (**page 208**)
- harm (**page 209**)
- aggravating factors (**page 210**)
- offences taken into consideration (**page 210**)
- plea in mitigation (**page 211**)
- pre-sentence report (**page 212**)
- totality principle (**page 214**)
- non-custodial sentences (**page 214**)
- custodial sentences (**page 214**)
- custody threshold (**page 215**)
- suspended sentence (**page 216**)
- Newton hearing (**page 222**)
- basis of plea (**page 223**)

■ SQE1-STYLE QUESTIONS

QUESTION 1

A woman was charged with murder but was convicted of unlawful act manslaughter having killed a man whom she suspected of killing her young daughter in a violent and frenzied attack. The woman sought counselling following her daughter's death and could not cope with the media attention and aftermath. She is a single mother who looks after a four-year-old son at home with no family support. This is her first conviction and she was previously of good character. The court now proceeds to sentence the woman following persuasive mitigation.

Which of the following best describes the likely sentence for the woman?

A. As the woman was charged with murder and has been found guilty of a related homicide offence, the court must pass a mandatory life sentence.

B. As the woman has been convicted of a serious offence, the court is likely to impose a custodial sentence. However, due to the woman's circumstances, the court may suspend the custodial sentence for a period not less than 14 days but not more than two years.

C. As the woman has been convicted of a homicide offence, she will receive a mandatory life sentence, but the term of release may be reduced due to her personal circumstances.

D. As the woman has been convicted of a serious offence, the court is likely to impose a custodial sentence. However, due to the woman's circumstances, the court must suspend the custodial sentence for a period not less than 14 days but not more than two years.

E. As the woman was charged with murder and has been found guilty of a related homicide offence, the court may pass a mandatory life sentence.

QUESTION 2

A man is charged with assault occasioning actual bodily harm, contrary to s 47 Offences Against the Person Act 1861. After co-operating with the police when the man was first arrested, he voluntarily confessed and took responsibility for his actions. At the first hearing at the magistrates' court, the man subsequently pleaded guilty. The magistrates adjourn for sentencing and the man asks his solicitor about whether he will get a reduced sentence for pleading guilty at the first hearing.

Which of the following best describes the advice which the solicitor should give to the man?

A. As the man voluntarily pleaded guilty at the earliest opportunity, which was the first hearing in the magistrates' court, the court must take these factors into account. As such, it is likely that the man will receive the full one-quarter reduction in sentence.

B. As the man voluntarily pleaded guilty and at the earliest opportunity, which was at the police station, the court must take these factors into account. As such, it is likely that the man will receive the full one-quarter reduction in sentence.

C. As the man voluntarily pleaded guilty and at the earliest opportunity, which was the first hearing in the magistrates' court, the court must take these factors into account. As such, it is likely that the man will receive the full one-third reduction in sentence.

D. As the man voluntarily pleaded guilty and at the earliest opportunity, which was at the police station, the court must take these factors into account. As such, it is likely that the man will receive the full one-third reduction in sentence.

E. As the man voluntarily pleaded guilty and at the earliest opportunity, which was the first hearing in the magistrates' court, the court may take these factors into account. As such, it is likely that the man will receive the full one-third reduction in sentence.

QUESTION 3

Having been convicted of burglary, contrary to s 9 Theft Act 1968, and an assault occasioning actual bodily harm, contrary to s 47 Offences Against the Person Act 1861, arising out of the same facts, a man is due to be sentenced. Before the hearing, the man asks his solicitor for advice on how the courts may approach his sentencing in light of the multiple offences.

Which of the following best describes the advice that should be given to the man?

A. The courts are required to adhere to the totality principle and impose a sentence which is just and proportionate to the man's overall criminality, and then decide whether the sentences will run consecutively or concurrently.

B. The courts are required to adhere to the totality principle and impose a sentence which is just and reasonable to the man's overall criminality, and then decide whether the sentences will run consecutively or concurrently.

C. The courts are required to adhere to the totality principle and impose a sentence which is fair and just to the man's overall criminality, and then decide whether the sentences will run consecutively or concurrently.

D. The courts are required to adhere to the totality principle and impose a sentence which is reasonable and proportionate to the man's overall criminality, and then decide whether the sentences will run consecutively or concurrently.

E. The courts are required to adhere to the totality principle and impose a sentence which is in the interests of justice, commensurate with the man's overall criminality, and then decide whether the sentences will run consecutively or concurrently.

QUESTION 4

A woman was convicted of theft, contrary to s 1 Theft Act 1968, and has a 12-month prison sentence suspended, with an operational period of two years. During the operational period, the woman allegedly committed an assault occasioning actual bodily harm, contrary to s 47 Offences Against the Person Act 1861, which she denies. The trial for the s 47 charge is yet to take place. The woman seeks advice on her suspended sentence.

Which of the following best describes the advice the woman should be given?

A. The s 47 charge constitutes an activation event, and the woman's suspended sentence will take effect immediately at the first hearing.

B. The s 47 charge constitutes an activation event, and the woman's suspended sentence must take effect as soon as the trial concludes.

C. The s 47 charge constitutes an activation event only if the woman is convicted or pleads guilty; if so, when being sentenced for that offence, the court may order that her suspended sentence takes effect immediately on its original terms, or altered terms, and pay a fine not exceeding £2,500.

D. The s 47 charge constitutes an activation event only if the woman is convicted or pleads guilty; if so, when being sentenced for that offence, the court may order that her suspended sentence takes effect immediately, or pay a fine not exceeding £2,500.

E. The s 47 charge constitutes an activation event only if the woman is convicted or pleads guilty; if so, when being sentenced for that offence, the court may order that her suspended sentence takes effect immediately on the original terms, or altered terms, or pay a fine not exceeding £2,500.

QUESTION 5

A man is currently serving a community order with an unpaid work requirement of 250 hours. When sentencing initially, the magistrates took the view that the offence did not pass the custody threshold. One day, the man wilfully refused to turn up for his day of unpaid work, and his probation officer issued him with a warning. Several weeks later, there was a second failure to comply, and the man was taken before the magistrates' court, which imposed a fine. One month later, the man persistently and wilfully failed to comply. The man has now been brought before the magistrates and seeks advice from his solicitor on what the magistrates may do.

Which of the following best describes the advice which may be given to the man?

A. As the custody threshold was not passed, the court cannot re-sentence the man to a period of custody for his failure to comply; they can only impose a fine not exceeding £2,500, or amend his current order.

B. Even though the custody threshold was not passed initially, the court is empowered to re-sentence the man and impose a custodial sentence as a result of the man's wilful and persistent failure to comply. The court must impose a custodial sentence and revoke his community order.

C. Even though the custody threshold was not passed initially, the court is empowered to re-sentence the man and impose a custodial sentence as a result of the man's wilful and persistent failure to comply. The court may impose a custodial sentence and, if so, they must revoke the community order.

D. Even though the custody threshold was not passed initially, the court can send the man to the Crown Court to re-sentence the man and impose a custodial sentence. The magistrates' court does not have the power in this instance to impose a custodial sentence.

E. Even though the custody threshold was not passed initially, the court is empowered to re-sentence the man and impose a custodial sentence as a result of the man's wilful and persistent failure to comply. The court may impose a custodial sentence and, if so, they must suspend the community order which would then resume on release from prison.

■ ANSWERS TO QUESTIONS

Answers to 'What do you know already?' questions at the start of the chapter

1) True. Murder is the only criminal offence on the SQE1 syllabus which, irrespective of the circumstances, requires the court to pass a mandatory life sentence. Other offences, such as robbery and aggravated burglary, carry *maximum* sentences of life imprisonment. However, these sentences are not *mandatory*.
2) False. The courts *must* follow the sentencing guidelines *unless* it considers that it is in the interests of justice not to do so. In addition, whilst there are occasions when departing from the guidelines may give rise to an appeal, it does not necessarily mean it will be a successful appeal.
3) A Newton hearing is best described as a hearing which takes place after a guilty plea, or conviction following trial, whereby the judge settles a factual dispute between the prosecution and defence before then sentencing on those facts.
4) The two broad categories of sentences which a court can pass are custodial sentences and non-custodial sentences.

Answers to end-of-chapter SQE1-style questions

Question 1

The correct answer was B. This is because the court *may* pass a suspended sentence, and it is not obliged to do so in any event; this is why option D is wrong. Options A and C are wrong because mandatory life sentences in this context only relate to a guilty plea or verdict to the charge of murder, not manslaughter, even though terms of release for those on life sentences can be altered. Whilst option E is accurate insofar as the maximum penalty for unlawful act manslaughter is a life sentence, it is not *mandatory*, and therefore it is incorrect.

Question 2

The correct answer was C. This is because the court *must* take the factors into account, and the full reduction available is that of one-third, not one-quarter; this is why options A and B are wrong. Option D is wrong because although the man admitted to committing the offence at the police station, and the fact that this may help him in mitigation, the earliest opportunity to plead guilty is at the first hearing; this is where the period for reductions in sentence for early guilty pleas starts. Option E is wrong because the courts *must*, not *may*, take the relevant factors into account.

Question 3

The correct answer was A. This is because the courts are required to adhere to the totality principle, and the wording of this answer accurately reflects the test for a sentence (sentences must be just and proportionate and reflect overall criminality). For this reason, options, B, C and D are wrong. Option E is wrong because the principle of totality is unrelated to the interest of justice test.

Question 4

The correct answer was E. This is because it best reflects the options available to the court regarding the suspended sentence if the woman is convicted of the s 47 charge, unlike option D. Options A and B are wrong because at this point, she has only been accused of committing the s 47 offence; it has not been proved. At this stage, therefore, it is not an activation event. Option C is wrong because the court need not activate the sentence *and* fine the woman. The option to fine is an alternative to activating the suspended sentence.

Question 5

The correct answer was C. This is because the courts are empowered to impose a custodial sentence for offenders who wilfully and persistently fail to comply with the terms of their community orders (hence why option A is wrong). If this occurs, the community order would be revoked. There is nothing to compel the court to impose a custodial sentence in these circumstances, however; this is why option B is wrong. Option D is wrong because the magistrates' courts do have the power to impose a custodial sentence in these circumstances if they imposed the initial community order. Option E is wrong because there is no power to reactivate the community order once the offender is released from custody having been re-sentenced.

KEY CASES, RULES, STATUTES AND INSTRUMENTS

The SQE1 Assessment Specification does not require you to know any case names, or statutory materials, for the topic of sentencing. Despite that, given that the SQE1 Assessment Specification refers to the Sentencing Council Guidelines, you are strongly advised to read through the overreaching guidelines and offence-specific guidelines relevant to SQE1.

9

Appeals procedure

MAKE SURE YOU KNOW

This chapter will cover the procedures and processes involved in criminal appeals.

For the purposes of SQE1, you are required to know:

- appeals from the magistrates' court
- appeals to the High Court by way of case stated
- appeals from the Crown Court.

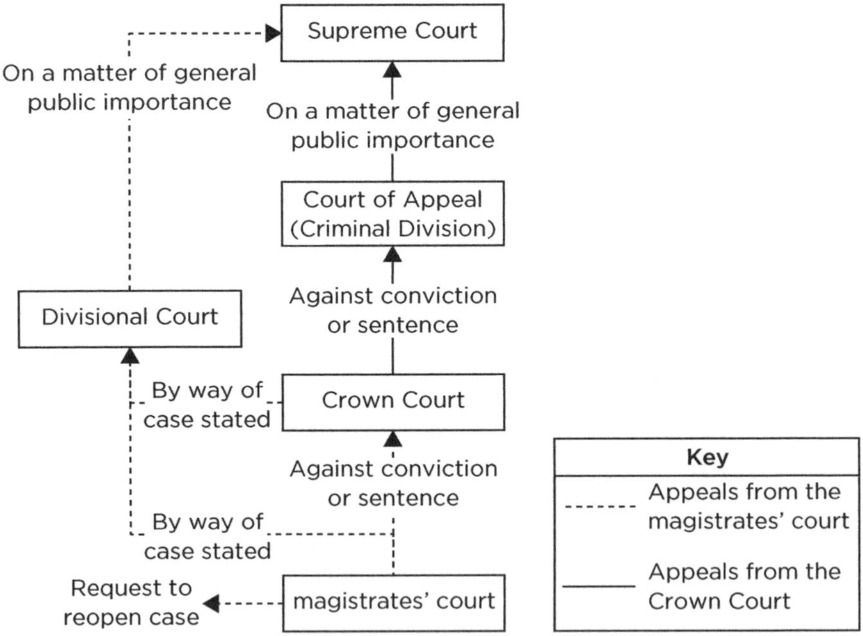

Overview of criminal appeals

■ SQE ASSESSMENT ADVICE

As you work through this chapter, remember to pay particular attention in your revision to:

- the routes to appeal dependent on whether the case was tried in the magistrates' court or the Crown Court
- the powers available to the appellate courts on hearing an appeal
- the limited circumstances by which the prosecution may appeal in a criminal case.

■ WHAT DO YOU KNOW ALREADY?

Have a go at these questions before reading this chapter. If you find some difficult or cannot remember the answers, make a note to look more closely at that area during your revision.

1) True or false? A defendant is acquitted in the Crown Court following a trial by jury. The prosecution, unhappy with this conclusion, can appeal to the Court of Appeal against the acquittal.

   [Appeals from the Crown Court, page 239]

2) Which court would hear an appeal against conviction following a trial on indictment in the Crown Court?

   [Appeals from the Crown Court, page 239]

3) Fill in the blank: A defendant's appeal against conviction will be allowed in the Court of Appeal if the Court considers the conviction to be

   ______________.

   [Appeals from the Crown Court, page 239]

4) A defendant has been convicted in the magistrates' court and wishes to appeal on the basis that the magistrates were wrong in law. Which court will the appeal be heard in?

   [Appeals by way of case stated, page 236]

INTRODUCTION TO APPEALS PROCEDURE

Following the conviction (and in limited cases, the acquittal) of a defendant, you may be faced with the issue of appeals. An appeal is a challenge against the decision or findings of the court below. The structure of appeals in England and Wales was demonstrated above in the **overview figure**. Importantly, you are not required to know appeals to the Supreme Court for SQE1, nor are you required to know of the circumstances where the magistrates' court can reopen a case to correct errors.

APPEALS FROM THE MAGISTRATES' COURT

If a defendant is convicted of an offence in the magistrates' court, there are a number of options available to them. The two forms of appeal relevant to SQE1 are:

- Against conviction or sentence: A convicted person may appeal to the Crown Court against the conviction or sentence.
- By way of case stated: If either party to the proceedings (prosecution or defence) believes that the magistrates were wrong in law, they may appeal to the Divisional Court of the High Court by way of case stated.

Importantly, these routes to appeal also exist for individuals convicted in a Youth Court (see **Chapter 10** generally). We shall now consider our first appeal route: from the magistrates' court to the Crown Court.

Appeals to the Crown Court

The main route available to a defendant convicted in the magistrates' court is to appeal to the Crown Court.

Exam warning

Do not get caught out; appeals to the Crown Court are *only* available to the convicted person; the prosecution has no right to appeal against acquittal or sentence. The prosecution's right to appeal is limited to appeals by way of case stated.

Procedure for appeal against conviction and/or sentence

In order to appeal, an appellant must serve an appeal notice on the magistrates' court and every other party involved in the case (normally, this just means the prosecution). This notice of appeal must be served not more than 15 business days after the magistrates pass or defer sentence. The appellant can submit an appeal at any time up to the 15-day time limit.

Exam warning

The appeal notice must be served not more than 15 business days after *sentence* and not *conviction*. Make sure you are not caught out by this in an MCQ.

It will be helpful to identify some further points relating to procedure:

- If the appellant is already remanded in custody and wishes to obtain bail pending appeal, they must include this application within their appeal notice. The presumption of bail does not apply to defendants appealing against conviction or sentence (see **Chapter 2**). If bail is refused by the magistrates' court, the appellant may apply to the Crown Court for bail.
- If the appeal notice is late, the appellant must include an application for an extension of time in their appeal notice.
- Provided notice is given within time, no leave to appeal is required (it is an automatic right of appeal).
- If the appeal is against conviction, and the appeal is contested, the respondent must submit a respondent's notice not more than 15 business days after service of the appeal notice.

- Once the notice of appeal has been served, the magistrates' court officer must notify the Crown Court of the service of the appeal notice. The court officer must do so as soon as practicable and must make available to the Crown Court all evidence and materials that were served on the magistrates' court as part of the summary trial.

Hearing the appeal

The nature of an appeal to the Crown Court is dependent on the type of appeal before it:

- Appeal against conviction: The appeal is a complete rehearing of the whole case (in essence, a retrial). Either party may call evidence not called at the magistrates, or omit evidence heard. There is no obligation on the prosecution to put their case in the same way as the lower court and the Crown Court may make a decision on this different basis.
- Appeal against sentence: The appeal is a complete rehearing of the sentencing hearing with the ability of the appellant to make another plea in mitigation (see **Chapter 8**). The Crown Court is not reviewing the sentence of the magistrates' court; the Court must form an independent view on all the evidence as to the correct sentence. The Crown Court may consider sentence on a different factual basis to that of the magistrates' court.

The appeal will be heard by:

- a judge (a High Court Judge, Circuit Judge or Recorder), and
- between two and four lay magistrates (none of whom took part in the decision under appeal).

Whilst the lay magistrates must accept the law from the judge, the decision is based on a majority vote, meaning that the lay magistrates are capable of outvoting the judge.

Powers of the Crown Court

Upon conclusion of the appeal, the Crown Court may confirm, reverse or vary any part of the decision appealed against. This means that if a defendant appeals against conviction, the Crown Court may find the defendant guilty, as the magistrates did (thus 'confirming' the decision of the magistrates), or may acquit them (thus 'reversing' the decision of the magistrates).

In the context of appeals against sentence, the Crown Court has the power to impose any sentence that would have been available to the magistrates' court. This means that the Crown Court could impose a sentence which is more or less severe than that imposed by the magistrates, so long as it is a sentence that could be imposed (thus allowing them to 'vary' the decision of the magistrates - see **Practice example 9.1**).

Practice example 9.1

James is convicted of common assault in the magistrates' court and is sentenced to two months' imprisonment. James accepts his conviction but wishes to appeal against his sentence, considering it to be harsh.

What advice would you give to James?

James may appeal against his sentence but runs the risk that the Crown Court could impose a harsher sentence of up to six months' imprisonment (the maximum available to the magistrates' court for a single summary offence). An unsuccessful appeal may also mean that James is required to pay prosecution costs (in full or part).

A further appeal?

Following a rehearing in the Crown Court, whether against sentence or conviction, both the prosecution and defence have the ability to appeal to the High Court by way of case stated. We consider this form of appeal immediately below; the principles and procedures are identical.

Appeals by way of case stated

The second form of appeal from the magistrates' court is an appeal by way of case stated. This form of appeal is restricted to an appeal based on law and not fact and is heard by the Administrative Court, sitting as a Divisional Court of the King's Bench Division (ie by the High Court sitting as an appeal court).

Appeals by way of case stated are open to both a convicted person and the prosecution. The appeal is brought on the basis that either party is 'aggrieved' by the conviction, order, determination or other proceeding of the magistrates' court (or Crown Court following an initial appeal from the magistrates' court). The grounds of appeal are twofold:

(a) that the decision made by the magistrates' court is wrong in law (eg the magistrates misapplied the law or admitted evidence that ought to have been excluded), or

(b) that the decision made by the magistrates' court is in excess of their jurisdiction (eg the magistrates heard a case for which they did not have jurisdiction).

Exam warning

Importantly, once an application to state a case to the High Court is made, the right to appeal to the Crown Court is lost. Given that the right to appeal by way of case stated is not lost when you appeal to the Crown Court, it is tactical to advise a client that the Crown Court may be the better option. Make sure an MCQ does not try to trick you into thinking that the defendant can subsequently appeal to the Crown Court following an appeal by way of case stated.

Procedure for appeal by way of case stated

In order to appeal by way of case stated, an appellant must apply in writing for the magistrates to state the case for the opinion of the High Court. This application must be made not more than 21 days after the decision that was made by the magistrates' court which the appellant wants to appeal. The appellant must serve the application on the court officer, and each other party.

The magistrates are not obliged to state the case and may refuse to do so where they find the application to be frivolous (ie having no possible prospect of success, because the case is unarguable). Any refusal must be made by a certificate of refusal and any such refusal is capable of being subject to judicial review. Where the magistrates' court decides to state the case for the opinion of the High Court, the court officer must serve a draft **statement of case** on each party not more than 15 business days after the court's decision to state the case.

Key term: statement of case

Also referred to simply as a 'case', this is a written document which specifies the decision in issue and the question of law on which the opinion of the High Court will be asked. The case will include a succinct summary of the nature and history of the proceedings, the court's relevant findings of fact and the contentions of the parties. If a question is whether there was sufficient evidence on which the court reasonably could reach a finding of fact, the case will specify that finding, and include a summary of the evidence on which the court reached that finding.

The parties to the case will then have opportunities to make representations as to any necessary amendments to the case. Once the case has been agreed, it will need to be lodged with the High Court by the appellant.

Hearing the appeal

The appeal is not a re-examination of the facts of the case heard in the magistrates' court. The hearing is confined to legal arguments made and no evidence may be called. Such appeals are often heard by three judges, though appeals can be heard by two judges (but no fewer than two). In cases where only two judges are sitting on the appeal, and the judges reach a stalemate (ie they cannot agree), the appeal fails and the decision of the magistrates' court stands.

Powers of the High Court

Upon conclusion of the appeal, the High Court will determine the question arising on the case and shall:

(a) reverse, affirm or amend the decision made by the magistrates' court, or

(b) remit (ie return) the matter to the magistrates' court with the opinion of the High Court, and may make such other order in relation to the matter (including as to costs) as it thinks fit.

The effect of these powers is that the High Court may conclude, on an appeal by the prosecution, that a defendant was wrongly acquitted and can remit the case back to the magistrates with a direction to convict and sentence. Likewise, on an appeal by the defendant, the High Court may rule that the defendant should be acquitted. The High Court could also remit the matter for a rehearing before a different bench of magistrates.

A further appeal?

Any appeal from the High Court is heard in the Supreme Court (bypassing the Court of Appeal). Both the prosecution and defence may appeal to the Supreme Court. In order to appeal, the High Court must certify that the case involves a point of law of general public importance and leave to appeal must be obtained from either the High Court or the Supreme Court.

Which route to appeal do I take?

By now, you should have identified that a defendant has two main options available to them upon conviction in the magistrates' court:

- appeal to the Crown Court
- appeal to the High Court by way of case stated.

It will be helpful to summarise the differences between these routes to appeal and consolidate our understanding to allow us to properly advise a client. We do this in **Table 9.1**.

Table 9.1: Crown Court or Divisional Court?

Factor	Correct court?
The defendant wishes to appeal against the magistrates' findings as to the facts of the case	Crown Court; the Divisional Court is restricted to appeals based on errors of law
The defendant wishes to appeal against the harshness of their sentence	Crown Court; unless the sentence is argued as being wrong in law, the Divisional Court will not entertain such an appeal
It is the prosecution wishing to appeal	Divisional Court; the prosecution has no right to appeal to the Crown Court

Simply put: if you are dealing with an appeal by the defence, preference should be given to the Crown Court as the venue for appeal.

APPEALS FROM THE CROWN COURT

We shall now move on to consider the appeals procedure where a defendant has been tried in the Crown Court. It is important to note that what we are going to discuss *only* applies to cases which are tried on indictment in the Crown Court, and *not* to cases which the Crown Court hears in its appellate capacity (ie appeals from the magistrates' court). For that, see above: **Appeals from the magistrates' court**.

An appeal may be brought by a defendant against their conviction or sentence at the conclusion of proceedings. The focus in this chapter will be on appeals brought by the defendant. In limited circumstances, the prosecution may also appeal, and this right shall be considered towards the end of the chapter.

Grounds of appeal

An appeal cannot be brought simply because a defendant does not agree with the decision of the arbiter of fact. Unlike appeals from the magistrates' court, permission (or 'leave') to appeal is required. This section shall briefly consider appeals against conviction, and appeals against sentence.

Appeals against conviction

If the defendant appeals against conviction, the Court of Appeal will *only* allow the appeal in the event of an **unsafe conviction**.

Key term: unsafe conviction

The test as to whether an appeal is successful is whether the defendant's conviction is 'unsafe'. This is the only basis upon which an appeal against conviction will be allowed. If the conviction is safe, the appeal must be dismissed.

There is no exhaustive list of what may give rise to an appeal. Despite this, we can identify a number of common arguments raised on appeal:

- The trial judge incorrectly rejected a submission of no case to answer.
- The trial judge misdirected the jury on a point of law.
- The trial judge permitted evidence to be adduced which should have been excluded (eg confession evidence) or excluded evidence which should have been permitted (eg hearsay evidence). See **Chapter 6** on evidence.
- The trial judge made an error in summing up.
- The trial judge made unnecessary interventions or comments.
- In limited circumstances, fresh evidence has been introduced (but this is greatly restricted).

Practice example 9.2 demonstrates what arguments could be made on appeal.

Practice example 9.2

James is charged with murder in the Crown Court. At trial, the judge directed the jury that if they found that James foresaw the result as being virtually certain, then he would *in law* have intended that end result. James is convicted of murder. James considers the judge to have misdirected the jury.

Will James' conviction be unsafe?

James would need to demonstrate that the misdirection would have such an impact on the conviction that it would not be safe to allow it to stand. Importantly, even if the Court of Appeal agrees that the trial judge did misdirect the jury, this does *not automatically* result in an unsafe conviction. The Court may be satisfied that despite the misdirection, the jury would not have changed their verdict (because of other compelling evidence in the case, for example). This is a vital distinction that you must remember for SQE1.

Hearing fresh evidence

It is important to remember that, as a general rule, an appeal will *not* be allowed on the grounds of introducing evidence which was not heard at trial. The Court of Appeal can, however, hear fresh evidence if it is in the interests of justice to do so. In particular, it will consider whether the fresh evidence is credible (ie capable of belief), affords a ground of appeal, would have been admissible at trial and whether there is a reasonable explanation for the failure to adduce it at trial.

Appeals against sentence

Where the defendant appeals against their sentence, they must demonstrate that the sentence is either:

- wrong in law (eg the judge had no power to sentence a defendant in a particular way), or
- manifestly excessive or wrong in principle.

Either of these grounds may be proven if, for example, the judge took the wrong approach in sentencing (eg by failing to give appropriate reductions in sentence or failing to take account of mitigating circumstances), the judge followed the wrong procedure before sentencing (eg the judge failed to undertake a Newton hearing (see **Chapter 8**) which was required), or there is a sense of grievance or disparity in sentencing.

Procedure for making the appeal

A defendant cannot automatically appeal against their conviction or sentence from the Crown Court; leave to appeal is *always* required. Leave may be granted by the trial judge at the conclusion of the trial by means of a certificate, or on an application to the Court of Appeal.

Figure 9.1 outlines the procedure when appealing to the Court of Appeal.

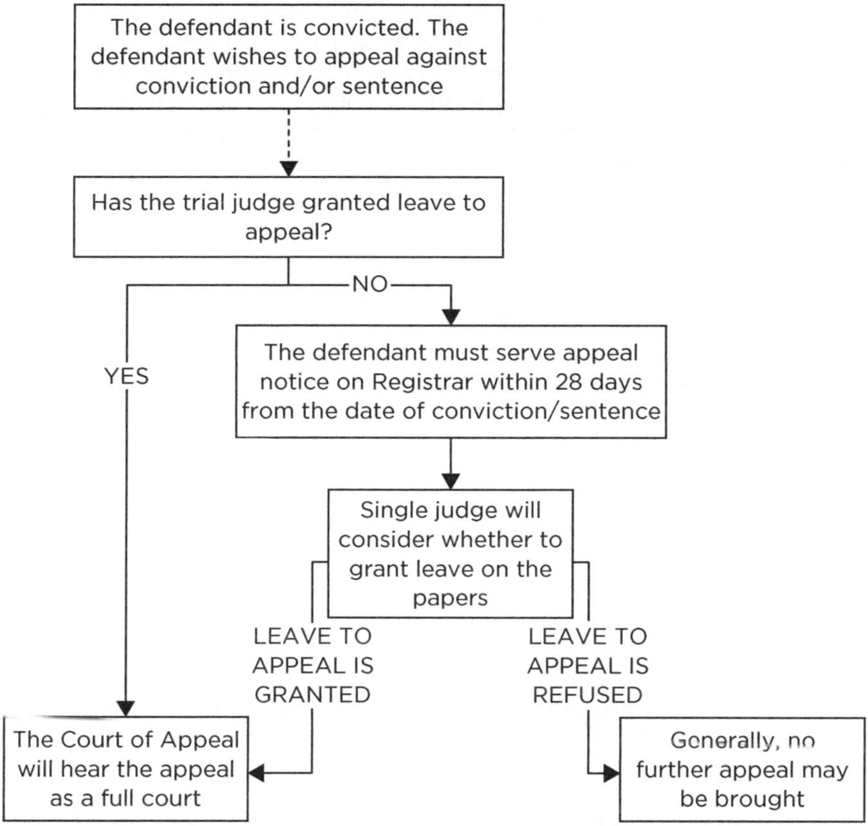

Figure 9.1: Procedure for appealing to the Court of Appeal

Obtaining leave to appeal

Following the jury delivering a verdict of guilty, leave to appeal may be obtained at this stage. The trial judge may grant a certificate on their own initiative, or an application will be made by defence counsel. If leave is granted by the trial judge, a certificate will be issued which details the question for the Court of Appeal's consideration. It is relatively rare for defence counsel to seek a certificate of leave to appeal; most applications are made directly to the Court of Appeal.

If leave is not granted by the trial judge, an application (known as an 'appeal notice') must be served on the Registrar of Criminal Appeals not more than:

(a) 28 days after the date of conviction (if the appeal is against conviction)
(b) 28 days after the date of sentence (if the appeal is against sentence).

Exam warning

If you are presented with an MCQ on appeals, and specifically when an application for leave must be made by, make sure you are clear on what the appeal is against. Remember, the court may adjourn for sentencing after the date of conviction; if you are appealing against conviction, the 28-day time limit starts *from the date of conviction*, even if sentencing takes place at a later date.

The appeal notice must be sent with the draft grounds of appeal. The Registrar will then place the application, along with a transcript of the evidence that was given at trial, before a single judge for their consideration. This is known as the 'filter stage' and will be considered separately now.

Consideration by the single judge

An application for leave to appeal will, in most instances, be initially considered by a single judge on the papers (ie without a hearing). The role of the single judge at this stage is not to consider the outcome of the appeal, but to consider whether leave should be granted. They will examine the grounds advanced by the appellant to see if they are cogent and if the case is suitable for an appeal hearing. If the case is suitable for appeal, then leave will be granted, and a hearing before a full court will take place. If not, leave shall be refused.

If there are multiple grounds of appeal, the single judge may grant leave for one ground, but dismiss others. If this is the case, then at the appeal hearing, an appellant may reapply for leave on the grounds which were dismissed by the single judge.

Hearing the appeal

After leave has been granted, an appeal will be heard before the full Court of Appeal. Generally, all appeals must consist of an uneven number of judges. Ordinarily, this will be a bench of at least three judges. Occasionally, a court of five or seven judges may sit if the case is of exceptional complexity or significance. A bench of two judges may sit in dealing with an appeal against sentence; an appeal against conviction must have a minimum of three judges, however.

Powers of the Court of Appeal

The powers of the Court of Appeal vary according to the type of appeal. **Table 9.2** demonstrates this distinction and **Practice example 9.3** demonstrates the application of these powers.

Table 9.2: Powers of the Court of Appeal

Appeal type and powers of the Court of Appeal	Further important details
Appeals against conviction At the conclusion of the appeal hearing, the Court of Appeal has several options available on how to proceed. It can: (a) Dismiss the appeal and uphold the conviction (b) Allow the appeal and quash the conviction (c) Allow *part* of the appeal, but dismiss the other part (d) Allow the appeal, quash the conviction and order a retrial (e) Allow the appeal and find the appellant guilty of an alternative offence (f) Make an order for loss of time	• A retrial will only be ordered if it is in the *interests of justice* to do so. The court will consider the length of time which has elapsed since the original trial, whether the appellant has been in custody, and if so, for how long, the superficial strength of any evidence and the degree of publicity which the case has invoked • The Court of Appeal may find the appellant guilty of an alternative offence if the jury could, on the indictment, have found the appellant guilty of some other offence; and providing it appears so to the Court of Appeal, the jury must have been satisfied of facts which proved the appellant's guilt of another offence • The Court of Appeal has the power to direct that any time spent in custody whilst an appeal is determined will not count towards the term of a custodial sentence which has been imposed. This is a discretionary, not mandatory, power
Appeals against sentence If the Court of Appeal considers an appeal against sentence, it may: (a) Dismiss the appeal and confirm the sentence passed (b) Allow the appeal and quash any sentence or order which the appeal concerns (c) Allow the appeal and substitute any sentence which was available to the Crown Court (d) Make an order for loss of time	• The most commonly argued ground in appeals against sentence is that the sentence was manifestly excessive or wrong in principle • A sentence is manifestly excessive if it is beyond the appropriate range for the offence(s). A sentence is wrong in principle if it may not be the most appropriate in the circumstances (ie a custodial sentence when non-custodial provisions were available and arguably more appropriate) • The Court of Appeal cannot increase the sentence imposed by the trial judge

Practice example 9.3

Mark is convicted of robbery, contrary to s 8 Theft Act 1968. Defence counsel offered credible and compelling mitigation which the trial judge ignored entirely, and a sentence was passed without due regard for the Definitive Sentencing Guidelines for robbery.

Is Mark's sentence likely to be upheld?

Mark would need to demonstrate that the sentencing judge imposed a sentence which was wrong in approach. A submission to support this contention could be made in respect of the trial judge failing to take account of the mitigation offered, and the appropriate provisions of the sentencing guidelines. Furthermore, whilst the following of the sentencing guidelines is advisory and not mandatory, the sentencing judge must state why they departed from the guidelines. In this instance, the Court of Appeal may substitute Mark's sentence for any sentence which the Crown Court could have imposed (though the Court of Appeal may not impose a more severe sentence).

A further appeal?

It is important to point out that a defendant has a single right of appeal. This means that if an appeal is heard by the Court of Appeal, and it is subsequently dismissed, there is generally no right to raise those grounds again. Any subsequent appeal will be to the Supreme Court.

Prosecution appeals

The prosecution's right to appeal from the Crown Court is heavily restricted. Generally speaking, the prosecution *cannot* appeal against the acquittal or sentence of a defendant. Below, we shall consider some of the limited circumstances in which the prosecution may appeal.

Terminating rulings

The prosecution may appeal against a **terminating ruling**.

Key term: terminating ruling

A terminating (or 'terminatory') ruling is one where the trial judge has effectively terminated the proceedings (eg accepting a submission of no case to answer).

If the prosecution wishes to appeal against a terminating ruling, it must inform the court, following the making of that ruling, that it intends to appeal. On appeal, the Court of Appeal may confirm, reverse or vary any ruling to which the appeal relates:

- to 'confirm' the ruling means that the defendant is acquitted of the offence
- to 'reverse' or 'vary' the ruling means that the proceedings should be resumed, that a fresh trial is ordered or the defendant should be acquitted.

Retrial of serious offences

An appeal against an acquittal, and ordering of a retrial, will only be permitted if:

- the defendant has been acquitted of a 'qualifying offence'
- the written consent of the Director of Public Prosecutions (DPP) has been obtained, and
- leave to appeal has been granted.

The qualifying offences (relevant to SQE1) include murder, attempted murder, manslaughter and aggravated arson. The DPP must only give their consent if there is 'new and compelling evidence' and if it is in the public interest for the DPP to give consent.

Revision tip

The SQE1 Assessment Specification is unclear as to the extent to which you are required to understand the additional routes to appeal (eg Attorney General's References). Given this uncertainty, it is recommended that you consult further reading around these additional routes to consolidate your knowledge.

■ KEY POINT CHECKLIST

This chapter has covered the following key knowledge points. You can use these to structure your revision, ensuring you recall the key details for each point, as covered in this chapter.

- Defendants convicted of an offence in the magistrates' court may appeal to the Crown Court against conviction or sentence, or to the High Court by way of case stated.
- The Crown Court and High Court may confirm, reverse or vary the decision of the magistrates' court.
- The prosecution may only appeal against a decision of the magistrates' court by way of case stated.
- Following trial in the Crown Court at first instance, a defendant may appeal to the Criminal Division of the Court of Appeal against their conviction or sentence.
- Leave to appeal to the Court of Appeal is *always* required but is not automatically granted. If the trial judge does not grant leave, an application for leave must be made.
- An appellant only has a single right to appeal; if an appeal is dismissed, there is generally no right to bring a second appeal on the same ground(s).

■ KEY TERMS AND CONCEPTS

- statement of case (**page 237**)
- unsafe conviction (**page 239**)
- terminating ruling (**page 244**)

■ SQE1-STYLE QUESTIONS

QUESTION 1

A man is convicted of assault occasioning actual bodily harm, contrary to s 47 Offences Against the Person Act 1861, following trial in the magistrates' court. The man is sentenced to a three-month term of imprisonment. The man accepts his conviction but wishes to appeal against his sentence.

Which of the following best summarises the position regarding the appeal against sentence?

A. The man may appeal against sentence to the High Court, which will take the form of a complete rehearing. The High Court may confirm, reverse or vary the sentence imposed on the man, including increasing the sentence up to the maximum term of imprisonment available to the Crown Court for that offence.

B. The man may appeal against sentence to the Crown Court, which will take the form of a complete rehearing. The Crown Court may confirm, reverse or vary the sentence imposed on the man, including increasing the sentence up to the maximum term of imprisonment available to the magistrates' court for that offence.

C. The man may appeal against sentence to the High Court, which will take the form of a complete rehearing. The High Court may confirm, reverse or vary the sentence imposed on the man, including increasing the sentence up to the maximum term of imprisonment available to the magistrates' court for that offence.

D. The man may appeal against sentence to the Crown Court, which will take the form of a complete rehearing. The Crown Court may confirm, reverse or vary the sentence imposed on the man, including increasing the sentence up to the maximum term of imprisonment available to the Crown Court for that offence.

E. The man may appeal against sentence to the Crown Court, which will take the form of a complete rehearing. The Crown Court may confirm, reverse or vary the sentence imposed on the man, but this does not include increasing the sentence up to the maximum term of imprisonment available to the magistrates' court for that offence.

QUESTION 2

A man is convicted of battery, following summary trial. The man disputes the verdict but does not identify any error in law on the part of the magistrates.

Which of the following is the best advice that can be given to the man regarding any appeal?

A. The man may appeal against his conviction to the Crown Court without leave being required.
B. The man may appeal against his conviction to the High Court without leave being required.
C. If the man chooses to appeal to the High Court, he cannot challenge his conviction, he can only challenge his sentence.
D. If the man chooses to appeal to the Crown Court, he cannot challenge his conviction, he can only challenge his sentence.
E. The man may appeal against his conviction to the Crown Court but must identify a point of law or evidence which was incorrectly decided during his summary trial.

QUESTION 3

A man has been convicted of robbery, contrary to s 8 Theft Act 1968 in the Crown Court. The trial judge adjourns for pre-sentencing reports, and the sentencing hearing takes place one week later. The man is remanded into custody until then. The man wishes to appeal against his conviction, and leave has not been granted.

Which of the following best describes the most appropriate advice to give the man?

A. The man, through his advocate, should make a renewed application to the trial judge at the sentencing hearing. If this is refused, he should apply for leave to appeal from the Court of Appeal, and should serve notice not more than 28 days from the date of sentencing.
B. The man should make an application for leave to appeal from the Court of Appeal not more than 28 days from the date of sentencing, as the proceedings have not been concluded.
C. The man should make a written application for leave to appeal to the Court of Appeal not more than 28 days after the date of his conviction, outlining the grounds of appeal. The application will be considered by a single judge on the papers.
D. The man should make a written application for leave to appeal to the Court of Appeal not more than 28 days after the date of his sentencing hearing, outlining the grounds of appeal. The application will be considered by a single judge on the papers.

E. The man should make a written application for leave to appeal to the trial judge not more than 28 days after the date of his conviction, outlining the grounds of appeal. The application will be considered by the trial judge on the papers.

QUESTION 4

A woman was charged with, and convicted of, murder in the Crown Court 15 years ago and is currently serving her custodial sentence. It has recently come to light that during the trial, the prosecution relied on evidence which is now known to be false. In addition, some crucially important fresh evidence has surfaced and there is a great deal of public attention on this case. The woman makes an application for leave to appeal out of time, and leave is granted. The Court of Appeal is now considering the outcome of the appeal.

Which of the following best describes the likely outcome of the appeal?

A. The Court of Appeal shall allow the appeal and order a retrial as, in the circumstances, it would likely be considered in the interests of justice to do so. The Court would quash the murder conviction and draft a new preferred indictment.

B. The Court of Appeal must allow part of the appeal on the ground of a misdirection but must dismiss the ground relating to fresh evidence as fresh evidence is generally inadmissible. The woman's sentence may be altered as a result.

C. The Court of Appeal must allow the appeal and order a retrial as, in the circumstances, it would likely be considered in the interests of justice to do so. The Court would quash the murder conviction and draft a new preferred indictment.

D. The Court of Appeal must allow the appeal and quash the conviction as it is unsafe. The woman's sentence would also be quashed, but a retrial would not be ordered as she has already served a large proportion of her sentence.

E. The Court of Appeal may allow part of the appeal on the ground of a misdirection, but dismiss the ground relating to fresh evidence due to the restrictions surrounding the introduction of fresh evidence. The woman's sentence may be altered as a result.

QUESTION 5

A man wishes to appeal against his conviction for manslaughter. He has applied for leave to appeal from the Court of Appeal on two grounds. A single judge, on the papers, has granted leave to appeal on the first ground, but has dismissed the second.

Which of the following best describes what the man should do?

A. The man may renew his application for leave to appeal on the second ground before the Court of Appeal at his appeal hearing. The Court of Appeal should grant leave following a renewed application.

B. The man can argue the second ground regardless, as leave to appeal has been granted for the first ground. The man does not need to do anything.

C. The man may renew his application for leave to appeal on the second ground before the Court of Appeal at his appeal hearing. The Court of Appeal may grant leave following a renewed application.

D. The man cannot take any further action; the single judge has refused leave to appeal on the second ground and this is a final decision that cannot be challenged further due to the single right of appeal principle.

E. The man may renew his application for leave to appeal on the second ground before the Court of Appeal at his appeal hearing. The Court of Appeal must grant leave following a renewed application.

■ ANSWERS TO QUESTIONS

Answers to 'What do you know already?' questions at the start of the chapter

1) False. The prosecution only has a right to appeal against a terminating ruling. Simple displeasure at the outcome of the trial is not a ground for appeal.
2) The Court of Appeal hears appeals against convictions from cases tried on indictment (ie in the Crown Court).
3) A defendant's appeal against conviction will be allowed in the Court of Appeal if the Court considers the conviction to be unsafe. The 'safety' test is used to determine all appeals against conviction in the Court of Appeal; it is the sole question to be considered.
4) An appeal on the basis that the magistrates were wrong in law may be heard in either the High Court, by way of case stated, or the Crown Court. Given that the Crown Court will involve a complete rehearing, without the need for leave to appeal, it is often the preferable route. Only points of law may be appealed to the High Court by way of case stated.

Answers to end-of-chapter SQE1-style questions

Question 1

The correct answer was B. This is because the appeal would be held in the Crown Court, which does have the ability to impose any sentence that would have been available to the magistrates' court (even if that means the sentence is increased). Options A and C are incorrect because any appeal against sentence would be heard in the Crown Court; appeals to the High Court are reserved for points of law. Option D is incorrect because the Crown Court cannot impose a sentence that would not otherwise be available to the magistrates' court. Option E is incorrect because the Crown Court can increase the sentence imposed, so long as it is a sentence that would have been available to the magistrates' court.

Question 2

The correct answer was A. This is because the man has an automatic right to appeal against his conviction to the Crown Court without the need for leave (thus option E is wrong), which will take the form of a complete rehearing. Option B is wrong because leave is required in the High Court and would not be the correct choice of court if the man wishes to appeal against his conviction and not on a point of law. Option C is equally incorrect because whilst the man could challenge his conviction, the High Court is reserved for points of law and not fact. Option D is wrong because the man can appeal against his conviction in the Crown Court.

Question 3

The correct answer was C. This is because the trial judge has refused leave to appeal, and he wishes to appeal against his conviction. The 28-day time limit for an appeal against conviction starts from the date of *conviction*. Option A is incorrect because once leave has been refused by the trial judge, an application is not renewed to the trial judge. Options B and D are wrong because the man is appealing against his conviction and not his sentence; therefore, the time starts to count down from the date of conviction. Option E is wrong because a written application is not made to the trial judge: it is made to the Court of Appeal.

Question 4

The correct answer was A. This is because this answer best reflects the wording of the relevant legislation ('the Court of Appeal *shall* allow ...') and, due to the fact that the new evidence is deemed 'crucial' and there is a great deal of public attention, a retrial is likely to be ordered in the interests of justice. Options B and C are wrong because there is no requirement that the court *must* allow an appeal and, whilst the rules on allowing fresh evidence are strict, it would likely be allowed in these circumstances. Option D is wrong, because although the woman has served a large proportion of her sentence, this is only one of the factors taken into consideration when ordering a retrial. Option E is wrong because whilst the Court of Appeal *may* allow part of an appeal, the evidential issues may be best explored by means of a retrial.

Question 5

The correct answer was C. This is because the man may, if he wishes, reapply for leave to appeal on the grounds which were dismissed by the single judge. The man must have leave to appeal if he wanted to argue the second ground (thus why option B is wrong). Options E and A are wrong because the Court of Appeal is not obliged to grant leave to appeal on a renewed application. Option D is wrong because the single right to appeal principle applies once an appeal has been determined; it does not apply to renewing applications for leave to appeal on grounds which have been dismissed by a single judge on the papers.

■ KEY CASES, RULES, STATUTES AND INSTRUMENTS

The SQE1 Assessment Specification does not require you to know any case names, or statutory materials, for the topic of appeals procedure.

10

Youth Court procedure and hearings

■ MAKE SURE YOU KNOW

This chapter will cover the procedures and processes involved when dealing with a youth offender. For the purposes of SQE1, you are required to know:

- jurisdiction of the Youth Court and grave crimes
- allocation of youth offenders
- sentencing of youth offenders.

The SQE1 Assessment Specification has identified that candidates are required to know and be able to use the *Sentencing Children and Young People Definitive Guideline* and the *Robbery – Sentencing Children and Young People* guideline.

■ SQE ASSESSMENT ADVICE

As you work through this chapter, remember to pay particular attention in your revision to:

- the differences between the procedure adopted in the criminal courts for adult offenders, and those adopted for youths
- the sentencing options available to all courts when dealing with a youth offender.

■ WHAT DO YOU KNOW ALREADY?

Have a go at these questions before reading this chapter. If you find some difficult or cannot remember the answers, make a note to look more closely at that area during your revision.

1) True or false? A man who committed an offence when aged 17, but turns 18 before his first appearance in court, *must* be dealt with in an adult court.
   [Jurisdiction and grave crimes, page 254]
2) What do you understand a 'grave crime' to be and what effect does this have on trial venue for a youth?
   [Jurisdiction and grave crimes, page 254]

3) Fill in the blank: A child jointly charged with an adult co-defendant, who has been sent forthwith to the Crown Court, may be sent to the Crown Court if ______________.

   [Allocation of youths jointly charged with an adult, page 259]

4) What is a Detention and Training Order and what length of time may be imposed for such order?

   [Sentencing, page 261]

INTRODUCTION TO YOUTH COURT PROCEDURE

In this chapter, we will turn our attention to youth offenders or 'youths', and the process that is taken when dealing with those youths in the criminal justice system.

Revision tip

Many of these matters are comprehensively covered in the *Youth Court Bench Book*, available at Judiciary.uk. The *Bench Book* provides guidance for magistrates who sit in the Youth Court and is an excellent resource for understanding the process to be adopted when dealing with youth offenders.

Aims of the Youth Court

The principal aim of the youth justice system is to prevent offending by children and young persons. Supporting this aim, every court must 'have regard to the welfare of the child or young person and shall ... take steps for removing them from undesirable surroundings, and for securing that proper provision is made for their education and training' (Children and Young Persons Act 1933, s 44).

Terminology in the Youth Court

The terminology adopted in respect of youths is vital. In particular, please note:

- 'youth'/'juvenile': anyone under the age of 18
- 'young person'/'young offender': anyone aged 14–17 (inclusive)
- 'child': anyone aged 10–13 (inclusive).

These terms are important as they will affect the procedure to be adopted, sentencing in particular.

Exam warning

Criminal responsibility begins at the age of ten in England and Wales. If an offence is committed by a child under the age of ten, no criminal liability exists.

JURISDICTION AND GRAVE CRIMES

The general rule is a simple one: A child or young person, charged with a criminal offence, must be tried in the Youth Court.

Revision tip

Keep this general rule simple: No matter what classification of offence is charged against the youth, the general rule is that they must be tried summarily (see **Chapter 3**) in the Youth Court. This means that no allocation hearing will be held, and the youth, even if they are charged with an indictable only offence, cannot elect trial by jury (see **Chapter 4**).

This general rule, however, is subject to a number of exceptions and may be affected by:

- the age of the offender at the time of trial
- the offence charged
- whether the youth is jointly charged with an adult.

We shall deal with the first two bullet points under this heading, and the third in **Allocation of youths jointly charged with an adult**.

Age of the offender

The jurisdiction of the Youth Court is founded upon the age of the defendant. There may be circumstances in which an offence is committed by an individual at the age of 17, but that individual turns 18 at some point during the proceedings. **Table 10.1** sets out how age may be determinative to the proceedings.

Table 10.1: Age of the offender during proceedings

Age and time of proceedings	Effect on procedure
The defendant is 17 when charged with an offence; the defendant turns 18 before their first appearance in the Youth Court.	The Youth Court has no jurisdiction. There is an obligation to remit the defendant to the adult magistrates' court. If convicted, the defendant will be subject to the full range of sentencing powers open to the adult magistrates' court. However, the court should take as its starting point the sentence likely to have been imposed on the date at which the offence was committed (ie when the offender was a youth).

Table 10.1: (continued)

Age and time of proceedings	Effect on procedure
The defendant is 17 when charged with an offence; the defendant turns 18 after their first appearance in the Youth Court, but before trial	The Youth Court has jurisdiction; the defendant may be tried in the Youth Court or remitted to the adult magistrates' court. This is a discretion to remit. • If the case is *retained* by the Youth Court, the court may sentence the defendant with the full range of sentencing powers available to the adult magistrates' court • If the case is *remitted* to the adult magistrates' court, there is no right to appeal against the order of remission and, if convicted, the defendant will be subject to the full range of sentencing powers open to the adult magistrates' court
The defendant is 17 when charged with an offence; the defendant turns 18 during trial, but before the conclusion of the trial	The Youth Court may deal with the case and make an order as if the defendant were still 17 Alternatively, the Youth Court may, at any time after conviction and before sentence, remit the defendant for sentence in the adult magistrates' court

Type of offence

Generally a youth offender should be tried in the Youth Court (even where the youth is charged with an indictable offence). There are, however, a number of exceptions to this rule. These are detailed below.

Exam warning

As we go through this list of exceptions, pay attention to the circumstances in which a youth is sent to the Crown Court *without* any indication of plea (ie 'forthwith'), and those where a plea before venue is undertaken (see **Chapter 4** generally on this). An MCQ may seek to test your understanding as to which cases require a plea before venue, and which cases do not.

Homicide offences

A child or young person charged with a homicide offence (eg murder or manslaughter) *must* be sent forthwith to the Crown Court for trial without an indication of plea being taken in the Youth Court. Attempts to commit homicide must also be sent forthwith to the Crown Court.

Firearm offences

A young person charged with a firearms offence (eg possessing a prohibited firearm), which is subject to a mandatory minimum sentence of three years, *must* be sent forthwith to the Crown Court for trial without an indication of plea being taken in the Youth Court. This exception only applies where the young person is aged 16 or over when the offence was committed.

Notice in fraud cases or cases involving children

In **Chapter 4**, we identified that in cases of serious or complex fraud, and some cases involving children, the case *must* be sent forthwith to the Crown Court, where notice is given by the prosecutor that the case is one that should be dealt with by the Crown Court. This same provision applies to youth offenders and, as with homicide and firearm offences, no indication of plea is taken.

Dangerous offenders

The Youth Court *may* send a youth to the Crown Court, without an indication of plea, where:

- they have been charged with a **specified offence** (not to be confused with the key term in **Chapter 7**)
- the court considers them to be a **dangerous offender**, and
- a custodial term (see **Chapter 8**) of at least four years would be imposed for the offence.

This is known as the 'dangerous offender provision'.

Key term: specified offence

A specified offence is a violent, sexual or terrorism offence listed in Schedule 18 of the Sentencing Code. Specified offences include, for example, manslaughter, wounding, robbery, rape and sexual assault. Some of these offences are also 'grave crimes' (see section below).

SQE1 will not expect you to know all specified offences listed in Schedule 18; rather, it is more likely that an MCQ will identify the offence as being 'specified'.

Key term: dangerous offender

A dangerous offender is one where the court is of the opinion that there is a significant risk to the public of serious harm caused by the child or young person committing further specified offences. A 'significant risk' is more than a mere possibility of occurrence.

In the majority of cases, it is likely to be difficult for the court to take a view on whether a child or young person could be considered a dangerous offender. In these cases, the Youth Court should retain jurisdiction. If, following a guilty plea or finding of guilt, the dangerousness criteria appear to be met, then the child or young person should be committed for sentence.

Grave crimes

Where a youth is charged with a **grave crime**, the Youth Court must determine whether to retain jurisdiction or send the youth to the Crown Court for trial.

Key term: grave crime

A grave crime is a serious offence, for which the sentence is not fixed by law, and is punishable with imprisonment of 14 years or more for an adult offender aged 21 years or over. Grave crimes assessed on SQE1 include:

- robbery (Theft Act 1968, s 8)
- causing grievous bodily harm or wounding with intent (Offences Against the Person Act 1861, s 18)
- aggravated criminal damage and arson/aggravated arson.

Unlike the above exceptions, in relation to grave crimes, the Youth Court must conduct a plea before venue in respect of youths charged with grave crimes.

- If the youth indicates a guilty plea, the offence should be treated as tried summarily and the court should proceed to sentencing (with the ability to commit the youth to the Crown Court for sentence).
- If the youth indicates a not-guilty plea (or does not enter a plea), the magistrates must then proceed to determine allocation.

In determining where the youth is to be tried, the test to be applied is a simple one: Is there a real prospect (and not merely a theoretical possibility) that a sentence in excess of two years' detention will be imposed on the youth?

Revision tip

The intention behind this test stems from the restrictive nature of a Detention and Training Order (DTO) (see below, **Sentencing**) that can be imposed by the Youth Court. Keep the following in mind:

- The maximum term of detention in the Youth Court is 24 months.
- There is no power to impose a sentence of detention on a child aged 10–11 years old in the Youth Court.
- There is no power to impose a sentence of detention in the Youth Court on a child aged 12–14 years old unless they are categorised as a persistent offender.

If the Youth Court considers that the youth should be imprisoned (either at an earlier age or for a longer period of time), the only option is to send the youth to the Crown Court. Keep this rationale in mind to assist in your revision on grave crimes.

Practice example 10.1 intends to bring all of these factors together to assist your understanding.

Practice example 10.1

Mark (14) is jointly charged alongside James (16) with robbery. The pair appear before the Youth Court. James has a previous conviction for robbery; Mark has no previous convictions. James pleads guilty to the robbery; Mark pleads not guilty.

Will Mark be subject to allocation proceedings and what factors would be relevant to the court's determination as to the appropriate trial venue?

Given that robbery is a grave crime, and Mark has indicated a plea of not guilty, Mark will be subject to allocation. Is a sentence beyond two years likely to be imposed? It would depend largely on the nature of the robbery and the facts of that case. Given that Mark has no previous convictions (it is his first offence) and without more information, it would seem likely that Mark's case would be retained in the Youth Court (though see immediately below).

Before deciding whether to send the case to the Crown Court or retain jurisdiction, the Youth Court will hear submissions from the prosecution and defence. The following is a brief summary of the relevant considerations in these cases:

- In most cases, it is likely to be impossible to decide whether there is a 'real prospect' that a sentence in excess of two years' detention will be imposed without knowing more about the facts of the case and the circumstances of the child or young person. In those circumstances, the Youth Court *should* retain jurisdiction.
- The Youth Court has the power to commit the child or young person to the Crown Court for sentence if it is of the view, having heard more about the facts and the circumstances of the child or young person, that its powers of sentence are inadequate.
- If the Youth Court does retain jurisdiction, it must warn the youth that all available sentencing options remain open and, if found guilty, the child or young person may be committed to the Crown Court for sentence.
- The youth has no right to elect trial by jury.

ALLOCATION OF YOUTHS JOINTLY CHARGED WITH AN ADULT

When tried alone, or with other young offenders, the youth will make their first appearance in the Youth Court. Where a youth and adult are jointly charged with a criminal offence, however, they *must* make their first appearance together before an adult magistrates' court. The process applied to the youth offender is dependent on the trial venue of the jointly charged adult offender (ie whether the adult will be tried in the magistrates' court or Crown Court) and the plea of the youth. The process can be quite confusing; **Figure 10.1** usefully summarises this process.

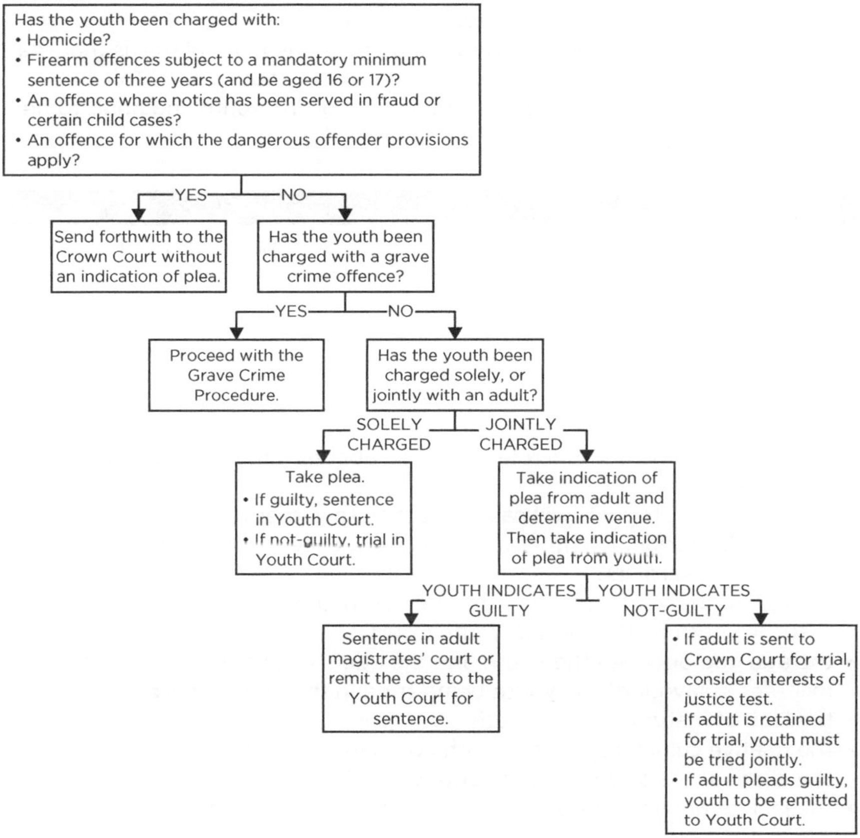

Figure 10.1: Allocation of youth offenders

> **Revision tip**
>
> The court will always deal with the adult defendant first before they deal with the youth. For your revision, use the same formula: identify the trial venue of the adult, then take the plea of the youth.

Adult tried in the Crown Court

If the adult is *sent for trial to the Crown Court* (whether this is an either way or indictable only offence - see **Chapter 3**), the court will then consider whether the offence charged is an offence listed above (see **Type of offence**). If the answer is no, a plea before venue (see **Chapter 4**) will be undertaken. The youth will be asked to indicate a plea:

- Guilty plea indicated: The youth is treated as having pleaded guilty and convicted summarily. The magistrates' court will proceed to sentencing or remit (ie return) the matter to the Youth Court for sentencing. In some limited circumstances, the magistrates may also commit the youth to the Crown Court for sentence.
- Not-guilty plea/no plea indicated: The procedure in s 51(7) CDA 1998 will be followed: an allocation hearing will be held; the general rule is that the youth offender should be tried separately in the Youth Court. This rule applies *unless* it is in the interests of justice for the youth and adult to be tried jointly.

Revision tip

The interests of justice test (not to be confused with the test of the same name in **Chapter 3**) will only be considered after the court has first determined whether the youth should be sent to the Crown Court for trial of a grave crime.

It is for the magistrates to determine whether the interests of justice test has been satisfied at the allocation hearing. In addition to the representations of the parties, and the general rule identified above, some factors that they will consider include:

- whether separate trials will cause injustice to witnesses or to the case as a whole (eg requiring witnesses to give evidence twice and the risk of inconsistent verdicts)
- the age of the youth: the younger the youth, the greater the desirability that the youth be tried in the Youth Court
- the age gap between the youth and the adult: a substantial gap in age militates in favour of the youth being tried in the Youth Court
- the lack of maturity of the youth
- the relative culpability of the youth compared with the adult and whether the alleged role played by the youth was minor
- the lack of previous convictions on the part of the youth.

Exam warning

The interests of justice test only applies where the adult defendant has been sent to the Crown Court for trial following a not-guilty plea. If the adult defendant pleads guilty, the youth will be remitted to the Youth Court for trial.

It is important to remember that even if the court does not send the youth offender to the Crown Court with the adult offender, the court may still commit the youth offender to the Crown Court for sentence where they have been convicted of a grave crime. This ability ensures that the same court deals with the sentences of both adult and youth offenders, even if tried separately. Should the magistrates' court send a youth to the Crown Court for trial with their adult co-accused under s 51(7), the court may also send any related indictable or summary only matter under s 51(8) CDA 1998.

Adult tried in the magistrates' court

If the adult is to be *tried in the magistrates' court*, the youth offender, pleading not guilty, should be tried with the adult. If the adult defendant pleads guilty, or the case against them is dismissed, the court will normally remit the youth to the Youth Court for trial. If the youth is convicted in the adult magistrates' court, they will normally be remitted to the Youth Court for sentence.

SENTENCING

When a case is proven against a youth, or following an admittance of the offence, the Youth Court (or whichever court is dealing with the youth) will proceed to sentence. The process is largely the same as that adopted in adult courts (see **Chapter 8**), though there are some key differences. The process is as follows:

- The prosecution will provide an overview of the offence and outline any previous convictions.
- This will be followed by a plea in mitigation by the defence advocate.
- The youth and/or their parent/guardian may be invited to make a statement to the court. The chair of the bench may wish to engage in a discussion with the youth to help them understand the reasons for their decision, and the effect that the youth's offending has had on the victim, their family or the community.
- Before the Youth Court sentences the youth, it must obtain a pre-sentence report prepared by the Youth Offending Team (YOT) (or a verbal report where no adjournment is ordered).

Role of the Sentencing Children and Young People Definitive Guideline

The Sentencing Council issued the *Sentencing Children and Young People Definitive Guideline* in 2017 to deal with children or young people, who are sentenced on or after 1 June 2017, regardless of the date of the offence.

The Definitive Guideline provides that when sentencing children or young people, a court *must* have regard to the principal aim of the youth justice system (ie to prevent offending by children and young people) and the welfare of the child or young person.

The Definitive Guideline emphasises that the approach to sentencing should be individualistic, as opposed to offence-focused. The sentence should focus on rehabilitation where possible; custody should be a measure of last resort. A court should also consider the effect the sentence is likely to have on the youth (both positive and negative) as well as any underlying factors contributing to the offending behaviour.

Determining sentence

The Definitive Guideline further provides that in determining the sentence of a youth, the key elements to consider are (in addition to the principal aim of the youth justice system and the welfare of the youth):

- the age of the child or young person (chronological, developmental and emotional)
- the seriousness of the offence
- the likelihood of further offences being committed
- the extent of harm likely to result from those further offences.

In **Chapter 8**, the principles adopted for determining sentence for adult offenders were considered. These principles largely mirror those of the youth justice system (eg the seriousness of the offence being the starting point) but with some modifications for dealing with youth offenders. In particular, the Definitive Guideline emphasises that when sentencing, courts must:

- avoid 'criminalising' youths unnecessarily; the primary purpose of the youth justice system is to encourage children and young people to take responsibility for their own actions and promote reintegration into society rather than to punish
- bear in mind the lack of emotional development and immaturity of a youth when compared with an adult.

Finally, when determining the appropriate sentence to be passed on a youth, the court should consider the **scaled approach** undertaken by the YOT.

Key term: scaled approach

The scaled approach refers to a model of interventions adopted by the YOT. It aims to ensure that interventions are tailored to the individual and based on an assessment of their risks and needs. The intended outcomes are to reduce the likelihood of reoffending for each child or young person by tailoring the intensity of intervention to the assessment, and more effectively managing risk of serious harm to others.

Using the scaled approach, the YOT will recommend an 'intervention level' to the court. These intervention levels include 'standard', 'enhanced' and 'intensive' and reflect the likelihood of the child or young person reoffending and the risk of the child or young person causing serious harm. This will affect the requirements imposed in the order. This intervention level will help the courts determine the length of a referral order, the duration and nature of any requirements imposed as part of a Youth Rehabilitation Order (YRO) and the nature of supervision following release on licence from custody under a DTO.

Role of the Robbery - Sentencing Children and Young People guideline

The *Robbery - Sentencing Children and Young People* guideline (June 2017) is designed to be read alongside the *Sentencing Children and Young People* guideline previously discussed.

Unlike traditional sentencing guidelines which use 'starting points' and 'category ranges', the *Robbery* guideline for children and young people is primarily focused on considering what the most suitable disposal is for a child or young person involved in robbery (see **Table 10.2** explicitly below).

As with other guidelines, the Sentencing Council recommends a number of 'steps' to be considered.

- Step 1 of the guideline requires the court to assess the seriousness of the offence, which involves considering the nature of the offence. In assessing the seriousness of the offence, the court will have regard to the factors provided in **Table 10.2**.

Table 10.2: Assessing the seriousness of the offence

A non-custodial sentence may be the most suitable disposal where one or more of the following factors apply:	A custodial sentence or youth rehabilitation order with intensive supervision and surveillance or fostering may be justified where one or more of the following factors apply:
• Threat or use of minimal force • Little or no physical or psychological harm caused to the victim • Involved through coercion, intimidation or exploitation	• Use of very significant force • Threat or use of a bladed article, firearm or imitation firearm (where produced) • Significant physical or psychological harm caused to the victim

The guideline is clear that these factors are merely 'examples' of the type of culpability and harm factors that may indicate that a particular threshold of sentence has been crossed. Furthermore, these factors must be balanced against each other to find the appropriate disposal in a given case.

- For Step 2, the court must have regard to the aggravating and mitigating factors, which are common amongst guidelines produced by the Sentencing Council.

- Step 3 then requires the court to consider the personal mitigation of the child or young person. The sort of factors relevant to the assessment of personal mitigation include the youth or immaturity of the child/young person, whether they had an unstable upbringing, and their current position or prospects in education, training or employment. Step 3 is essential to the court's assessment in that it may reduce what would otherwise be a custodial sentence to a non-custodial one, or a community sentence to a different means of disposal.
- Step 4 requires the court to consider what credit for guilty plea is available as in all cases.
- Step 5 is key to the uniqueness of the guideline: having now considered the seriousness of the offence, and the mitigation of the child/young person, the court must now review the sentence to ensure it is 'the most appropriate one for the child or young person'. This will include an assessment of the likelihood of reoffending and the risk of causing serious harm. The guideline goes on to provide a summary of the orders available to the court, including referral orders, youth rehabilitation orders (with or without intensive supervision and surveillance or fostering), and custodial sentences. We consider all of these orders in the next section.

Orders available

The SQE1 Assessment Specification identifies three orders that are examinable on SQE1. Whilst there are more powers and orders available to the sentencing court, we shall focus only on those orders stipulated in the Specification. These are referral orders, DTOs and YROs. We shall consider each in turn.

Referral orders

The majority of youth offenders, for whom an order has been made upon a finding of guilty, will receive a **referral order**.

Key term: referral order

A referral order is an order requiring the youth offender to attend meetings with a Youth Offender Panel (YOP), established by a YOT. The order will require the youth to agree a 'contract' with the YOP. As part of this contract, the youth must comply with a programme of behaviour designed to prevent reoffending. The programme will address the causes of offending behaviour and will allow the youth to take responsibility for the consequences of their actions.

A referral order can be made by the Youth Court and adult magistrates' court; it cannot be made by the Crown Court (unless the Crown Court judge reconstitutes themselves as a youth court or magistrates' court and sits as a district judge). A referral order will be *mandatory* in cases where:

- the youth has no previous convictions
- the youth pleads guilty to an imprisonable offence

- the court is not proposing to impose a custodial sentence, or make an absolute or conditional discharge, and
- the offence is not one for which sentence is fixed by law.

If these conditions for a compulsory referral order apply, a referral order must be imposed *unless* the court is considering imposing a discharge, hospital order, or custody.

A referral order *may* also be available in a number of limited circumstances, where the youth:

- pleads guilty to a non-imprisonable offence
- pleads guilty to some offences, but not guilty to others and is convicted of those offences following trial
- has previous convictions but has never had a referral order made against them, or
- has had a referral order made against them, but the YOT recommends a further referral order and the court finds 'exceptional circumstances to justify this course of action'.

A referral order can last 3–12 months; the more serious the offence is, the longer period of time will be imposed in the order. The *Sentencing Children and Young People Definitive Guideline* states the suggested length of a referral order for a low-seriousness offence as being 3–5 months and for a very high-seriousness offence as being 10–12 months. The court determines the length of the order, but a Referral Order Panel determines the requirements of the order.

Detention and Training Orders

The second order available is a **Detention and Training Order.**

> **Key term: Detention and Training Order**
>
> A DTO is the only form of custodial sentence available to the Youth Court. A DTO will result in the youth being held in a young offenders' institution before being released into the community under supervision. A DTO cannot be made unless the court is of the opinion that the offence (or combination of offences) was 'so serious that neither a fine alone nor a community sentence can be justified for the offence' (ie it must be a measure of last resort).

Please note the following about DTOs and the age of the youth:

- Aged ten or 11: DTOs *cannot* be made in respect of offenders aged ten or 11 at the date of conviction.
- Aged 12–14: DTOs *can only* be made in respect of offenders aged 12–14 at the date of conviction if they are a **persistent offender**.
- Aged 15–17: DTOs *can* be made in respect of offenders aged 15–17 at the date of conviction.

Key term: persistent offender

A persistent offender does not have a static definition; it is for a court to determine whether a youth can be classed as a 'persistent offender' on the facts. The Definitive Guideline provides that:

- A youth who has committed *one* previous offence cannot reasonably be classed as a persistent offender.
- A child or young person who has committed *two or more* previous offences should not necessarily be assumed to be one.
- If there have been *three findings of guilt* in the past 12 months for imprisonable offences of a comparable nature then the court could certainly justify classifying the child or young person as a persistent offender.
- When a child or young person is being sentenced in a single appearance for a series of separate, comparable offences committed over a short space of time, then the court could justifiably consider the child or young person to be a persistent offender, despite the fact that there may be no previous findings of guilt.

To determine if the behaviour is persistent, the nature of the previous offences and the lapse of time between the offences would need to be considered.

A DTO no longer needs to be imposed for a fixed period (ie 4, 6, 8, 10, 12, 18 or 24 months), providing that the period is between 4 and 24 months. This gives the sentencing court more discretion as to the applicable period, and to pass the right sentence in the interests of the child and the interests of justice. Any time spent on remand or bail, where the youth is subject to a qualifying curfew condition and an electronic monitoring condition, is counted as 'time served'. This means that such time will be credited against the custodial section of the DTO. Only the Crown Court has the power to sentence offences to longer than 24 months, and only where the offence is a 'grave crime'. A DTO cannot be imposed unless the youth is legally represented (unless they have refused to apply for legal aid/have had such funding withdrawn).

There are other forms of custodial sentence for young offenders (known as 'detention') which exist for young offenders convicted of grave crimes. These sentences, however, are not featured in the SQE1 Assessment Specification.

Youth rehabilitation orders

The final order that can be made is a **Youth Rehabilitation Order.**

Key term: Youth Rehabilitation Order

A YRO is a community sentence imposed on a youth offender. A YRO involves the imposition of one or more 'youth rehabilitation requirements' which are designed to punish the youth, protect the public, reduce reoffending and to make reparation.

A YRO may only be imposed where the court is of the opinion that the offence was 'serious enough to warrant the making of such an order'. Such orders are discretionary. The maximum period of time for a YRO is three years, from the date on which the order comes into effect (and there is no minimum period). There are different levels of intensity available to the court under a YRO, including 'standard', 'enhanced' and 'intensive', which are based upon the likelihood of reoffending and the risk of serious harm.

Examples of such rehabilitation requirements include (see **Chapter 8** for details of these requirements given their similar nature):

- curfew requirement (up to 20 hours per day; 112 hours per week)
- activity requirement (maximum of 90 days)
- supervision requirement
- unpaid work requirement (40–240 hours).

Exam warning

Be aware that the requirements included within the order and the length of the order must be *proportionate* to the seriousness of the offence and *suitable* for the child or young person. The court should take care to ensure that the requirements imposed are not too onerous so as to make breach of the order almost inevitable. Look out for these practical considerations in an MCQ assessing the suitability of a particular order, or its requirements.

Practice example 10.2 allows you to apply your understanding of these various orders to a scenario.

Practice example 10.2

James is a 14-year-old boy with a difficult family situation. James has two previous separate convictions, for theft and assault respectively, when he was 12 years old. James received a referral order for both offences and has not been in trouble with the law for over 12 months. James has now been convicted of assault occasioning actual bodily harm, contrary to s 47 Offences Against the Person Act 1861.

What is the likely order that will be made against James?

James has already received two referral orders. It is doubtful that a third referral order will be issued. As a 14-year-old, James is capable of being issued with a DTO, but he must be considered to be a 'persistent offender'. Given that this is James' third offence, he may be considered a persistent offender and thus subject to a DTO. However, it is more likely that James will be issued with a YRO, though this depends on the seriousness of the offence and whether that justifies the imposition of a YRO.

The court may also impose a YRO with Intensive Supervision and Surveillance (ISS) or a YRO with Fostering. Both orders may only be made where the court is of the opinion that the offence has crossed the custody threshold and custody is merited. The SQE1 Assessment Specification does not list this specific type of YRO and so we shall not consider it any further here.

Crossing a significant age threshold between commission of offence and sentence

There may be occasions when a child commits an offence at a certain age and yet is a different age at the time of sentencing (for example, a defendant commits an offence at 14 but is 15 at the date of being found guilty). The age of the youth at the point of sentencing will affect the orders that the courts can make (as demonstrated in **Table 10.2**).

Table 10.2: Sentencing youths

Orders available	Age of child or young person (inclusive)		
	10–11 years	**12–14 years**	**15–17 years**
Referral order	✓	✓	✓
Youth Rehabilitation Order (YRO)	✓	✓	✓
Detention and Training Order (DTO)	×	✓ *If they are a persistent offender*	✓

The Definitive Guideline states that when any significant age threshold is passed, it will rarely be appropriate that a more severe sentence than the maximum that the court could have imposed at the time the offence was committed should be imposed. This means that a 15-year-old who committed the offence at the age of 14 should be treated, as a starting point, as if they were still 14 for the purposes of sentencing. As we can see above, this would impact on whether a DTO could be imposed (go back to **Practice example 10.2** to appreciate this fully).

■ KEY POINT CHECKLIST

This chapter has covered the following key knowledge points. You can use these to structure your revision, ensuring you recall the key details for each point, as covered in this chapter.

- The Youth Court is a specialist court dealing with offenders aged 10–17 (inclusive). The general rule is that all youth offenders are to be tried summarily in the Youth Court.
- A youth *must* be sent to the Crown Court for trial in a number of circumstances (eg where charged with homicide offences). When

considering rules on allocation, remember to consider whether a plea before venue must be conducted.
- A grave crime is a serious offence for which an adult aged 21 or over may receive a custodial sentence of 14 years or more. Where a youth is charged with a grave crime, they must be sent to the Crown Court for trial if the Youth Court considers that a custodial sentence longer than 24 months is appropriate, or the Youth Court may retain the case for summary trial.
- A youth charged with an adult must be sent with the adult to the Crown Court if it is in the interests of justice to do so, and must be tried with the adult in the magistrates' court. The youth will normally be remitted to the Youth Court for sentencing.
- The Youth Court must follow the *Sentencing Children and Young People Definitive Guideline* when dealing with youths and the *Robbery - Sentencing children and young people* guideline when specifically sententencing children and young people for crimes of robbery. The court may make a referral order, a YRO or a DTO.

KEY TERMS AND CONCEPTS

- specified offence (**page 256**)
- dangerous offender (**page 256**)
- grave crime (**page 257**)
- scaled approach (**page 262**)
- referral order (**page 264**)
- Detention and Training Order (**page 265**)
- persistent offender (**page 266**)
- Youth Rehabilitation Order (**page 266**)

SQE1-STYLE QUESTIONS

QUESTION 1

A female (aged 17) is charged with theft, contrary to s 1 Theft Act 1968. The female is jointly charged with a male (aged 22). The pair plead not guilty to the offence at their first appearance in the magistrates' court. The male consents to summary trial.

Which of the following statements best describes the trial venue of the female?

A. The female is an adult and must therefore be tried in the magistrates' court alongside the male.

B. The female is a youth and must therefore be tried in the Youth Court.

C. The female is a youth but is jointly charged with an adult, and therefore must be tried in the magistrates' court alongside the male.
D. The female is an adult and as she is charged with an either way offence, may be tried in the magistrates' court or the Crown Court.
E. The female is a youth but is jointly charged with an adult, and therefore the magistrates' court has discretion to retain the case or remit it to the Youth Court.

QUESTION 2

A girl (aged 16) appears before the Youth Court charged with inflicting grievous bodily harm contrary to s 20 Offences Against the Person Act 1861. The defence has been served with initial details of the prosecution case and the girl intends to plead not guilty. The girl has never been in trouble with the police before and the magistrates do not consider her to be a dangerous offender.

Which of the following is the most likely procedure that the magistrates will adopt to decide the venue for the girl's trial?

A. The magistrates must conduct a plea before venue procedure before deciding whether they should try the girl.
B. The girl should be sent forthwith to the Crown Court for trial, without an indication of plea.
C. The girl's plea should be taken, and the matter adjourned for trial in the Youth Court.
D. The girl should be asked in which court, if the matter were to go to trial, she would wish to be tried.
E. The girl's plea should be taken, and the matter adjourned for trial in the adult magistrates' court.

QUESTION 3

A boy (aged 14) appears in the Youth Court charged with burglary, contrary to s 9 Theft Act 1968. The boy has eight previous findings of guilt in the past six months. Based on the sentencing guidelines, the prosecution and defence agree in their assessment that if the boy receives a sentence of detention after trial, it is likely to be no more than four months. The boy intends to plead guilty.

Which of the following most accurately describes the likely outcome?

A. The Youth Court will impose a Detention and Training Order on the boy for a period of four months.
B. The Youth Court could impose a Detention and Training Order on the boy, but only if they deem him to be a persistent offender.

C. The Youth Court cannot impose a Detention and Training Order on the boy as he is too young for such an order to be made.
D. The Youth Court could impose a Detention and Training Order on the boy, but this is unlikely due to the sentencing assessment made by the prosecution and defence.
E. The Youth Court will impose a Detention and Training Order on the boy, which may be for any period of time up to 24 months.

QUESTION 4

A girl (aged 16) is charged with criminal damage in the Youth Court. The girl is alleged to have inflicted a large number of scratches on the car belonging to one of her schoolteachers, causing extensive exterior damage. The girl intends to plead guilty to the offence and the court has identified that it is not proposing to impose a custodial sentence or make a discharge. The girl has previous convictions but has never had a referral order made against her.

Which of the following best describes the legal position regarding a referral order?

A. The Youth Court must impose a referral order on the girl as she has pleaded guilty to an imprisonable offence and the court is not proposing to impose a custodial sentence or make a discharge.
B. The Youth Court must impose a referral order on the girl as she has previous convictions but has never had a referral order made against her. As the girl has not already had a referral order imposed, it is mandatory for the court to impose one now.
C. The Youth Court may impose a referral order on the girl but only where the Youth Offending Team recommends the referral order, and the court finds exceptional circumstances to justify this course of action.
D. The Youth Court cannot impose a referral order on the girl as such orders could only be made if the girl did not have any previous convictions.
E. The Youth Court may impose a referral order on the girl as she has previous convictions but has never had a referral order made against her. As the girl has not already had a referral order imposed, it is at the discretion of the court whether to impose one now.

QUESTION 5

A boy (aged 17 and with learning difficulties) is charged with robbery (a grave crime). The boy makes his first appearance before the Youth Court and indicates a not-guilty plea. At the allocation hearing, the prosecution submits that the boy is likely to be sentenced to a minimum of three years' imprisonment given the seriousness of the offence and the boy's previous conviction. The defence submits that a three-year sentence is excessive given that the boy only has one previous conviction and the Youth Court is best placed to deal with his learning difficulties.

Which of the following is the most likely outcome of the allocation hearing?

A. The Youth Court is likely to send the boy to the Crown Court for trial on the basis that there is a real prospect that a sentence in excess of two years' detention will be imposed.

B. The Youth Court is likely to retain jurisdiction and try the boy summarily. If the Youth Court chooses to try the boy summarily, they may then commit the boy for sentencing to the Crown Court if it becomes appropriate to do so.

C. The Youth Court is likely to send the boy to the Crown Court for trial on the basis that there is a strong possibility that a sentence in excess of two years' detention will be imposed.

D. The Youth Court is likely to retain jurisdiction and try the boy summarily. If the Youth Court chooses to try the boy summarily, they cannot thereafter commit the boy to the Crown Court for sentencing.

E. The Youth Court must send the boy to the Crown Court for trial as he will likely turn 18 before the end of proceedings.

■ ANSWERS TO QUESTIONS

Answers to 'What do you know already?' questions at the start of the chapter

1) True. If an individual turns 18 prior to their first appearance, the Youth Court does not have jurisdiction to try the case. The man must be tried in an adult court. The Youth Court may retain a case if the individual reaches the age of 18 during the proceedings.
2) A grave crime is a serious offence which is punishable, in the case of an adult offender aged 21 or above, by a minimum term of 14 years' imprisonment and is an offence for which the sentence is not fixed by law. If a youth is charged with a grave crime, and pleads not guilty, the Youth Court *may* send them to the Crown Court for trial if there is a real prospect that a sentence of imprisonment over two years will be imposed.
3) A child jointly charged with an adult co-defendant, who has been sent forthwith to the Crown Court, may be sent to the Crown Court if the youth has pleaded not guilty and it is in the interests of justice that the adult and youth should be tried together.
4) A DTO is the only form of custodial sentence available to the Youth Court. The youth will be held in a young offenders' institution before

being released into the community under supervision. A DTO no longer needs to be imposed for a fixed period (ie 4, 6, 8, 10, 12, 18 or 24 months), providing that the period is between 4 and 24 months.

Answers to end-of-chapter SQE1-style questions

Question 1

The correct answer was C. This is because where an adult co-accused (the male) pleads not guilty and consents to summary trial, if the youth also pleads not guilty, they must be tried in the adult magistrates' court with their co-accused. Options A and D are wrong as the female is a youth since she has not yet attained 18 years of age. Option B is wrong as although the female would generally be tried in the Youth Court, she must be tried with an adult co-defendant in the magistrates' court. Option E is incorrect because the magistrates' court has no such discretion in this situation.

Question 2

The correct answer was C. This is because there is a general rule that all offences allegedly committed by a youth must be tried summarily in the Youth Court. There are no exceptions to that general rule present in this case (such as a homicide offence). Option A is wrong as a plea before venue would only be required if the girl was charged with a grave crime or jointly charged with an adult. Option B is wrong because none of the circumstances in which a youth can be sent forthwith to the Crown Court for trial apply. Option D is wrong because a youth never has the right to choose where their trial is to take place. Option E is wrong because the girl is not an adult, and she should be tried in the Youth Court unless she is sent to the Crown Court. A youth will only be tried in the magistrates' court if jointly charged with an adult who is to be summarily tried.

Question 3

The correct answer was D. This is because a DTO is capable of being imposed. Based on the assessment of the prosecution and defence, the boy faces a four-month DTO if convicted after trial. If the boy pleads guilty, he will receive a discount which will take the sentence below the minimum four-month period for which a DTO can be imposed. Option A is incorrect because it supposes that the court will definitely impose a DTO and ignores the guilty plea. Option B is not the 'most likely' outcome: although this answer is factually correct (the boy will likely be classed as a persistent offender), it does not best address the issue of whether the boy will be awarded a DTO. Option C is incorrect as a DTO can be imposed on a 14-year-old child, so long as they are deemed to be a persistent offender. Option E, which is technically correct, is not the best answer as it fails to consider the guilty plea of the boy.

Question 4

The correct answer was E. This is because a referral order is available to the Youth Court at its discretion in circumstances where the youth has previous convictions but has never had a referral order made against them. Given that the girl has a previous conviction, a referral order is not mandatory (therefore options A and B are wrong). Option C is incorrect because the 'exceptional circumstances' test is only applicable where the youth has had a referral order made against them already. Option D is wrong as referral orders can be made in this circumstance, though such orders are not mandatory.

Question 5

The correct answer was B. This is because the 'real prospect' test is a high threshold to pass and the Sentencing Children and Young People Definitive Guideline suggests that in most cases, it is likely to be impossible to decide whether there is a 'real prospect' that a sentence in excess of two years' detention will be imposed without knowing more about the facts of the case and the circumstances of the child or young person. As such, the Youth Court is *most likely* to retain jurisdiction and then has the power to commit the boy to the Crown Court if they are satisfied of the real prospect test at that point (ie it is appropriate to do so). Option A is wrong as it ignores the principle in the Definitive Guideline; given that we are told of the potential learning difficulties of the boy and the dispute of the defence as to the minimum sentence, the real prospect test is unlikely to be satisfied at this stage in the proceedings. Option C is wrong as it uses the incorrect test ('strong possibility' as opposed to 'real prospect'). Option D is wrong given that, whilst the Youth Court is likely to retain jurisdiction, it does have the power to commit for sentence. Option E is wrong as the boy has made his first appearance at the age of 17 and the Youth Court retains a discretion to try his case, even if he turns 18 before the conclusion of proceedings.

■ KEY CASES, RULES, STATUTES AND INSTRUMENTS

The SQE1 Assessment Specification has identified that you need to know and be able to use the Sentencing Children and Young People Definitive Guideline, in relation to its role in sentencing youths. The SQE1 Assessment Specification does not require you to know any case names, or statutory materials, for the topic of Youth Court procedure.

Index